The Piano: *A History*

Cyril Ehrlich

THE PIANO
A History

London

J. M. Dent & Sons Ltd

First published 1976
© Text, Cyril Ehrlich, 1976

Made in Great Britain
at the
Aldine Press · Letchworth · Herts
for
J. M. Dent & Sons Ltd
Aldine House · 26 Albemarle Street · London

This book is set in 11 on 13 point Garamond (156)

ISBN 0 460 04246 7

Contents

Acknowledgments

Grateful acknowledgment is made to the Houblon Norman Fund and the Social Science Research Council for grants in aid of research. I am indebted for encouragement and advice to Professor F. J. Fisher, John Steinway, James Vincent, Professor Klaus Wachsmann, and to my colleagues Ken Brown, Leslie Clarkson and Max Goldstrom. For help in illustrating this book I am grateful to the British Library, the Mary Evans Picture Library, the Victoria and Albert Museum, Bösendorfer Pianos Ltd and Steinway and Sons. The staffs of the British Library, the Victoria and Albert Museum, the Library of Congress, New York Public Library and the Bibliothèque Nationale have rendered indefatigable assistance. Finally I must express my appreciation to my family, for years of forbearance, and to Andrew Roberts for stimulus and tactful criticism.

List of Illustrations and Tables

Plates run between pages 96 and 97.

Plates

Tables

FOR FELICITY

Chapter 1

Introduction

The early history of the piano is familiar, or easily accessible. Scrupulously documented with a mass of technical detail by Rosamund Harding, it has been summarized in many reference books, and more recently explored in a growing literature which reflects a new cult of old keyboard instruments.[1] But the richness of this material, its concentration upon the period before 1850, and the antiquarianism of its more recent practitioners, threaten to distort our view of the piano's development. Especially is this so if we consider its place in the broad stream of cultural, economic and social history. For the piano was not merely a prince of instruments, 'a mirror reproducing whatever is most characteristic of the general state of music'.[2] In its golden age it became the centre of domestic entertainment, of musical education and, not least, a coveted possession, symbolic of social emulation and achievement, within reach of an ever-widening circle of eager purchasers. A primary aim of this book is to depict the rise, and ultimate fall, of an instrument once recognized as the 'household orchestra and god', the 'highly respectableising piece of furniture'.

A first step in this task is to reassess the chronology of the piano's technical development, remembering that, from society's viewpoint, widespread adoption of new techniques is more important than invention, quantitative advance more significant than isolated achievement. It is commonly assumed that the piano's history culminates in the middle of the nineteenth century, its basic repertoire established, its technology settled, apart from a few minor improvements, its influence already pervasive, and even that 1851 was 'the annus mirabilis of pianoforte manufacture'.[3]

These beliefs have little basis in fact. In 1851 good pianos were still luxury goods, produced by craftsmen along traditional lines without machinery, and therefore expensive. 'Square' pianos shaped like a clavichord were still popular: Broadwood made approximately 1,000 a year throughout the first half of the nineteenth century. They were by no means cheap—a Broadwood or Stodart cost between sixty and seventy guineas—but they were probably the best choice for musicians who could not afford money or space for a grand. The design of 'uprights' was in

its infancy—few had an adequate tone or a mechanism which, in its relia-
bility and responsiveness to the player's touch, could be regarded as
satisfactory. Yet these too were costly—fifty to a hundred guineas,
roughly equal to the annual income of a clerk or school teacher. Some
cheaper instruments were available—one was shown at the Great Exhibition—but they were perforce shoddy makeshifts. The total world output
was probably about 50,000 pianos a year, nearly half of them made in
England, which shared a generally acknowledged leadership of the industry
with France, though many musicians still preferred the simpler Viennese
instruments. Neither German nor American production was yet significant.

Fifty years later the industry and its product were utterly transformed.
World output had increased tenfold, with a new geographical distribution of industrial power and technological leadership. Both concert and
domestic pianos had developed into modern instruments, overstrung
with iron frames, indistinguishable in any significant respect from those
we use today. Many Steinways and Bechsteins built during the first decade
of this century still command high prices and are bought for everyday use.
Moreover, the gulf that had once separated the best makers from the rest,
and the musician's grand from the 'cottage' piano, had narrowed per-
ceptibly by 1900. Durable instruments of real musical quality were now
available at modest prices, rendered even more attractive by a widespread
system of hire purchase. The price, say £25, though much cheaper instruments were available, was now roughly equivalent to three months' income of a clerk or school teacher, and ownership was by no means limited
to such white-collar workers. This was a modest but significant part of that
social revolution, based upon industrial and commercial progress, which
the Victorians celebrated and later generations have derided. Since it
symbolized respectability, then 'the sharpest of all lines of social division',[4]
the piano was at the centre of social change. Its history cannot therefore
be appreciated purely in musical terms.

Predecessors and beginnings

But if the golden age did not begin until the 1870s, what had been
achieved during the first 150 years of the piano's existence? To understand this we must now retrace our steps and examine the evolution of
its technology. This should not be conceived as a series of giant steps by
'great inventors'. Rather was it a cumulative process of relatively simple
improvements, with many unsuccessful or eccentric experiments and
occasional brilliant innovations, in which the pattern of change depended
ultimately upon the nature of challenge and response.

The first craftsmen to make pianos were attempting to correct the inherent deficiencies of existing keyboard instruments. The clavichord was simple and cheap to construct, and it allowed the player an intimate control over the intensity and quality of its sound. Sensitive gradations of tone, even a vibrato—the *bebung*—could be achieved. But the clavichord was quiet, and therefore a private instrument. The harpsichord, by contrast, was sufficiently loud and brilliant for hall, theatre and church, but could not produce subtle gradations of volume, offering instead a 'terraced dynamic', which was produced mechanically rather than through the immediate control of the player's fingers. This is not to say that the instrument was ineluctably soulless. No less an authority than François Couperin has often been misquoted in support of this misleading view. In his seminal *L'Art de toucher le clavecin* (1717) the following passage appears: 'Since the sounds of the harpsichord are isolated and cannot be increased or diminished il a paru presqu'insoutenable, jusqu'à présent, qu'on put donner de l'âme à cet instrument"' (p. 15). It is surely misleading to take these words out of context as confession of an unavoidable inexpressiveness. Wanda Landowska rightly chides those who do so and reminds us that dry playing was the player's fault.[5] C. P. E. Bach, who wrote the other great eighteenth-century manual for keyboard instrumentalists, takes a similar line: 'Tones will sing on the harpsichord as well as on the clavichord if they are not detached from each other, although one instrument may be better constructed for this purpose than another.' He admits that it is difficult to 'give a singing performance of an adagio without creating too much empty space' or 'a silly caricature . . . through an excessive use of rapid notes'.[6] But these intrinsic deficiencies can be concealed by the musician's artistry and the sensitive response of intelligent listeners who 'replace losses mentally'.

The argument has a much wider relevance, and should be borne in mind throughout the following pages. Keyboard players have always been urged to 'sing'; yet in a literal sense this is impossible for in all keyboard stringed instruments each note fades from the moment that it begins to sound. The complex aesthetic relationship between instrument, performer and audience, and the frequent suspension of disbelief which it entails, is an essential part of musical experience. There has always been a gap, as well as a mutually enriching relationship or tension, between musical expression and technical resources. In the second half of the eighteenth century this gap appeared to be widening, and it is in this sense that makers of keyboard instruments could be said to have faced a challenge.

• Some reacted by attempting to give the harpsichord a *crescendo* and *diminuendo*, by means of rapid changes of register, or by hinged slats which gave a 'swell' effect. None of these devices was really successful, and their proliferation could indeed be regarded as compromising the essential nature of the instrument which they were designed to improve. For 'deficiencies' or 'limitations' in an instrument, provided its design and workmanship are of high quality, can only be understood in relation to changing musical requirements and taste. The very 'limitations' of the harpsichord were a stimulus to its magnificent literature. The relevant solo works of Couperin, Scarlatti and Handel are obvious examples, and in orchestral music the instrument's sparkling incisive sound stood out clearly from the orchestral texture, of which it was the centre. The harpsichord was an indispensable feature of baroque music and the accompaniment to *secco recitative* in eighteenth-century opera. Its replacement by the piano in nineteenth-century performances of such music was a retrogressive step which continued into the 1930s and beyond, as can be heard in otherwise distinguished recorded performances by such artists as Busch and Casals.[7] The point need not be laboured, for the revival of the harpsichord has re-educated musicians and listeners: today the use of a piano in, say, Bach's Fifth *Brandenburg* Concerto is no longer acceptable.

But to return to the eighteenth century, the fact that instrument makers experimented so widely is evidence of new musical requirements which grew more insistent as the style of musical composition became increasingly homophonic, rather than contrapuntal. Musicians required more nuance and dynamic inflexion, a greater ability to mould a phrase and separate melody from accompaniment. One possible solution was to replace the harpsichord's plectra by hammers. The idea had been described (*c.* 1440) by Arnault [8] and there were various later claimants to the invention, but the earliest successful instruments, three of which survive, were made by Cristofori for the Court at Florence between 1698 and the 1720s. They were described as *gravicembali col piano e forte*, a clear indication of their purpose. The piano made little further progress in the country of its birth, and no later Italian manufacturer ever attained international prominence. Musical, social and economic factors account for this. After Scarlatti, Italian music was dominated by the opera. As Max Weber has explained, in southern Europe the growth of bourgeois demand for 'home comforts' was severely limited by climate and culture. Moreover, a modern industrial base, which soon became indispensable both for the growth of demand and for the resources of manufacture, was not established in Italy until late in the nineteenth century. It is therefore 'no accident that the representatives of pianistic culture are Nordic peoples, climatically house-bound and home centred'.[9]

The creation and diffusion of a new technology took place through spontaneous experiment in several Northern European centres, and by transmission through printed and verbal accounts and the work of migrating craftsmen. Thus an enthusiastic description of Cristofori's instrument, with a sketch of its action, was published in Venice in 1711 and translated into German in 1725, assisting Gottfried Silbermann in Freiburg to construct similar instruments. One was tried by J. S. Bach, who found its action heavy and treble register weak. Although he is said to have approved a later model, Bach, of course, remained loyal to the harpsichord and clavichord.

Several of Silbermann's apprentices, including his nephew Johann Heinrich, and Christian Ernst Friederici, continued these experiments. A significant departure was Friederici's manufacture of little 'square' pianos. He called them *fortbiens* and they were said to be 'famed and scattered over half the world'.[10] These pianos were obviously cheap, simple modifications of the clavichord, a natural development in Germany where the harpsichord had never been as popular as its more modest contemporary. By contrast with France, where formal music-making tended to centre upon the court and the harpsichord was dominant, German music, typified by J. S. Bach, was firmly based in church, school and home, with organ and clavichord as the dominant keyboard instruments.

In 1760 a group of instrument makers arrived in London from Saxony. Their exodus is commonly attributed to the Seven Years War; but migrations are seldom so simply explained, and the attractions of the English market (to which we shall return) were probably an equally significant motive. Among these 'twelve apostles', as they became known in the trade, were Pohlmann and several of Silbermann's apprentices, including Johann Christoph Zumpe. After a short period of employment with Shudi, the founder of Broadwood's, Zumpe built up a successful business by specializing in the manufacture of square pianos for which his name practically became a synonym in England. Abroad, they were commonly known as 'pianos anglais'. Like Friederici's squares they were simple, small—about four feet long—and sold for upwards of £20. One of Zumpe's instruments, dated 1767, can be seen at the Victoria and Albert Museum (Plate I). Heard on a gramophone record, it is, in the writer's experience, rarely identified as a piano: uninitiated listeners describe it as a spinet or harpsichord.

In the late 1760s pianos were still a novelty. In 1767, a Covent Garden performance of the *Beggar's Opera* included a song which was advertised as being 'accompanied on a new instrument called Piano Forte'. [11] Its London debut as a solo instrument took place in the following year, when Johann Christian Bach played a Zumpe square, for which he had paid £50, at a benefit concert.[12] J. C. Bach was the instrument's first distinguished advocate. A new phase had begun.

An established instrument 1770–1830

Until about 1770 pianos were ambiguous instruments, transitional in construction and uncertain in status. As modified harpsichords or clavichords their outward appearance and quality of sound betrayed their origins. Makers were not yet specializing exclusively in their manufacture, for there were as yet few buyers, even among the prosperous English middle classes. Support came predominantly from amateurs; among professional players, composers and musical journalists, complaint still tended to outweigh advocacy. Although surviving evidence often reveals as much about the critic's prejudices and preoccupations as it does about an instrument's shortcomings, the conclusion is inescapable that the piano had not yet 'arrived'.[13] After 1770 the period of gestation is over, the pace quickens and pianos enter a phase of rapid technical and commercial advance. During the next sixty years, according to one authority, they acquired 'power and expressiveness', were 'scientifically designed to work efficiently and to continue to do so,' and generally underwent a transformation 'never exceeded in rapidity by the development of any other musical instrument'.[14] Each one of these statements is open to challenge: during the 1860s unprecedented improvements in power, durability and the application of science were effected by Steinway, achieving a fundamental revolution within two decades. But if enthusiasm for the 'classical grand pianoforte' requires modification in the light of later developments, it nevertheless conveys a correct impression of substantial progress.

Having emerged as a distinct instrument in its own right, the grand piano went on to supplant its rivals, acquiring greater structural and tonal strength, and a magnificent repertoire. The logic of its physical development was approximately as follows. In order to get a bigger and brighter sound, thicker strings were used at higher tensions, two or three to each note, except in the bass (hence the terms 'bichord' and 'trichord'), with improved methods of fixing. Overspun strings were used for the lower notes and the instrument's compass was increased. A typical keyboard of 1750 ranged over five octaves from F′ to F‴ (the third F below middle C to the third F above). By 1810 it commonly extended upwards to F⁗, and by 1820 downwards to C′—this was the compass of Beethoven's 1825 Graf. Larger hammers were used, covered with a variety of different materials. These changes greatly increased the strain on the instrument's frame, which therefore had to be reinforced, first with wooden braces and struts, later with metal. Actions, the complex mechanisms which transmit a player's touch from keys to hammers and dampers, were much improved.

This transformation took many years to complete, and even by the 1850s did not lead to uniformity of design. In describing its ramifications, it is difficult to strike a reasonable balance between the minimum technical and acoustical information required for general understanding, and a bewildering plethora of detail. Attempts at verbal description soon defeat their purpose, particularly in the case of actions, and diagrams or photographs are usually either too simple to be accurate or too complicated for any but specialist readers. We shall therefore attempt to keep discussion at a general level, adding further details at various stages of the narrative.

By 1780 two clearly defined types of grand piano had emerged, the German or Viennese, and the English. The former was lightly built (about one tenth the weight of a modern concert grand) and bichord, with a thin flat soundboard and tiny leather-covered hammers. Its beautiful, even but thin tone suggests a louder clavichord. The touch was shallow, only half the depth of a modern piano, and requiring much less force. English pianos were more substantial in structure and sound, trichord with thicker strings and soundboard, the latter convexly shaped. Damping was less efficient, touch deeper and more cumbersome, tone louder, resembling a harpsichord, and unevenly balanced between bass and treble. Their actions were of totally different design, the Viennese simpler and more direct. The mechanical details and the continuing debate about their respective merits need not detain us, for one fact is of overriding significance to the history of music. Whereas the English piano required and was capable of further development, the Viennese instrument was already good enough for Mozart who, within a decade, created for it a series of masterpieces, most notably the piano concertos, 'the peak of all his instrumental achievement'.[15] All authorities agree that these works, at least after K. 414 (1782), were intended for the piano not the harpsichord.[16] The best evidence is in the music: flowing melodic lines, uncluttered by embellishment, compete and blend with the most lyrical of instruments, woodwinds and horn. Even more remarkable is the *scena*, 'Ch'io mi scorda di te', for soprano, piano and orchestra, K. 505. Einstein regards the piano part as 'a souvenir of the taste and depth of his playing' but it is also a tribute to the Viennese piano's ability to sing. Nine years earlier, Mozart had expressed his delight in a much quoted but indispensable letter. Writing from Augsburg on 17 October 1777, he describes the instruments of Johann Andreas Stein. Their tone is even, with clean damping, because they have an escapement which obviates jangling and vibration. The knee pedal is sensitive, without the least reverberation. Stein's love of music leads him to finish each instrument with infinite patience 'until it can do anything'. Every soundboard is deliberately cracked by exposure to rain and sun, then wedged and glued so that it will never crack again. Thus the supreme artist pays tribute to a master craftsman.[17]

Meanwhile, John Broadwood was redesigning the English piano. A Scottish carpenter who had joined the Swiss harpsichord maker Shudi in London in 1761, his subsequent career is a classic example of pioneering craftsmanship and enterprise. In 1769 he married his master's daughter and was taken into partnership. Shudi's son succeeded to the partnership in 1773 and possibly acted as a brake on the progressive Scot; but he withdrew some twenty years later, leaving Broadwood in sole command of a firm which was soon to become the largest piano manufacturer in Europe. Broadwood's activities were influenced by science, market opportunities and music. His energies were first devoted to the square piano. Despite their manifest inadequacies, Zumpe's instruments had become sufficiently popular for him to subcontract work to Pohlmann, a business practice which became increasingly common thereafter. According to Dr Burney, there was 'scarcely a house in the kingdom where a keyed instrument had ever admission but was supplied with one of Zumpe's pianofortes, for which there was nearly as great a call in France as in England'.[18] Attracted by these prospects Broadwood entirely reconstructed Zumpe's primitive design. By 1780 he had shifted the wrest plank and pins from the right, as in the clavichord, to the back of the case, straightened the keys, improved the dampers and replaced Zumpe's hand stops by 'loud' and 'soft' pedals.

After patenting his improvements to the square in 1783, Broadwood turned to the design of grand pianos. This was a return to old interests, for during the late sixties he had worked with Backers and Robert Stodart on modifications of Cristofori's action. The precise authorship of the so-called 'English' grand action is uncertain,[19] but the improved mechanism was firmly established by Broadwood, along with trichord stringing and the *una corda* pedal, borrowed from earlier makers. His original and vital contribution was to design a new string scale and striking point for the hammers. Whereas in the past these crucial aspects of the instrument had been decided arbitrarily, Broadwood sought the advice of two acousticians, Gray and Cavallo. By 1788 he had produced a vastly improved instrument, with enhanced sonority, greater evenness throughout the range and increased dynamic flexibility.

Like all successful entrepreneurs, John Broadwood had a sense of market opportunity and the capacity to exploit it. The unique advantages of the English market derived less from the quality of musical life than from the affluence and social ambitions of a prosperous middle class. It was essentially a matter of income and spending power which was greater, more widespread, and growing faster in Britain than anywhere else. In every European country there was a small, circumscribed market for luxury goods and services—jewellery, fashionable clothing, fine furniture, theatre and music. But only in Britain was there a large and expanding middle class, eager to spend for prestige, enjoyment and self-improvement.[20] Its demands were increasingly felt in England by the 1770s. In Scotland the piano became popular during the 1780s, and in Dublin several piano-makers started business before 1790.[21] Not yet a mass market, it was expanding rapidly enough to attract pianists, teachers and pianomakers, who could exploit a new commercialization of leisure with a potent symbol of social emulation. Possession of a piano was evidence of gentility, ability to play it a necessary feminine 'accomplishment', recognized everywhere as 'one of the primary ornaments in the education of women'. The quotation is from Diderot's *Encyclopédie* and refers to the harpsichord in France, although it was also true of high society in Russia, Europe and America. In Britain the piano usurped this function; aspiration started lower in the social scale, and was therefore more widespread and more vulgar. Teachers and pupils were assisted by a proliferation of instruction books, compiled with a callowness which betrays their cultural milieu: 'New Guida di musica, or book of instructions for beginners on the pianoforte, 7/6d.'; '*The Musical Assistant* . . . theory and practice of the pianoforte', an album of trumpery snippets, facile melodies with a rudimentary bass, and emasculated 'duettino' arrangements from *Figaro* and Haydn's *Surprise* Symphony! The same compiler, James Coggins, presented a 'Companion to *The Musical Assistant*, containing all that is . . . necessary for the information of young performers on that fashionable instrument'. The *British Lady's Magazine* highly recommended it to 'those to whose superintendence the musical practice of young ladies is so generally entrusted'. There was even a *Pianoforte Magazine*, published each week between 1797 and 1802, at 2*s* 6*d* a copy. Buyers of the complete set were promised a free piano, but the project did not survive. All this is a far cry from Bach's Notebook for Anna Magdalena, or the extensive elementary solo and duet repertoire by the Viennese masters, but it was a rich market, easy to exploit.

For piano makers the attractions of this domestic market were augmented by the proximity of France. We have already referred to the popularity of *pianos anglais* during the 1770s. It became fashionable to identify the new instrument as quintessentially English. The castrato singer Albaneze celebrated 'l'arrivé du forte-piano': 'How now, dear friend, thou comest to us from England: Ah then, how could anyone declare war upon her?' To the Chevalier de Piis its very tone suggested the 'phlegmatic English' and, 'like an ungrateful child, jeers at the frail harpsichord'.[22] In a list of instruments confiscated during the French

Revolution half the pianos, but only one harpsichord, came from England.[23] Ease of transport was obviously a contributing factor to the success of London makers. We can appreciate the comparative isolation of Vienna by recalling the journey endured by the instrument which Broadwood sent to Beethoven in 1818—by ship to Trieste and then carted 360 miles over the Alps and along primitive roads. Few Viennese instruments travelled in the opposite direction. French makers, of course, were better located, but their progress was disrupted by revolution and war: several, including Erard and Pape, fled to London, with results to be described in the following pages.

Broadwood stopped making harpsichords for a dying market in 1793 when the younger Shudi left the firm, and vigorously expanded the production of pianos. In addition to improving the instrument's technical quality, his technical innovations were a step towards rationalizing its mode of production and expanding output. During the subsequent decade he made over one hundred grand pianos a year, in addition to some three hundred squares. The implications of this expansion are significant, not merely for the history of the leading and therefore untypical firm, but as indicating an important change in the productive process. The leading craftsmen of the eighteenth century produced, with the assistance of half a dozen apprentices, about twenty instruments a year. Both Shudi and Stein operated on this scale. Kirkman (1710–92), whom Fanny Burney described as 'the first harpsichord maker of the times', made some forty instruments a year at the peak of his activity.[24] One of Stein's best pupils, J. D. Schiedmayer (1753–1805), whose son was to establish a famous German house, usually worked alone, and must therefore have produced even fewer clavichords and pianos.[25] Stein's daughter, Nanette Streicher, who became one of Vienna's leading manufacturers, was making about fifty pianos a year by 1815. Broadwood's output was about eight times larger in quantity, and probably even greater in value. Does this mean that the piano had now become, as Max Weber suggests, a product of 'machine-made mass production'?[26]

It is a commonplace in the economic history of this period that increased production of a variety of goods at lower prices was achieved by specialization and mechanization, which were in turn dependent upon widening markets. By this process of industrial revolution the productivity, and therefore the earning power, of labour was increased while consumers got better and cheaper products. Several of these factors were at work in English piano manufacture, particularly in Broadwood's factory, with an important exception: machinery was almost wholly absent. The prevalence of hand labour throughout the industry must not be exaggerated. Even the eighteenth-century harpsichord maker was not required to reduce tree trunks to planks, and plane 'great shaggy timbers to thickness'.[27] There was already some division of labour. A highly organized international timber market supplied a bewildering variety of special woods. Hinges, metal work and wire could be purchased from specialist firms: not that such 'buying out' was always indicative of industrial progress for, particularly in France, it was commonly enforced by rigid and minute guild regulations which restricted various processes to particular trades. As Hubbard justly remarks, this imposed a 'milieu so legalistic and categorized' as to be 'extremely discouraging to the inventive worker'. Here, as in other respects, London manufacturers gained by working in a comparatively open society where guild regulations had long been dead. Several of them were therefore more efficient and progressive than their continental rivals, though not wholly free of conservative practice and entrenched tradition. Most significant is the fact that even in Broadwood's factory the manufacturing process could not be described as undergoing an industrial revolution; *pace* the impressionistic view of several writers.[28]

The neglect of machinery is remarkable at a time when other industries were rapidly adopting new technology, and woodworking machines were being developed. A planing machine invented in 1779, circular saws and slide rests, were adopted by the Navy and manufactured under Samuel Bentham's direction during the French wars. Whatever deterred John Broadwood and his sons, who joined the firm in 1795 and 1807, from adopting such devices, it was certainly not lack of capital. The business was sufficiently profitable to leave considerable funds for investment in property and shipping. Between 1785 and 1797 these disbursements amounted to nearly £8,000 which, nurtured by compound interest, made a substantial contribution to the family fortune.[29] Such activities followed the tradition established by Jacob Kirkman, whose progress was almost a caricature of the genre. According to the indispensable Dr Burney he captured the widow of his employer, the harpsichord maker Herman Tabel, one month after the latter's death, proposing at breakfast and marrying the same morning, 'without loss of time, or hindrance of business'. The lady died two years later but Kirkman prospered greatly, doubling 'the profits of his instruments by becoming a pawnbroker and a usurer'.[30] Since Burney was wrong about the date of Kirkman's death, which actually took place in 1792, and almost certainly exaggerated the value of his estate, which he put at £200,000, these stories must not be taken literally. But their general import is clear: the manufacture of keyboard instruments was highly remunerative for those who could establish a 'name', though they were apparently not wholly committed to reinvestment in the productive process. This does not mean that the leading makers were foolish or inefficient. In fashionable trades the salesroom is commonly more important than the factory, and price-cutting less desirable than, and possibly inimical to, a reputation for quality and exclusiveness: 'An article is likely to be dropped from the list of those used to express social standing when it has been once firmly seized upon by machine industry.' [31] In piano manufacture, without machinery and a far more rational division of labour, productivity remained low and prices therefore high. Even at Broadwood's where output (not productivity) was greatly increased, the second generation was probably less concerned with the organization of production than with their fashionable clientele. More generally, despite the appearance of a few large firms, piano-making remained a craft, expanded to be sure, but not yet a factory industry.

Musical influences: composition, technique and technology

It was a paradox that London should become a centre of piano manufacture for, despite those apologists who purport to see oases in the desert which separates Purcell and Elgar, by continental standards England was then 'the land without music'. No English composer of the period achieved more than a modest competence, and no instrumentalist, if we exclude the Irishman Field, a more than parochial reputation. Perhaps it is unduly naïve to attribute the banality of English music to the weakness of formal musical education [32]—what did any great composer learn at music college? But the absence of professional training—scarcely affected by the foundation of the Royal Academy of Music in 1822—reinforced a tradition of amateur mediocrity among composers and performers which remained pervasive for the rest of the century. What England did offer was an attractive platform for visiting pianists, and therefore for native instruments. This is a rare example of a simple relationship between musical and technical developments. The new emphasis upon contrast in music, an essential feature of sonata form, was reinforced by the technical demands of virtuoso pianists who converged upon London. Steibelt, Dussek—said to have been the first pianist to place the instrument sideways to his audience so that they might admire his profile—Hummel and Cramer all played the new Broadwoods in London, stimulating and demonstrating technical improvements. Clementi above all epitomized the new style in his playing and compositions: a proliferation of octaves, heavy chords and widely expressive shading. Mozart's well-known disparagement of Clementi, which followed their pianistic 'duel' at the Emperor's Vienna Court in 1782, is relevant here. [33] For in later years Clementi attributed the subsequent refinement of his style to the study of good singing, and to 'the perfected mechanism of English pianos, the construction of which formerly stood in the way of a *cantabile* and *legato* style of playing'.[34] It was in London, more than any other city at the turn of the century, that manufacturers and pianists impressed their techniques of construction, composition and performance upon each other, and the image of an exciting new instrument and musical experience upon the public.

Such concerts became increasingly popular, to the frequently expressed disapproval of the more solemn critics and equally common acclaim of their gushing contemporaries. In 1835 the *Musical Magazine* was particularly incensed by Henri Herz, 'the great musical mountebank, whose new grand concerto in D minor is anything but new or grand'.[35] Herz both played and made, or at least attached his name to, pianos. A few years later the *Musical Journal* was urging piano manufacturers to 'testify their gratitude to Thalberg for the rapid destruction of instruments which the practice of his music has occasioned—the sale, we hear, is recently increased thirty per cent'. Thalberg's yearly income was variously estimated between £3,000 and £10,000, and confidently totalled at £24,000 by 1840, at least half of which had been earned in England.[36] In fact he was a comparatively gentle pianist, well mannered and a darling of the Victorian public. When this 'prince of piano players ... gave a concert to the gentry residing in the vicinity of Blackheath' it was noted that he played an Erard grand.[37] More obviously in the grand tradition of charlatan-virtuoso was Leopold de Mayer, 'the great Lion Pianist .... When he is first heard attentively, you feel a sort of thankfulness he has concluded ... the greatest instrumental marvel we have ever listened to ... his fantasia from *Semiramide*, his *Lucia*' (Donizetti's opera). The Lion was about to roar in America, where we shall join him in a later chapter. A London puff (presumably placed by his agent) was breathlessly convinced of 'the immense sensation he must create in Yankeeland'.[38] On at least one occasion there was an apparently genuine attempt to let the public judge the relative merits of different instruments. In 1823 Moscheles gave a recital in Vienna on a piano by Conrad Graf (1782-1851), doyen of the Viennese makers, and Beethoven's Broadwood. The verdict was predictably equivocal, the audience preferring the Graf's clear, bright tone, while at least one Englishman present admired the Broadwood's greater power. Doubtless it was an unfair match, for the London instrument had endured an arduous journey and five years of agonized maltreatment by the deaf composer. But the dispute continues to the present day: one authority is convinced that Beethoven preferred the Broadwood to all his other pianos—and he had a wide choice.[39] Another remarks that the composer praised the instrument before its arrival, that it meant no more to him than a prestigious gift, and that in 1826, a year before his death, he regarded not only the Broadwood but all contemporary pianos as inadequate. He wanted 'a heavier action, a sturdier instrument, and a bigger tone'.[40]

It was common practice for concert pianists to give lessons. In 1836 the young Charles Hallé explained to his parents how the system worked in Paris. Chopin and Liszt charged twenty francs a lesson; good teachers could command twelve francs, and even 'second-rate lessons' cost five. Since one could live comfortably on two hundred francs a month Hallé was optimistic about his prospects. Twelve years later he fled from revolution to London, only to find the circus stars already there: among the pianists appearing that season were Chopin, Kalkbrenner, Pixis, Pillet, Prudent and Thalberg. But the market was still large enough for a competent teacher, and in Manchester there was no shortage of paying pupils.[41] The espousal of a chosen instrument at public concerts, commonly financed by the manufacturer, and its recommendation to pupils, was an important link between makers and professional pianists. Despite obvious abuses it was a healthy, indeed an essential relationship, for how else could the quality of the best instruments and incentives to improvement be assured? Probably the best example is the friendship between Bechstein and von Bülow described in Chapter 4. The lack of such relationships in the English industry after about 1860 was both a symptom and, arguably, one cause of its subsequent decline.

Since every concert pianist at that time was a composer, with results descending from Liszt's sonata to de Mayer's *Lucia*, one might expect there to have been a fruitful relationship between the instrument and its music. We have already touched upon the early history of this connection, in terms of challenge and response, but further discussion is elusive and controversial. At one extreme we have the view that 'instruments came first, the music followed';[42] or, as expressed by Tovey, that 'the compass of the piano hampered Beethoven in all his works for it'.[43] At the other extreme no less an authority than E. J. Dent was convinced that only 'second rate composers . . . are stimulated by mechanical inventions'— the great composer leads and instrument makers try to follow.[44] The divorce of opinion is too complete to allow an anodyne conclusion: the truth lies somewhere between. If the discussion is merely about technique and technology then fairly clear relationships can be established. It is when we consider the possibility of a more fundamental interaction between musical composition and 'mechanical invention' that Dent's view becomes persuasive.

There are fairly obvious links between a particular mechanical improvement and the pianist's ability to execute certain kinds of *bravura* passage. One example is Sebastien Erard's invention of the 'double escapement' action, patented in 1821. This enabled any note to be repeated quickly without its key having to return to the full height (level with the keyboard) before restriking. Moreover, such repetition could be achieved not as a dull reiteration, which had previously been exploited by several earlier makers and players, but with a controlled rhythmical emphasis. It extended the performer's vocabulary, making possible such virtuoso compositions as Liszt's Paganini Studies, including the revised version of *La Campanella*, 'unthinkable without Erard'.[45] But to describe it as providing the essential basis for modern pianoforte technique is to exaggerate the capabilities of the pre-Steinway piano.[46] Modern technique for performance to large audiences was developed by such powerful players as von Bülow and Anton Rubinstein—who were notorious for smashing instruments—and further extended by the later Russian and American schools. No piano built on the old system could meet such demands: virtuoso technique and the work of the best piano makers advanced together, achieving enormously increased sonority, responsiveness and control.

As John Ogdon explains in an illuminating essay on the romantic tradition, new styles of piano playing developed very slowly.[47] An exclusively digital technique was first extended by greater reliance upon the wrist and forearm. When Saint-Saëns (1835–1921) looked back to the playing standards of his youth he remembered that Liszt's compositions 'seemed impossible to play, except by him, and such they were if you recall the old method which prescribed complete immobility, elbows tucked into the body and all action of the muscles limited to fingers and forearm'.[48] Later development gave freedom to the upper arms and shoulders, in quest of greater power and dexterity.

The extent to which these improvements can be based upon scientific analysis is demonstrated in Ortmann's massive 'Physiological Mechanics of Piano Technique',[49] but elsewhere there is a fair measure of mystique and still much disagreement. Thus, a standard work on the physics of music dismisses the books of Tobias Matthay, whose many pupils included Myra Hess, as very high in 'nonsense content'. Particular scorn is reserved for Matthay's discussion of forty-two distinct piano touches, for science 'proves' that a pianist cannot influence the quality, as distinct from the loudness, of single notes by the way he strikes the keys.[50] Yet music critics use an all too familiar vocabulary to distinguish the singing (pearly, velvet, beautiful, or harsh, percussive, ugly) touch of individual performers. In 1951, eight leading English pianists were asked in an elaborate questionnaire if they thought they could influence tone; only one, Denis Matthews, accepted the verdict of science.[51] By far the best discussion of this thorny question is in Backus' indispensable book. As he explains, physicists do not argue that all pianists sound alike on the same piano. 'Touch' involves an infinitely complex amalgam of qualities—evenness, legato, emphasis of individual notes in a chord—but loudness and tone are interdependent and are determined simply by the speed of the hammers.[52] Yet most pianists and many listeners will remain unconvinced.

Turning from technique to composition, it is an amusing, but ultimately profitless exercise to trace examples where a composer has been 'limited' by the instrument at his disposal. Beethoven's *Waldstein*, *Appassionata*, and *Les Adieux* sonatas display successive increases in the piano's compass, while opus 106, the *Hammerklavier*, required the six and a half octaves of his Streicher instrument. This is not to say that earlier works were restricted, in any meaningful sense, by a reduced keyboard. Thus in the 'cello sonata, opus 69, a comparison between bars 55–57 and 192–194 of the first movement reveals modifications in the piano part which were apparently dictated by 'running out of notes' at the top of the keyboard. But in this and similar passages, conjecture about how they might have been written for a bigger instrument can rightly be dismissed as 'idle speculation'.[53]

For Chopin and Liszt there were no comparable limitations of compass: a full seven octaves were available, from the fourth A below middle C to the fourth G above. Indeed some contemporaries regarded this extension of the keyboard as excrescent. In 1840, the *Musical Journal* dismissed instruments by Stodart, Wornum and Collard with keyboards shorter than a modern piano's because the extreme notes were 'nearly out of the reach of performers of ordinary dimensions'—an extraordinary comment on early Victorian physique.[54] A more serious weakness was the thin wooden sound of the upper notes. In saying this we touch upon another controversy, or rather a new conventional wisdom which must not go unchallenged. In recent years it has become fashionable to extol the merits of old pianos with an unguarded enthusiasm which goes much further than Gough's praise of the classical grand (quoted on page 14). The modern piano is said to 'sound elephantine by comparison', to 'falsify the musical sense of what Schubert wrote'; the accompaniments to the *Winterreise* and *Schöne Müllerin* song cycles apparently 'cry out for the early instrument'. Recordings are eagerly anticipated of the *Hammerklavier* on an early nineteenth-century Broadwood, of Chopin on an 1840 French piano, and Schumann on a German instrument of the 1850s.[55] One is tempted to ask if such critics have ever listened to Britten accompanying Schubert songs, Brendel playing a Mozart concerto, Perlemuter in Chopin, or Richter in Schumann. No doubt musical criticism has progressed since Huneker's conjectures about what Chopin would have 'accomplished with the modern grand',[56] but the new antiquarianism is not wholly acceptable as a substitute for the old belief in inevitable progress. In the first place it ignores the late ninetenth century's rejection of the old technology, or implicitly regards it as an aberration. Since later chapters deal with this we shall not discuss it further at this stage. But secondly, the new fashion assumes too ready an acceptance of the old instruments' alleged superiority, and a disregard for their manifest inadequacies.

It must be admitted that instruments cannot be assessed with complete objectivity, for players and listeners have different preconceptions and requirements. Modern attempts to understand past sound through reconstructed instruments add a further veil of obscurity, for pianos, unlike violins, deteriorate with age and use. No doubt present-day craftsmen have greatly increased their knowledge and skill in rebuilding old instruments, but acceptance of their offerings is by no means unequivocal. The same pianos which lead one enthusiast to proclaim a golden age of rediscovery earn from another expert critic the comment that their 'sound is painfully bad, and no amount of reconstruction has brought the instruments, long dead, back to life'.[57]

Readers can judge for themselves by examining the finely reconstructed Broadwoods in Edinburgh's Russell Collection, or the more extensive private collection of C. F. Colt at Bethersden in Kent. Several excellent recordings have been issued, but their availability changes so rapidly that no details will be listed here. Special mention, however, must be made of a BBC recording of Malcolm Binns playing Schubert's *Wanderer* Fantasy on a piano by the Viennese maker Haschka (*c.* 1825) from the Colt Collection. This unbraced, wooden-framed instrument has a warmth of tone and a silvery treble which are the most convincing testimony for the old technology known to the present writer. Nevertheless it must be noted that Paul Badura-Skoda, probably the most distinguished scholar-performer in this field, is least dogmatic in his claims for old pianos. He even reminds us that Curt Sachs, the eminent musicologist, used to say that the more he had to do with old instruments the less desire he had to hear them![58]

If we juxtapose these considerations of technology and technique it may be agreed that comparisons between old and new instruments have little meaning without reference to methods and standards of performance. For example, it is said that early pianos 'speak' more easily and clearly, particularly in the bass, where individual notes of a chord are heard with a clarity denied to the 'woolly' modern instrument. Yet the technique of Arrau or Michelangeli makes nonsense of these claims. Any piano music can be satisfactorily played on a modern instrument by an artist with adequate technique and a sense of style. In Schubert's posthumous B-flat Sonata the low bass trills are executed with perfect clarity by Brendel or Serkin, and the textures of his *Wanderer* Fantasy never sound muddled in the hands of a Richter or Pollini. Sometimes a composer demands effects no longer possible on modern instruments, but these tend to be peripheral and their fulfilment not vital to satisfactory performance. An interesting example occurs in the second movement of Beethoven's Fourth Concerto, which calls for the use of a true *una corda* pedal, leaving the hammer to strike only one string. The sound is charming, but scarcely indispensable.[59] Few established concert pianists are willing to relearn their technique in order to play old instruments. Their lack of enthusiasm, like that of the general musical public, reflects broad satisfaction with the far more versatile and reliable modern piano. The 'Forte-piano' is likely to remain a minority cult.

Ironically it is the modern economics of the recording industry—mass production, high productivity and low prices—which give old pianos their widest audience. And this is as much to be welcomed as the earlier revival of the harpsichord, for it engenders a greater awareness of the composer's requirements and a better sense of style. Sometimes it is a matter of detail. We now know, as presumably Tovey did not, that the pianos of Beethoven's day were capable of sustaining tone and that the pedal could not therefore be held down through changes in harmony. Since literal reading of the pedal markings in such passages as the opening of the *Moonlight* Sonata, or the Third Concerto's slow movement, gives a meaningless jumble of sounds—on both old and new pianos—it must be because indications were imprecise and required the player's common sense.[60] But there are wider benefits from playing and listening to the old instruments. The anachronisms of bad style, although they persist, are more easily assessed: elephantine performances of the Beethoven concertos (available in a currently popular album of records), brutal assaults upon Chopin, inflated (once popular) or 'Dresden china' (all too common) interpretations of Mozart. The remedy for these solecisms lies less in a return to the pianos which, for reasons to be discussed in later chapters, were discarded a century ago, than in the intelligent and informed playing of modern instruments. It is a striking fact that some of the most 'orchestral' music in the piano repertoire was written before the birth of the modern piano, i.e. before the Steinway revolution: Schumann's *Fantasia* (1836), the Liszt Sonata (1853) and Brahms' First Piano Concerto (1858), to name only a few familiar examples, demanded a power and tonal range beyond the resources of contemporary instruments. We return therefore to Dent: the great composers led, and instrument makers tried to follow.

Chapter 2

The Victorian Piano

Visitors to the Great Exhibition of 1851 were probably impressed by the range of pianos on display. Table I lists the numbers and nationalities of the exhibitors. Among them were a few old English firms, including Broadwood and Kirkman, and many newcomers. The great French tradition was represented primarily by Erard, with instruments from both its Paris and London factories. There was also an entry by Henry Pape, whose mechanical ingenuity and profound influence upon a generation of craftsmen were never matched by success in business. Among the German contingent were instruments by J. L. Schiedmayer, Breitkopf and Härtel, the renowned music publishers, and a modest square piano by Lipp. Remarkably, there were no Austrian pianos of quality: although prizes were abundant, even for modest or eccentric achievement, no Austrian maker received even an honourable mention. The American entry, in prophetic contrast, was led by the iron-framed instruments of Jonas Chickering. Here were the best products of American industry, claimed *The Times*, their excellence compensating for the country's poor showing elsewhere in the Exhibition.

Several of these names were to survive into the twentieth century, some, like Schiedmayer and Lipp, with enhanced reputations; others merely as names. But the modern reader of the Exhibition catalogue will be struck by the absence of familiar makers. Some, like Pleyel of Paris (the instrument on which Chopin made his debut) and Bösendorfer of Vienna, who made pianos that could withstand even the young Liszt, did not exhibit. But the three most eminent firms of modern times did not appear because they did not yet exist. The statement is more than a gratuitous truism because it focuses attention upon a theme to be explored in later pages: the advantages of a late start. If there is an *annus mirabilis* in pianoforte history it must be 1853, when Steinway (New York), Bechstein (Berlin) and Blüthner (Leipzig) all commenced business.

The catalogues,[1] jury report and contemporary comment upon the Exhibition are useful guides to the state of the industry, its products and potential customers. In external appearance the fashion, like that for furniture,[2] was for ornate decoration, ranging from a grotesquely carved,

Table I   Pianos at the Great Exhibition of London in 1851

Country of origin	Makers exhibiting	Instruments	Makers gaining prize medals or 'honourable mention'
England	38	66	12
France	21	45	9
Germany *	18	26	8
Belgium	6	16	5
United States	6	10	4
Austria	5	6	–
Switzerland	3	3	1
Canada & Nova Scotia	2	2	–
Russia	1	2	1
Denmark	2	2	1

* States of the German Zollverein.

thousand-guinea Erard grand, to Metzler's 'small cottage with ornamental shell front'. Elaborate casework might conceal a useful musical instrument, but an apparently unbridgeable gulf separated the skilled, if idiosyncratic, craftsmanship of the great makers from the freakish 'invention' and pretentious nomenclature which prevailed elsewhere. Thus Greiner showed a 'semi-grand on the principle of the speaking trumpet'; Smyth and Roberts a cottage (i.e. a small upright) instrument, backed 'on the principle of the violoncello'; and Luff the 'registered tavola pianoforte' in which a 'drawing room table stands upon a centre block or pedestal, and contains a pianoforte (opening with spring bolts) on the grand principle, with a closet containing music composed by the inventor'. There was a vocabulary of puff to impress the gullible: microchordan, registered compensation, lyra cottage, microphonic, utiliton. For another half century eccentric claims and pseudo-scientific terminology were to litter advertisements and the patent lists. Charles Hampton of Fitzroy Square offers a representative example in a full-page advertisement, with illustrations of nine models priced at twenty to sixty-five guineas which appeared in *The Musical Monthly* in December 1864. His 'compressed pianofortes' were said to embody an 'invention dating from 1860 . . . acknowledged to be the most important improvement of the present day in the construction of cottage pianos'. Each instrument had five metal tubes and was subjected to 'ten tons pressure in the direction of the strings for one month'. Such technomongering can obscure the history of genuine technical development, unless we understand something of the instrument's mechanics.

Mid-nineteenth century technology

This is not a technical treatise on pianoforte construction; nor is economic and social history to be equated with the history of technology. Nevertheless, the process and impact of technological change cannot be described without some explanation of the instrument's basic construction. The attempt should, however, be understood as an amateur guide for amateurs. Piano technicians should no more seek enlightenment here than would an engineer expect accuracy of detail in a history of iron and steel in the industrial revolution.

We can begin with the 'scale' or stringing of the instrument, the correct design of which requires a grasp of certain basic acoustical principles.[3] When a string is struck it vibrates as a whole, but it also separates itself into nodes, or resting points, and internodal lengths. The note which is heard consists of the fundamental tone plus a series of upper partials, the first five of which make up the notes of a common chord and are thus consonant. It is therefore desirable, as Helmholtz explained in 1862 and as generations of piano makers worked out empirically both before and since, to 'develop' these partials in a string, but to suppress as far as possible the seventh, ninth and tenth, which are dissonant.[4] The pitch of a note and its quality, determined by the relative intensities of the various partials (including the fundamental), depend upon the length of the string, its thickness, stiffness, weight and tension. To design a good piano one must therefore select a number of strings of different lengths and thickness between bass and treble, in gradations which ensure not merely correct pitches but a smooth transition in tone quality through the register. Carefully weighing these qualities the designer attempts to choose a perfect set of metal strings. Modern practice tends to favour steel wire for the treble and steel overspun with copper for the bass, but brass, silver, platinum and gold have all been used in the past.[5] A string selected for appropriate pitch may be too thin to survive adequate blows from the hammer and will therefore give a feeble tone, or break. An increase in weight might yield insufficient partials and thus inadequate tone. During the late nineteenth century, the thickness and tension of strings were greatly increased, giving strength and brilliance, particularly in the treble. Pianos before the 1860s were singularly lacking in these qualities—strings broke frequently and the top octave degenerated into a wooden knock. A significant advance was made by Horsfall who, in 1854, introduced an 'incredible new process' which effected 'a complete revolution in the trade' of wire manufacture.[6] Before this wire could only be drawn to a tensile strain of sixty to seventy tons per square inch. Horsfall's piano wire was much stronger and was seized upon for a wide range of industrial purposes. The scalemaker's problems do not end when he has successfully juggled with length, weight, thickness and tension. He must next lay the strings in appropriate position. Traditional practice was to place them in parallel lengths, but there were obvious advantages to be gained from crossing bass over treble. This procedure of 'overstringing' allowed the alternatives of saving space, obviously important in designing upright or small grand pianos, or using longer strings with better tonal results. It also offered the possibility of more effective use of the soundboard (see below). Successful application of this principle awaited a designer of genius.

Meanwhile there were many experiments. Pape introduced a cross-strung 'pianino' only one metre high in 1828 [7] and was said by 1842 to be getting 'extraordinary power and tone' from small instruments.[8] A cross-strung semi-grand by the Belgian maker Lichtenthal, who had settled in St Petersburg, received 'honourable mention' at the 1851 Exhibition, but is dismissed by Hipkins as a 'curiosity' designed for symmetry of case rather than improved tone.[9] There was wide-spread prejudice against overstringing, particularly among conservative English and French makers, which is difficult to disentangle from their simultaneous condemnation of iron frames. But a clear distinction should be made at this stage between the ultimate success of overstringing—brilliantly applied by Steinway as part of an integrated scientific design—and its earlier, and often subsequent misapplication by inept manufacturers attempting to cram an ill-brewed quart into a cracked pint pot. In such cases bass strings gave an unpleasant 'tubby' sound and there was a distinct 'break' in tone at the point of crossing, which could only be camouflaged by skilled treatment of the hammer surfaces. Both these weaknesses can be detected, even in some of today's small uprights and baby grands, and help to explain the persistence of vertical stringing into the first decade of the twentieth century among some conservative makers of quality. Harding suggests another practical reason for the unpopularity of early attempts at overstringing. When professional tuners were rare, the amateur found broken cross strings very difficult to replace. For the same reason there were several unsuccessful attempts to simplify tuning; one such device was advertised, with a testimonial from Thalberg, as indispensable 'in country places and warm climates'.[10]

Quality of tone is also affected by the point at which the string is struck, the material used to cover hammer heads, and the weight and decisiveness of the blow. Deciding the best point of impact requires careful selection of a position where dissonant partials are effectively eliminated and consonant partials retained; the nearer the centre of a string, the greater the intensity of the lower partials and the more 'hollow' the tone. Shifting towards the end of a string increases the intensity of dissonant partials and makes the tone more piercing which, after a little wear, results in a 'tinpan' quality, sometimes exploited today for commercial effect. Mid-nineteenth-century pianos, even concert grands, had small hammers, not markedly different from the 'tiny light shapeless implement of the eighteenth century'.[11] Their covering had to withstand the cutting force of continual impact against the string, but materials were also selected for their influence on tone. These requirements encouraged experiments with an incredible range of substances, including cork, rubber, sponge, various kinds of cloth, even tinder, singly and in combination.[12] Leather, the traditional material, was still common enough in 1851 to merit a special display at the Exhibition by an Austrian manufacturer.[13] Felt was already much in use, but its existing forms were even less durable than leather. Several firms in England, France and Germany began to specialize in the manufacture of felt which was both durable and sufficiently elastic not to 'block' the hammer on the string. But hammers were still covered by hand, a slow and therefore expensive process which had the additional disadvantage of stretching the felt and damaging its elasticity.

A clean, precise blow and effective damping are also essential for good tone. The complex mechanism which transmits finger stroke to hammer and damper is known as the action, fairly described as a 'triumph of nineteenth-century technical ingenuity'.[14] Apart from keys and hammers, it consists essentially of two elements: 1. A device which allows a key to throw its hammer at the string, called the escapement. 2. A mechanism which raises the damper at the moment of touch, thus freeing the string to sound, and then returns it and stops the note immediately the finger leaves a key. The (horizontal) grand pianoforte's dampers fall back by their own weight as keys are released, but in (vertical) uprights they have to be pressed back against the strings, adding fresh difficulties to an already cumbersome device. Early actions were deficient in many respects: clumsy, tending to 'block' or bounce, and requiring frequent skilled attention. The quality of an action is judged by its ability to avoid these faults, to impart rapidly a clean start and tidy finish to each note, and to continue so for many years. Without this no instrument is satisfactory. Erard's 'repetition' action (see page 22), later simplified by Herz, solved most of these problems for grand pianos before 1850 and was copied by many makers. Uprights proved more intractable. The clumsy 'sticker' action is illustrated in Plate 3. Broadwood made nearly 9,000 of these absurdly tall 'cabinet' pianos between 1812 and 1856,[15] and variants of the sticker were still used in cheap English pianos until late in the nineteenth century. Robert Wornum's 'tape check' action, invented *c*. 1840, was more compact and successful, forming a working basis for modern upright mechanisms, but it took several decades to develop effectively.[16]

In 1850 inadequate and expensive actions were one of the principal
impediments to the manufacture of good cheap domestic pianos.

The soundboard is an amplifier, without which the vibrations of a
piano's strings transmitted to it by the bridge would be practically in-
audible. So that it can resist the string's pressure, a soundboard must be
supported by carefully positioned ribs: sufficient in number to prevent it
from sagging and weakening the tone; not so many as to render it unduly
stiff and resistant to vibration. It must be well seasoned for, since it cannot
normally be replaced, the useful life of an instrument depends upon the
soundboard's durability. We have already referred to Mozart's description of this traditional process at its laborious best. The design and preparation of soundboards have always been regarded as one of the great
'mysteries' of the craft, subject to endless experiment in the selection and
treatment of woods and placing of ribs, much skill and, on occasion, much
'mumbo jumbo'. The scope for standardized mass production was nevertheless self evident.

Beneath a grand and behind an upright lies a system of wooden bracing,
like the beams and rafters of a house. Its function changed with the adoption of the iron frame. The traditional craftsman built his frame with
massive timbers and dovetailed cross braces, attaching a wrest plank ('pin
block' in America) which held the tuning pins taking the strings. The
strain was enormous and grew rapidly as the instrument's compass was
extended, its pitch raised and string weight increased. The total force on
the frame of a concert grand increased from about sixteen to thirty tons
between 1860 and the 1930s. Wood was expensive, difficult to replicate,
and ill-suited to such burdens: clumsy and sensitive to climatic change,
its frequent expansions and contractions ruined string tensions and tuning.

In an age of rapidly advancing metallurgy and its application to a
widening range of industrial and domestic use, it was inevitable that piano
makers should experiment with iron bracing, but its obvious advantages
had to contend with effects, real and imagined, upon tone. For a quarter
of a century or more after its introduction, metal was looked upon as a
necessary evil.[17] It is important to distinguish between the various earlier
attempts at reinforcing wood with metal, and the overall cast-iron frame,
'one of the most far-reaching improvements that have ever been applied
to the pianoforte'.[18] Moreover, it is essential to realize that the iron frame
was 'far reaching', not merely in a technical sense, but with profound
economic implications, to be considered below.

The overall cast-iron frame was essentially an American achievement.
It was first applied to square pianos by Alpheus Babcock of Boston in
1825. Many writers fail to give due weight to this significant development,
probably because it was misinterpreted by Hipkins in the 1885 edition of

the *Encyclopædia Britannica* and, despite subsequent correction, the error was repeated in *Grove* until 1946.[19] At the 1851 Exhibition Chickering displayed a grand with 'the whole framing consisting of string plate, longitudinal bars, wrest block and drilled bridge . . . of iron cast in one piece'.[20] A few years later Steinway was to clinch the matter of iron framing, as of overstringing. Meanwhile, European makers, apart from Hornung of Copenhagen who acknowledged and followed 'the American plan',[21] continued to experiment with composite frames of metal and wood. The Exhibition jury was particularly impressed by Broadwood's use of metal tension bars, and argued that the simplification of such bracing would 'eventually enable the public to obtain first rate instruments at a comparatively moderate price'.[22] Even that firm, however, acknowledged that tension bars were 'but make shifts', to be superseded if only an alternative way could be found of strengthening the case. Many French and some British pianos shown at the Melbourne Exhibition of 1882 still had wooden frames.

Enough has been said to establish the main features of mid-nineteenth-century technology and its potential areas of growth. This evolution was, of course, primarily the work of a few talented men whose innovations were adopted when (often long after) they had been simplified or had proved their commercial value. A wide gulf separated best practice (which naturally gets most notice from the technical historians) from the norm. Indeed, the industry's greatest achievement in later years was to narrow this gap. The initial timidity of most piano makers can be explained, at least in part, by the fact that good design required, in addition to mechanical skills, a knowledge of acoustics which was then an infant science. Helmholtz published 'On the sensation of tone' in 1862. The first English translation (of the third German edition) did not appear until 1875. Meanwhile the craft of piano making, particularly in England and France, developed empirically, with the inherent defects of such methods. It is for this reason that Theodore Steinway, able to communicate with Helmholtz and embody new science, engineering and musical sensitivity in his instruments, deserves a unique place in the piano's history.

But long after the successful general application of rational techniques, piano building remained a craft. Even by 1965, the author of a formidable treatise was urging manufacturers to 'do away with pure guess-work and trial and error' and acquire 'a basic knowledge of mathematics'.[23] There were economic as well as technical reasons for conservatism. The typical firm was small and poor, depending upon the pace makers not only for ideas but for supplies. As the new technology proved its superiority and was accepted, it encouraged entrepreneurs to supply standard units—iron frames, soundboards, actions—profiting from the economies of scale which a large market could provide. This process had tentatively begun before 1850, as firms like Goddard (1842) and Brooks began to supply pre-cut timber, veneers, and an assortment of 'piano supplies'; but its extension had to await that standardization which the new technology would both demand and fulfil.

Mid-Victorian production

In 1851, the English pianoforte industry consisted of some two hundred firms, most of them very small and concentrated overwhelmingly in London. In 1843 George Dodd remarked that there was 'perhaps not one occupation, throughout the whole range of industry, in which the metropolis maintains a more marked pre-eminence'.[24] Although there was considerable division of labour in the biggest factories, even these worked very slowly, enjoyed few economies of scale and were without machinery. Costs were therefore high and productivity was very low. Pianos, like furniture, clothing and most of the 1851 exhibits, were typical products of a pre-industrial revolution system of manufacture: they were either the expensive artifacts of skilled craftsmen or shoddy substitutes from the sweatshop. The highly seasonal nature of the piano trade, and an antiquated system of distribution with large profit margins and low turnover reinforced these tendencies towards inefficiency and high cost.

A few makers could be found outside London, enjoying a growing advantage of lower rents, defying obvious difficulties of access to materials and skilled labour, supplying a local market, and leaving scant record for the historian. J. B. Cramer had been a familiar name in Liverpool since 1820. Locke and Son were Manchester importers and makers established in 1849. The tiny Aberdeen firm of Marr and Co. started in 1847 and was entitled to use the royal arms as 'makers to the Queen', a distinction which occasioned wry comment from the London trade but was later to be put to good commercial use by an enterprising American manufacturer (see page 141). Charles Begg also opened shop in Aberdeen in 1849 and was said to be producing several hundred pianos a year before he emigrated to New Zealand in 1861. Muir Wood in Edinburgh made perhaps twenty instruments in a year. McCullough of Belfast, operating on a similar scale, claimed that his pianos were entirely Irish, exhibited 'several splendid specimens' at the 1853 Dublin Exhibition, and continued to pick up silver medals from the Royal Dublin Society until his death. A number of provincial 'makers' merely attached 'stencils' of their names to all or most of the instruments they sold, a procedure adopted more legitimately by many shopkeepers. None, with the possible exception of Cramer, gained a national reputation for quality or extent of manufacture.

There was, however, one important exception: Pohlmann and Sons commenced business in Halifax in 1823 but claimed origins back to the 'twelve apostles' (see page 13).

Various London directories list about two hundred 'makers', many still in the traditional centre around Soho Square, but there were already signs of a shift northwest. Like the coach builders of Long Acre, the Soho piano makers were one of the few trades in Central London which needed considerable space, and there was a general tendency to move out where rents were lower, perhaps leaving a showroom at the old address.[25] Some of the two hundred were mere shopkeepers 'stencilling' other men's instruments, and others were described by a contemporary observer as 'workmen in some single branch only of the trade'.[26] An additional fifty names are clearly identified as makers of parts.[27] Ten key makers were listed, five fret cutters and five makers of hammer rails. Two firms offered 'pins', one cloth for hammers and dampers, and five 'pianoforte silkers', all women, supplied fronts for uprights. There were twenty-one string makers who cannot be distinguished from suppliers of strings for other instruments; and twenty-one tuners complete the 1851 list. A pattern of manufacture can be discerned in which the piano maker is already able to buy partly processed materials and components. The system was as yet rudimentary; even the humblest manufacturer still needed to be master of, or to employ men with, a wide range of skills. It is notable that complete actions were not yet offered for sale. Only four years later the leading English 'supplies' firm of T. & H. Brooks, hitherto offering rails, keys and frets, took this momentous step.[28] A few months earlier Jean Schwander, already completing a decade of action-making in Paris, took as his partner Joseph Herrburger, and in Germany Adolf Lexow started in the same line of business.

Meanwhile, the larger piano manufacturers undertook every operation from raw material to finished product. By far the greatest firm was Broadwood's, admired in 1843 for its associations with great composers, its large labour force embodying high skills, 'not likely to be supplanted by any automatic machinery', and its conservative ways personified in a venerable octogenarian foreman who had been with the firm for sixty years. With an enthusiasm typical of the period, G. Dodd marvelled at actions which contained '3,800 separate pieces of ivory, woods, metals, cloth, felt, leather and vellum, all fashioned and adjusted by hand'.[29] This was indeed a big enterprise by the standards of contemporary London industries. The 1851 census indicated that eighty-six per cent of London entrepreneurs employed less than ten men. Only twelve factories were recorded as employing more than three hundred, and Broadwood's was one of these. Its workforce of between three and four hundred performed a bewildering range of operations which were strictly demarcated. A grand piano, remarked E. F. Rimbault, 'passes under the hands of upwards of forty different workmen'.[30] He was referring to documents prepared by Broadwood's for the Exhibition as a proud demonstration of the industry's advanced state. We must follow their rather tedious enumeration of processes as a necessary indication of the existing division of labour:

1   The *Key maker* prepared a complete keyboard from one piece of lime-tree wood, fixed ivory and ebony, bored holes, and cut into separate keys. He is shown in Plate 4.

2–5   The *hammer maker, check-maker, damper maker*, and *damper-lifter-maker* constructed their appropriate parts of the action.

6, 7   The *notch-maker* covered the ends of the hammer shanks with doe-skin and leather cloth. The *hammer-leatherer* covered each hammer head with leather and felt, shaping them individually.

8   The *beam maker* cut the rail extending across the action and covered it with brass.

9–15   The following 'music smiths' performed various specialized operations:
(a) *Brass-stud maker, brass-bridge maker*, and *wrest-pin maker.*
(b) *Metallic-brace maker, plate maker, steel-arch maker*, and *transverse-bar maker*, all of whom constructed parts of the metallic bracing for what was still fundamentally a wooden frame.

16   *Spun string maker.*

17–21   The instrument's body was constructed by the *sawyer, bent-side maker, case maker, bracer*, and *bottom maker.*

22, 23   The *sounding-board maker* and *belly man*, both highly skilled operations.

24   The *marker-off* marked out the scale, finished the beech bridge and fixed its pins, inserted the upward bearing bridge and bored it for the tuning pins, fixing the metallic bracing.

25   *The stringer.*

26   The *finisher* assembled and fixed the action, bringing the whole mechanism into playing order.

27, 28   The *rougher-up* gave the instrument its first tuning, and was followed by the *tuner.*

29, 30   The *regulator of action* and *regulator of tones.*

Twelve additional operations were performed by individual craftsmen during the course of the instrument's construction. These were the top maker, plinther, fronter, canvas-frame maker, lyre maker, leg-block maker, leg maker, turner, carver, gilder, scraper and polisher. Several of the thirty processes are illustrated in Plate 5.

Annual production at Broadwood's during the 1850s was about 2,500 instruments, a total approached by no other firm. Chickering, the leading American manufacturer, was making about one thousand instruments a year. In France, Pleyel, soon to become one of Turgan's 'Grandes Usines',[31] was of similar size and output; Erard rather smaller. In England Collard occupied second place with some 1,500 instruments a year, followed by perhaps eight firms whose annual output probably ranged between three and five hundred: Allison, Brinsmead, Challen, Chappell, Grover and Grover, Hopkinson, Kirkman and Pohlmann. Out of an approximate total of two hundred English firms that leaves some 190 small men who probably each made about thirty instruments during the busy season, when rapid sales enabled them to survive with little capital. Our phraseology is deliberately tentative for reasons, elaborated in Chapter 8, which are particularly relevant for the 1850s, half a century before the first census of production. Although the names, dates and addresses of most makers are known, quantitative information about their activities, poor even for the big firms, is non-existent for the small. Nevertheless, informed guesswork gives an estimate of total English production in 1851 as between 15,000 and 20,000 instruments. Contemporary writers, using even more dubious methods, guessed slightly higher and probably exaggerated. The annual production of instruments in London was estimated [32] at more than 23,000, of which five to ten per cent were grands, a similar proportion squares, and the remaining eighty to ninety per cent uprights. This output was valued at £955,000 made up as follows:

1,500 grands, bichords and small grands at, say, £110	£165,000
1,500 squares at, say, £60	£90,000
20,000 uprights of various kinds at, say, £35	£700,000
	£955,000

Such estimates are subject to wide margins of error in an industry both innocent and distrustful of statistics. But even if actual production were double our assessment, it would still have been modest in relation both to later achievements and to potential home and foreign markets. Foreign trade was very small. In 1851, imports of musical instruments amounted to a mere £62,000 of which probably less than half were pianos. Therefore scarcely one thousand pianos could have entered England, most of them from France. British exports certainly exceeded this figure, but there were large, untapped markets. Even more attractive were the opportunities at home. At least a million English men were employed in 'middle class' occupations and their numbers were growing rapidly.[33] They or their wives and daughters could reasonably be expected to aspire to the new, perhaps the principal, status symbol of mid-Victorian times. If we add the enormously greater number of skilled artisans, with similar aspirations, it will be apparent that large, growing markets awaited enterprising manufacturers of reasonably priced, durable instruments.

Prevailing economic conditions in the industry made this an unattainable objective. Even Broadwood's elaborate division of labour achieved an annual productivity of only about seven pianos per man, no higher than that of small firms; indeed, one well-informed observer argued that it was considerably lower! [34] Clearly there were few internal economies of scale. Moreover production was very slow, tying up large capital sums in raw material and instruments on the long road to the ultimate buyer. The natural seasoning process required that wood be stored for several years (stocks equivalent to two years throughput were customary), and a grand piano remained 'in hand upwards of six months' before it was pronounced fit for the showroom. Machinery was still, thirty years after the death of James Watt, notable by its absence.

It was a deficiency remarked by contemporaries who drew contrasts with American practice. The distinguished engineer Joseph Whitworth explained in 1854: 'In no branch of manufacture does the application of labour-saving machinery produce by simple means more important results than in the working of wood.' [35] A visiting committee was particularly impressed by the manufacture of pianos and harmoniums in 'a building similar to an English cotton mill . . . with steam engines and special machinery applied to the production of every part'.[36] In England there had been no further progress in the mechanization of woodworking since the coming of peace in 1815, and existing machinery was virtually ignored for forty years.[37] During this period Americans, with abundant cheap wood and a shortage of iron and skilled labour, developed a wide range of machines for sawing, planing, boring, mortising and tenoning, and introduced hundreds of special modifications for the manufacture of carriages, ploughs and furniture. In 1844 the Liverpool firm of William Furness began importing and patenting American machinery, but with little success. When G. L. Molesworth read a paper on 'The conversion of wood by machinery' to the Institute of Civil Engineers in 1857, he was charting virtually unknown territory in England. Resistance to the machine stemmed from a combination of mutually reinforcing circumstances—ingrained conservatism, the small size and limited market of the typical firm, and an abundance of skilled craftsmen throughout the country. Such conditions were pervasive wherever men worked with wood. Until the 1860s even cabinet making, despite large markets, 'could hardly be described as an industry'. It was ignored by the Select Committee of the School of Design in 1849, presumably because of the lack of large firms, most furniture being made by 'individual local craftsmen, working for their own town or village'.[38]

Apart from its concentration in London, piano making shared these characteristics and weaknesses. Even the dominance of London arose not from economies of large scale production, but because of the concentration of metropolitan demand, the availability of recondite skills, the prestige which assisted even humble makers, and, not least, the transport advantages of a great port. As provincial markets expanded, an improving railway system helped London firms, tending to offset the cost advantages of proximity which local makers might enjoy, though the allegedly high level of railway freights was a frequent source of complaint. Without economies of scale or machinery, productivity continued to be low and prices high. Broadwood grands were priced at £135, and 'good' uprights at forty-five to eighty guineas. Instruments by obscure makers were advertised in *The Musical World* for little less, though no doubt there were discounts for favoured customers willing to pay cash. Prices were always quoted in the dignifying unit of guineas: six-octave 'piccolos' (small uprights) at forty to sixty; 'cottages' at forty-five to seventy; 'cabinets' and 'semi-grands' (about six feet long) were priced at ninety to 110, and full grands upwards of 120 guineas.[39] Similar prices ruled throughout the 1850s and 1860s, even rising in some cases without improvements in quality. Cheaper instruments were also available. Collards showed at the 1851 Exhibition two 'microchordans, semi-cottage pianofortes . . . superior instruments of their class' at the 'very low price' of thirty guineas, in a plain deal case. Hopkinson proudly quoted the opinions of Thalberg and Sir Julius Benedict, composer of 'The lily of Killarney', that their instruments were 'unsurpassed in tone and touch', and promised to 'greatly surprise such as imagine that the art of making first class grand pianos is confined to the *favoured few* old established houses'.[40] The tone of *lèse-majesté* is unmistakeable in this early attack upon the cult of a 'name' by a firm which was eventually to profit from that cult. Meanwhile Hopkinson's 'boudoir cottages' or 'piccolos' started at twenty-five guineas, but their grand pianos commanded similar prices to those of Broadwood. Another firm destined for success was Brinsmead, offering a 'piccolo semi-cottage' at thirty-eight guineas. There were also a number of bizarre constructions from C. Cadby, whose name was to survive in more appetizing circumstances—Cadby Hall being acquired by J. Lyons.

Adorned with such 'extras' as 'patent truss bracing', Cadby's pianos started at thirty-eight guineas, achieved a rapid obsolescence, but earned their maker enough for him to leave £26,000 in 1884 to his seven daughters. 'Absence of male issue has brought down many a fine piano business' lamented a veteran of the trade many years later.[41]

Several makers offered even greater bargains. John C. Jones of Soho Square presented 'a piano for the people' at twenty guineas, but particularly recommended his twenty-five guinea model, 'extremely elegant . . . all the requisites of a really good instrument'. Readers of the Royal Academy of Music Calendar in 1854 were also assured by J. H. R. Mott in the Strand that his 'patent, everstanding, and *ne plus ultra* pianos surprise all who are acquainted with their beautiful qualities'. Near the bottom of the market was James Stewart whose advertisement appealed to country dealers. After twenty-six years with Collard he was now 'prepared to TREAT for the SALE of instruments of his own make, from his new manufactories' in Old St Pancras Road. Grand pianos (he surely meant large uprights) were offered at £20 and uprights at £10 'besides a liberal allowance to the trade'.[42] None of these articles survive or have left any evidence of their qualities, but records of the Exhibition again provide some guidance. An 'artisan piano' was a makeshift object of reduced compass with plain wooden keys, presumably deemed adequate for calloused hands. Another shoddy substitute was Harrison's 'piccolo utilitarian boudoir piano' with only one string to each note, instead of the customary bichord, or trichord, shortened keys, and a very primitive action. Probably the 'best buy' among legitimate instruments in the lower price range were the little 'pianettes' from France which gradually began to establish a reputation for neat workmanship. Among the makers entering this market, by far the most important was Antoine Bord who started in 1843 and was making over five hundred a year by the early fifties. Van Gruisen of Liverpool began importing them, rapidly defeating the prejudice which reigned against French instruments among everyone 'except those who had purchased them and discovered their merits'.[43] Bord was a pioneer in many directions and was to become the largest piano manufacturer in French history, making over 4,000 instruments a year by the 1880s, of which some two thirds were exported.

Despite some ambitious claims, none of these cheaper pianos—not even Bord's—were really satisfactory instruments. So much can be deduced both from those few which have survived and from the admittedly confused and conflicting evidence of contemporary opinion. Nor were they cheap: Collard, for example, was praised for his 'little Quaker-like pianos of white wood, fine tone and most moderate price . . . offered to the public of small means—the needy clerk, the poor teacher, the upper class mechanic'.[44] But since skilled craftsmen were earning about thirty shillings a week, and £150 a year qualified men for the middle-class privilege of paying income tax, such enthusiasm for thirty-guinea instruments was clearly overstated. Even wider of the mark was the same writer's proclamation of cheap pianos as a social revolution: 'as glorious a transition . . . from the rare and royal virginals, as is the daily press and cheap literature of the nineteenth century from the chained Bible'. A more realistic if less prescient commentator welcomed attempts to lower prices by using plain materials, but lamented that nothing could 'make this a cheap instrument; the mechanism is too intricate and delicate for us to hope to realize pianofortes for the millions.'.[45]

The lack of a cheap serviceable action was probably the most serious impediment to lowering costs, but there were more general weaknesses. Manufacturing techniques were, as the Broadwood example demonstrates, complex, labour intensive, and suffused with the 'mysteries' of the craft. Processes tended to be *ad hoc* rather than based on explicit analysis, and therefore inappropriate for repetition or simple adoption. The implications were explained by William Pole, professor of engineering at London University and a Doctor of Music: 'the *engineering* of the construction is not so well studied as it ought to be and the application of acoustical science . . . is yet more behindhand'. Successful exploitation of a potentially large market required that 'means should be found to bring a class of instrument equal to the ordinary grand within the reach of persons by whom it is now quite unattainable'. Other consumer goods had achieved precisely such an industrial revolution: 'the expediency of combining cheapness with excellence in quality has long been acknowledged and acted upon in almost every other branch of manufacturing', concluded Pole with pardonable exaggeration, and he urged a similar course upon piano manufacturers, rejecting shoddy substitutes: 'Although advocating cheapness, we cannot consider it desirable to obtain it by depriving the pianoforte of the improvements it has received, or by any other means calculated to deteriorate its quality'.[46] It is a curious fact that Pole, despite his perceptive appraisal of the industry's present weaknesses and future opportunities, nevertheless shared his contemporaries' prejudice against the use of iron, and failed to appreciate the great contribution it could make to cheap mass production. The 'growing tendency to use too much metal', he argued, harmed tone and added to weight and cost.

Mid-Victorian distribution

These production inefficiencies were compounded by a distributive system which was at best costly to and at worst a conspiracy against the defenceless customer. Since its inadequacies were responsible for doubling the retail price of most instruments, their origins and persistence require some examination.

In the early years of pianoforte manufacture most instruments were sold directly from the craftsman's workshop to a client who was probably musical and understood something of what he was buying. Distribution was a simple matter, requiring little capital or organization because pianos were usually made to specific order and payment was, if not immediate, at least a matter of clearly defined responsibility. Gradually this relationship became more elaborate and tenuous, and its participants less well informed. Max Weber's claim that by 1800 the piano was already 'a standard commercial object produced for stock'[47] identifies an important transition but is misleading in two ways. Pianos were not yet 'standardized' in any meaningful sense. Without a degree of standardization not only were costs high, but it was impossible for purchasers of so complicated a machine to distinguish good from bad in the absence of unprejudiced knowledgeable guidance. Consumer ignorance and bewilderment prevailed for many years and to some extent persist today. Weber also tends to antedate the decline of bespoke manufacture: a considerable element remained in the work of even the bigger firms, although customers' requirements were commonly a matter of exterior ornament, rather than a basic design. The great London manufacturers continued to retail directly to local buyers as well as supplying provincial dealers, to whom they granted long credits and substantial discounts. Much capital was inevitably tied up in stocks of finished instruments, for turnover was slow and highly seasonal, the peaks occurring at Christmas and, to a lesser extent, during the spring wedding season. Dealers attempted to keep their profit margins sufficiently high to offset this slow turnover, earning additional income from sales of music, with a similarly high mark up, tuning, repairs and, perhaps, musical tuition and performance. Edward Elgar's father was such a man.

Most music traders occupied a humble position in the cultural and social scale of a severely ranked society. Elgar was humiliated by this ubiquitous snobbery[48] which is best illustrated by an episode in the career of a quintessentially Victorian figure, Munby. When he heard that a clergyman's daughter was employed as maidservant to a Tooting music seller, Munby thought the case scandalous enough to investigate immediately. His relief at discovering that her father had been merely a dissenting preacher was offset by sadness at the plight of the tradesman's wife, 'a *lady* who married beneath her'.[49] This commonplace of Victorian snobbery helps our understanding of the relationships between the great English piano makers and the rest of the trade, in which economic factors frequently took second place to social ambition and an acute and finely-judged sense of class. A fashionable directory of 1860 listed six Broadwoods, headed by Henry Fowler, whose residence in Bryanston Square was near the Greek Minister and opposite the Turkish Ambassador.[50] Less august but still worthy of inclusion were the Collards and Joseph Kirkman. By 1873 H. F. Broadwood had moved to St George's Square where his neighbours included titled ladies and a major general.[51] Thomas Brinsmead, living off Fitzroy Square, was in the lower company of architects and sculptors but was climbing fast. For such men, hobnobbing with the elect was a delightful and essential perquisite of their business, more important than those close relationships with musicians and craftsmen which their predecessors had carefully nurtured. This position in society was not to be sullied by too familiar a relationship with dealers or lesser piano makers. There was cause here for much inefficiency and bad feeling in the trade.

Although the net returns to provincial dealers were generally modest, the high level of profit margins was a constant attraction to anyone with spare cash and some knowledge of local demand who could get access to a supply of instruments. With negligible overheads, such 'intruders' as publicans, furniture dealers, 'professors' of music, even factory clerks, could sell at much lower prices than the 'legitimate' traders and still make a profit. Thus, typically, a forty-pound piano could be procured for eighteen and sold for twenty-five pounds cash. Another common practice was the advertisement of new instruments as second hand for individual enforced sale by a 'recently bereaved widow' or 'gentleman about to emigrate'. Some were genuine bargains, other meretricious rubbish, deliberately assembled and falsely labelled to impress the gullible. The pervasiveness of this subterranean market suggests a widespread demand for cheap instruments which legitimate practice could not satisfy. The piano was in vogue, 'fashion in a town mansion, respectability in a suburban cottage, alike demand it', announced the *Pall Mall Gazette*.

How did consumers exercise their choice? For most buyers, and not a few sellers, the selection of an instrument was a mysterious rite, dependent upon mysterious unmeasurable qualities of 'tone' and 'touch' which few could honestly judge. Shop keepers anxious to dispose of stock, 'professors' eager for their commission, 'musical' friends ignorant of technical matters, would proffer advice, but the customer was bereft of disinterested expert guidance. In 1854 an anonymous booklet suitably entitled *The Guard*[52] promised to 'convey secrets worth knowing to the intending purchaser', and warned of many pitfalls. Provincial customers were particularly at risk for 'many London dealers despise (them) and sell rubbish through their travellers or country dealers'. 'The sudden advancement of music' offered great opportunities of profiting from ignorance for 'the mothers of nineteen families out of twenty, in certain distant counties, know nothing whatever either of music or musical instruments' and responsibility for choice fell upon daughters. Moreover a poor instrument, once bought, remained unassessed, since musical friends would keep a polite silence. Newspapers were 'teeming with advertised unsound pianos', many of which although allegedly second-hand were in fact new. Indeed a migratory pattern could be discerned—bad new pianos left London for the provinces, good old ones travelled in the opposite direction. A twenty year old piano, argued *The Guard*, was often better than a new one because it dated from a time when 'music had not dawned upon the million, consequently only first rate, high priced instruments were manufactured'. One should be wary of music 'professors', the majority of whom 'have sadly lost caste . . . not content with commission from good makers they certificate, for a valuable consideration, the mushroom instruments that spring up from the metropolitan hot-beds of fraud'. Some even recommended the new seven octave keyboards with treble notes which Moscheles had likened to throwing needles against a milestone. Others pretended to tune instruments, an arrogation also assumed, with grievous results, by 'housepainters, carpenters, wheelwrights and blacksmiths'. Only a London tuner of experience should be employed, and paid ten and sixpence. The writer was particularly upset by 'the condition of pianos in ladies' seminaries' and urged mothers, presumably from the metropolis and therefore knowledgeable, to inspect them as they would the beds. In the unlikely event that a reader might still decide to buy, *The Guard* offered only one practical bit of advice: 'A purchaser may enter the establishment of Erard, Broadwood, Collard, Wornum, or Stodart; these are respectable makers and their names carry with them an indisputable warranty'. Only thus could one escape the 'host of inferior manufacturers and dealers who catch the unwary with a gilded counterfeit'.

It is possible though unlikely that this precursory consumers' guide was not wholly disinterested—unlikely because such enterprise would have been beneath a 'great' maker's dignity, although Brinsmead was soon to tarnish that code. A simpler interpretation is that, despite a certain excess of caution, the writer was a well-informed and accurate observer, giving no succour to the impecunious because there was none to give. Good pianos were expensive: one either paid heavily for a 'name', bought shoddy, or courted fraud.

Fifteen years later little had changed. An article in the *Musical Standard* offers a rare statement of the consumer's viewpoint in a trade where *caveat emptor* had degenerated into an implicit conspiracy against him.

The price of good instruments, it argued, was 'preposterously high. One third might come off and still leave the manufacturers a good profit'. The cause was attributed to inefficient distribution, with too many commissions 'direct and indirect . . . always at the purchaser's ultimate cost'. It was therefore possible for 'shrewd individuals' to sell good pianos at thirty per cent below prevailing retail prices by working on 'quick returns and moderate profit'. No improvement could be expected 'until greater facilities are given for the competition of the best class of French or German-made instruments'.[53]

Why were existing 'facilities' unable to provide this necessary competition? There was no longer even the ten per cent duty, and free trading England raised no legal barriers to imports, which doubled between the mid fifties and 1870, French instruments being joined by a few hundreds from Germany. The answer lies partly in the nature and finance of retailing and partly in the productive process. As the *Musical Standard* implied, distributive outlets were limited and rigid. Relying upon makers for the financing of their stocks, most retailers were tied to established English makers by strong cords of indebtedness. Cutting loose from this dependence required alternative sources of finance and a product which would repay such risk by ready sale. A successful challenger had to be sufficiently cheaper or better to overcome the prejudice and ignorance of traders and consumers whose conservatism was deeply entrenched. Despite the attractions of French pianettes and faint stirrings from Germany, no new instrument yet offered such unequivocal advantages. Change also required a new assessment of potential markets: a belief in the expansibility of demand. Like most tradesmen of the period, piano manufacturers and retailers tended to adopt traditional attitudes, assuming implicitly that demand curves were inelastic in a fixed market.[54] A 'good trade' with regular patronage was therefore preferred to an impersonal drive for wider custom, which would be antisocial or self-defeating. Advertising was non-existent among the 'great' firms, minimal and tentative lower down and crass at the bottom. In the legitimate trade, goodwill, tranquillity and respectability were the supreme virtues, competition less than energetic. Such activities had a certain charm: when in 1856 Hopkinson had a serious fire, he was helped by Collard and Broadwood with loans of benches and tools to enable him to complete orders.

For this quiescence the public paid dearly, while English piano manufacturers remained unperturbed by occasional criticism. Such arrogance was perhaps inevitable. Both France and Germany were novices in the skills of modern technology and industry. In the middle of the nineteenth century Germans were just beginning to design their own machines rather than copy those from England.[55] It was natural that English manufacturers should find nothing fearful in a threat of competition from the continent. In so far as a piano was an item of furniture, the appeal of French cabinet-making skills and Gallic accomplishments in pretty fashion might be admitted. But as a piece of machinery, so they reasoned, the best instrument was bound to come from the workshop of the world. French products were considered elegant but lacking in robustness, German beneath notice. The self confidence of innate superiority bred an attitude of lofty indifference in all but a few perceptive minds. Like British car manufacturers disdainfully surveying the ruined Volkswagen works in 1946, or German camera makers contemplating their Japanese infant competitors, equanimity was a pardonable if dangerous state of mind.

Chapter 3

Steinway and the New Technology

In the history of the modern piano one firm has been pre-eminent. Its rise to a position of world leadership in the industry was meteoric, its influence upon standards of technology and quality pervasive. Within two decades, the Steinway family emigrated to America, transformed the instrument's technology, establishing the essential features of the pianos we use today, assumed leadership of the American industry and then returned to conquer Europe. Pianos made before the Steinway revolution are of interest today primarily to music historians, antiquarians and collectors of furniture. Those made since have adopted the Steinway's main features or earned a rapid obsolescence. The verdict of the market is unequivocal. Steinways dating from the 1880s are still in regular use by practical musicians, and those a little younger are eagerly sought. Of no other maker can this be said. Other fine pianos, notably Bechsteins, find a ready market after up to sixty years (older models are usually suspect) but their price on the second-hand market is invariably lower than a comparable Steinway.

The 'American system'

An ideally qualified piano manufacturer would possess technical knowledge and flair, musical sensitivity and awareness, business acumen and thrust. Few firms have been endowed with all these qualities; some, including those inheriting and living solely upon a previously established reputation, have survived with none. The remarkable fact about Steinway is that all these desiderata were available for several generations within a closely knit family; specialization through kinship goes far to explain the firm's rapid emergence in the 1850s and 1860s and has been consciously exploited until very recently. The beginning could hardly have been more modest. Heinrich Engelhard Steinway was born in Wolfshagen, Duchy of Brunswick, in February 1797, the youngest of twelve children. At fifteen he was the family's sole survivor, at eighteen he fought at Waterloo and, on his discharge four years later, set up as a cabinet maker. Interested in building and playing organs he soon turned to the piano, completing an instrument, still possessed by the Steinway family, in the kitchen of his house at Seesen in 1836. Three years later he exhibited a grand and two squares at the Brunswick state fair. A photograph of the house, where five sons and three daughters were born, indicates that it was a substantial bourgeois residence, and implies a degree of business success. The emigration of Charles, the second son (born 1829) in 1849 was not in itself momentous. Like many of his generation he sympathized with the revolution of 1848, and found German society uncongenial thereafter. It was extraordinary, however, that he should have persuaded his father and younger brothers to join him in New York only a year later. The firm's official history suggests that, had there been no revolution in 1848, the family 'would probably have headed towards the New World in due course of time',[1] but it can equally be argued that a successful business-man in his early fifties who has survived privation in childhood and youth might be expected to settle with equanimity into provincial respectability. Instead, the family uprooted itself and moved into a New York tenement, Heinrich and his sons taking jobs at the bench. Only Theodore, the oldest son (born 1825) remained in Germany, taking F. Grotrian as his partner in 1856. In 1853 his father and brothers, now 'Henry Steinway and Sons', had opened a modest workshop and made a thousand instruments in their first three years.

They were starting business in an environment which greatly favoured innovation and expansion. Good timber was abundant and cheap, metallurgy and engineering advanced and highly responsive to new needs.[2] Workers with appropriate skills were highly paid, but since most of them were recent immigrants—German remained the common language in Steinway's factory for many years—they tended to be younger, more energetic and less inclined than European craftsmen to resist new procedures and techniques. Conditions of demand were equally encouraging: a large and rapidly growing market in which intrinsic quality and ruggedness were as much appreciated as an established name, and modernity could be a positive selling point even for a product which, in Europe, was stifled by tradition.

A curious feature of the American market was its continuing preference for square pianos long after they had become practically obsolete in Europe. Even the ultra-conservative Broadwood's discontinued their manufacture in 1860 except for a few made for the tropics, and these were also stopped in 1864. In America squares were still common twenty years later. During the early fifties an annual output of some 9,000 pianos of all kinds included few uprights and a mere handful of grands, notably those of Chickering. A few hundred pianos were imported annually, mainly high quality Erards and Pleyels from France. The square's persistence has no simple explanation, but at this stage it was still superior to the upright as a musical instrument if not as a piece of furniture, for the American squares were far more substantial than their European predecessors, as can be seen in Plates 1 and 2. Their appearance apparently displeased Henri Herz, one of the first concert pianists to visit the country (whose own compositions do not suggest a rarefied aesthetic sensitivity), but they were better instruments than contemporary English and French uprights. Moreover they were built to withstand the rigours of American climate and domestic heating, a test which no contemporary and few later European instruments could survive.

The limited American market for grands is more easily explained. As yet there were comparatively few elegant drawing rooms, and no outstanding concert pianists requiring fine instruments and creating further demand through the influence of their performances. America 'had no Liszts or Thalbergs, had not even seen or heard feebler examples of this species of performer before 1845'.[3] The first visiting pianists were, if not feeble, scarcely prepossessing, and they brought European instruments with them. Their artistic and commercial influence was thus minimal. Leopold de Meyer, 'the lion' (see page 21), whose claims to have performed before Louis Philippe and Queen Victoria were as spurious as the musical content of his programmes, arrived in 1845 with a couple of Erards. In the same year Henri Herz touted his own instruments, selling a number of wooden-framed uprights which soon became total wrecks, reinforcing the American prejudice against upright pianos.[4]

During the fifties, musical life and the industries associated with it began to improve. In 1853 Louis Gottschalk, 'the American Chopin',[5] returned from Europe with two Pleyel grands for his first tour of the United States. Two years later, needing funds, he sold them in New Orleans, but was soon approached by Chickering and agreed to use his instruments. Meanwhile Thalberg brought American audiences their first experience of fashionable European standards of performance. Schumann once wrote of this celebrated pianist, nicknamed 'Old Arpeggio', that if anyone were to criticize him 'all the girls in Germany, France, and the other European countries would rise up in arms'. Now, at hundreds of concerts given between 1856 and 1858, American girls could join the legions. Thalberg played his first tour on an Erard which was badly mauled by transportation and climate. In 1857 he too changed to Chickering. A golden age was beginning, with immediate opportunities of profit for makers of concert instruments and immeasurable 'spin off' for the rest of the trade. There were other sources of stimulus: the influx of German immigrants whose culture ranked music highly in the pleasures to be bought from a new prosperity; the sprouting of conservatories, orchestras and opera; the migration of earnest young Americans in search of European music and their return with a mission to pass on the faith; [6] and underlying all this, the rapid growth of population and income which made this a golden age for American manufacturers of pianos, as of so many other products. The Steinways could not have chosen a better time and place to start business.

Within a year they were awarded a prize for a square piano exhibited at a Washington fair,[7] and in 1855 were again successful at the American Institute Exhibition in New York, with an overstrung iron framed square. Having established a reputation with the traditional American shape of instrument, they turned next to grands, and finally to uprights. Within a decade the firm had emerged as the only serious rival to Chickering in America, and was ready to assert its supremacy in Europe. The rapidity, persistence and quality of innovation were astonishing, not merely in its technical achievement, but in its perception and exploitation of market opportunities. Between 1857 and 1872 sixteen patents were registered, most of them substantial. The next fifteen years saw another thirty-nine patents, some for minor improvements or exterior design, but none eccentric or gratuitous. The details need not detain us: since many Steinway instruments of that period survive and pianos dating from the 1880s are still commonly in use they can easily be examined. We shall merely indicate a few leading features of the Steinway or 'American system',[8] as it came to be known in Europe. Although we are concerned, of course, with its application to piano manufacture, it will be appreciated that the term had a wider industrial connotation, referring to the large scale assembly of interchangeable parts and the use of machine tools, first demonstrated by Colt's guns at the 1851 Exhibition.[9]

The early Steinway grands of 1856 were iron framed but straight strung. In 1859 an overstrung grand was first played at a public concert and was patented in December. The first upright in which the bass strings crossed the others in a fan-like pattern was built in 1863. This instrument, Number 7765, marks a watershed in the history of modern piano manufacture: the first really adequate upright, on which virtually all later instruments of quality were based. The new system of overstringing was wholly different from and superior to earlier experiments which had either crowded the strings or, as in Pape's uprights and the Russian grand exhibited at the London Great Exhibition in 1851, been forced to use separate soundboards for the two sets of strings. Steinway's method used one soundboard and also enabled the bridges to be moved nearer to its centre, greatly intensifying the tone. As the iron frame was cast in one piece and covered the wrest plank, string tension could be vastly increased—threefold on concert grands by the 1870s—taking advantage of improved metallurgy and further enhancing the tone. Much heavier hammers were fitted with thick felt, and the action was modified to give pianists control over the unprecedented power now at their command.

Numerous other innovations included an 'agraffe' attachment patented in 1859—modifying one of Pierre Erard's inventions [10]—which strengthened the strings' resistance to the hammers' blows. This fundamental reworking of the instrument is described by Spillane, quaintly but with insight, as 'the outcome of patient experiment and great elementary knowledge'.[11] The basic principles were indeed elementary, but they were grasped and applied with infinite care by educated minds open to new ideas and subservient to neither conventional wisdom nor traditional practice. Henry Steinway Junior was responsible for the first seven patents, all connected with grands, but his sudden death and that of Charles in 1865 precipitated a crisis which was met by Theodore, the oldest and most formidable of the brothers. Selling his Brunswick business to Grotrian, Heifferich and Schulz, he joined his father and surviving brothers in New York.

Theodore now took over the technical side of the business, creating a tradition of research and development without parallel in the industry's history. In the royal line of great piano makers—Stein, Pape, Erard, John Broadwood—he brought to his craft a rare combination of qualities: meticulous concern for every detail of the instrument, tempered by that indispensable ability (which Pape had lacked) to distinguish between technical advance and mere ingenuity. His papers, including letters to the family written before he joined them in America, are crammed with scientific notes and diagrams. Most notable is his correspondence with Helmholtz in which the great scientist acknowledges his practical achievements. On 9 June 1871, Helmholtz writes, 'With such a perfect instrument as yours . . . I must modify many of my former expressed views regarding pianos.' Two years later he praises the new 'duplex scale', its tone 'even more liquid, singing, and harmonious', an improvement which 'being based upon scientific principles is capable of still greater development'. Since the principle of overstringing was to be continually under attack by conservative critics as leading inevitably to unevenness of tone through the register, one final opinion of Helmholtz is worth quoting. On 16 March 1885, he welcomes further improvements which have led to 'the tone throughout the entire scaling being remarkable for its evenness, and its wonderful sweetness, richness and volume'. Such testimony from the progenitor of modern acoustics goes far to establish Theodore's position as one of the greatest of all piano makers.

His arrival in America was also significant for quite another reason. Coming from Europe where the square piano was obsolete and the design of a good upright the greatest challenge, he entered an environment where squares were the standard instrument and grands the new priority among leading makers. Against considerable opposition from his own workmen Theodore, while continuing to improve the concert grand and make large splendid square pianos (Plate 2), turned his attention first to the creation and then to the mass production of the modern upright. In this he was anticipating the future trend of American production: whereas, up to 1866, 97 per cent of the annual output of pianos were squares, by 1896 this proportion had fallen to one per cent, and ninety-five per cent were uprights.[12] The changing emphasis at Steinways can be traced in successive catalogues, and in the firm's choice of instruments for display at American industrial fairs. The first upright design of 1863 was steadily improved and output increased during the early 1870s, by which time total production of all styles was running at 2,000 a year, surpassing even Chickering's output. At the Philadelphia Centennial Exhibition in 1876 Steinways displayed four concert grands, a 'parlor grand' (six feet eight inches), and three uprights (two were four feet eight inches high, one three feet ten inches). An 1888 catalogue lists four grands, seven uprights and only one square, the last of which was built in 1888. All models were highly priced, ranging from $850 for the square illustrated in Plate 2, to $1,800 for an eight feet ten inches concert grand. Uprights were priced from $700 for a four feet ten inches model, to $1,500. Plate 7 is taken from this catalogue. An 1881 announcement in the English press says that high prices have hitherto debarred them from the 'household market' and introduces a 'moderately priced upright grand' four feet six inches high, retailing at 105 guineas.[13] Moreover these prices held firm in the second hand market, whereas the pianos of Steinway's predecessors and contemporaries behaved like the modern motor-car, falling sharply in value as soon as they left the showroom. In 1888 a London correspondent was astonished to find one of the 105-guinea models after six years' use selling for £86.[14] It became common practice for the firm's agents to investigate advertisements for 'cheap Steinways', usually to discover that they were not genuine instruments. But this is to anticipate Steinway's adventures in Europe, to which we must now turn.

Marketing

While Theodore Steinway was remoulding the piano's technology, his younger brother William transformed its marketing. His personality and abilities were ideally suited to this task, complementing the introverted Theodore who stayed in his workshop using only his native tongue and who retired eventually to Germany. William was a confident, extrovert

American with wide business and political interests which led to friendship with President Cleveland, partnership with Daimler, whose premises, in 1892, were next door to Steinway Hall, and active participation in land companies, transport and banking. He was also a knowledgeable music-lover who kept in touch with concert-life, forging links which were of inestimable benefit to the firm. His diaries, written between 1861 and a few weeks before his death in 1896, provide abundant evidence for these remarks. He even enjoyed the New York recitals of von Bülow, whose services he had lost to his principal business rival Chickering.[15] His marketing techniques were analogous to those which had been pioneered a century earlier by Josiah Wedgwood to capture the world of fashion with a luxury product. In 1779 Wedgwood had reasoned that 'fashion is infinitely superior to merit in many respects . . . if you have a favourite child you wish the public to fondle and take notice of, you have only to make choice of proper sponsors'. Wedgwood chose monarchs, nobles, connoisseurs of art, and used puffing articles, advertisements, exhibitions and travelling salesmen.[16] Similar techniques of promotion had been employed by piano makers before Steinway—Erard's instruments for Marie Antoinette, Broadwood and Graf for Beethoven—but never with such dedication and panache.

William Steinway's targets fall into three interconnected groups: the aristocracy and *haute bourgeoisie*, eminent musicians and habitués of artistic salons, and, not least, the new emporia of international commerce, the great exhibitions. The approach to the first group is simply illustrated by a select list of blue-blooded purchasers or recipients of Steinway pianos:

1867   A Paris Exhibition grand to the Baronesse de Rothschild.
       Lionel and James de Rothschild of London.
1868   The Queen of Spain.
1872   The Empress of Russia—concert grand number 25,000 and two
       other instruments for the Imperial Court.
1875   The Sultan of Turkey.
1879   Queen Victoria—for Balmoral.

Enlistment of the musical world was equally calculated to impress. A brochure printed in 1876 lists ninety-four 'eminent artists' who 'have used and prefer to use Steinway pianos' and have addressed complimentary letters to the firm. Most of the leading French composers appear: Auber, Berlioz, Gounod, Thomas, Saint-Saëns. But apart from the latter artist, French pianists such as Planté, the country's leading virtuoso at that time, appear to have held aloof. German representation was similarly weighted more towards general musical, rather than keyboard, eminence, including Wagner and Joachim (the latter inevitably comparing the Steinway with a Stradivarius) but excluding Brahms and the Schumanns. The Austrian musical establishment was not represented, but from Russia came support which offered both immediate prestige and longer term influence. Leschetitzky, the most influential piano teacher of his age, Nicholas and Anton Rubinstein—directors respectively of the Moscow and St Petersburg Conservatories and founders of the Russian style of playing—all sent ardent testimonials. During the 1872–3 season Anton Rubinstein toured America for Steinway, giving 215 concerts and receiving enormous publicity and 200 dollars per concert, in gold. Thus was inaugurated a uniquely American method of sales promotion: the barnstorming tour by a flamboyant virtuoso whose exotic presence and much publicized eccentricities made people talk about, and perhaps buy, pianos. Rubinstein's tour even inspired a popular piece of folksy prose 'Jud Browning hears Ruby Play' which was much recited for the next thirty years.[17] During the 1890s these frenzied events, forerunners of 'pop' enterprises in our own time, reached their culmination in the American tours of Paderewski, a pianist of moderate ability and enormous charisma whose fees, popular reputation, and commercial influence were quite unrelated to his musical achievement.[18]

The most fulsome testimonials came from Liszt and Wagner. The doyen of pianists praised both the concert grand [19] and an upright which 'served under my fingers as Vice-Orchestra'.[20] Confessing his ignorance of the piano's mechanism, he marvelled at the 'magnificent result in volume and quality of sound' and enclosed sketches of two compositions, the third *Consolation* and a transcription of the *Danse des Sylphes* from Berlioz's *Damnation of Faust*.[21] The latter piece made use of Steinway's middle 'sostenuto' pedal which retains the dampers of notes already held down. Thus selected notes can be sustained without the general blurring which results from using the normal sustaining pedal. Invented by Montal in 1862, it was improved and patented by Steinway for squares in 1874, and for uprights and grands in 1875. It is now a standard fitting on most concert and many smaller instruments. The recently expressed opinion [22] that it 'is now seldom met with' is inexplicable. But it was Richard Wagner whose praise for Steinway pianos predictably scaled the heights of eloquence. Deprived of his piano while it was fitted with the new 'tone pulsator' he lamented its loss 'as one misses a beloved wife' and when it returned penned this massive tribute:

I do indeed find it humiliating for so many other branches of art that the art of building pianofortes alone should so closely approach undeniable perfection. I know of nothing in painting, sculpture, architecture, literature, and unfortunately also music, which—since I have comprehension of this—could compare with the masterly perfection reached in pianoforte building. Our great tone masters, when writing the grandest of their creations for the pianoforte, seem to have had a presentiment of the Ideal Grand Piano, as now attained by yourselves. A Beethoven Sonata, a [*sic*] Bach Chromatic Fantasy, can only be fully appreciated when rendered upon one of your pianofortes.[23]

The contrast with modern ideas of 'authentic' performance on 'contemporary' instruments (discussed in Chapter 1) could hardly be greater.

Uncritical acceptance of these eulogies would be ingenuous: Liszt also played Bösendorfers and Erards, and praised Chickerings. But we need not be unduly censorious about the use of relevant testimonials.[24] Their validity when musicians support musical instruments is scarcely open to reasonable objection. The views of a virtuoso whose livelihood depended upon the quality of his tool of trade were relevant to intending purchasers; the opinions of singers, who, in any case, usually preferred accompaniments to be barely audible, were less so. The public could reasonably be expected to distinguish useful testimony from those too eagerly proffered by such artists as the famous prima donna whose activities earned her the unkind sobriquet 'Testimonial Patti'. Merit by association, like guilt, is neither intrinsically true nor false, but depends on the individual case. Steinway, like Wedgwood, offered good wines which still needed a bush. More help came from the informed gossip of the salons, which could persuade those who never deigned to read an advertisement or be persuaded by a puff. Here William found a great ally in the artist Gustave Doré, whose studio in the Rue St Dominique was a gathering place for the most celebrated writers and musicians of the day.[25] It is an exaggerated claim that his endorsement made Steinways '*de rigueur* in French society and thereby in all Europe'[26] for this ignores the entrenched position of the leading European makers, and exaggerates the ease with which conventional attitudes were changed. Nevertheless, Doré had great influence and was an extraordinary capture for an American parvenu.

The activities so far described were continuous and cumulative in their effect upon Steinway's public image: a general association with high quality. Easier to document and more precise in its impact was the firm's appearance at the great international exhibitions. Their catalogues and the jury reports provide abundant evidence for the history of technology —a particularly useful source for the piano historian because the most important exhibitions happened to take place at the time of the instrument's most rapid technical advance. We shall therefore make considerable use of this material, but must first enter a *caveat* against the assumption that it is always representative of typical firms. Frequently, and particularly during a period of rapid technical change, it tends to indicate peaks of achievement, or at least of activity, against a background of traditional practice and inertia. Nevertheless, the exhibitions played a unique role in the diffusion of technology during the second half of the nineteenth century. They were meeting places for technicians and businessmen 'where the latest developments were discussed and publicized'.[27] They were markets where the greatest splash could be made before a large public, with ripple effects of even wider commercial significance. Approximate numbers, in millions, attending the principal European exhibitions were as follows:

1861 London 6	1867 Paris 6.8	1886 London 5.5
1855 Paris 5.1	1873 Vienna 6.7	1889 Paris 32
1862 London 6.2	1878 Paris 16	1900 Paris 39

They were arenas for gladiatorial combat where new and ambitious firms could gain immediate recognition, and old established houses earn fresh laurels or court ignominious defeat. Juries, including qualified experts and others, were subject to national and commercial pressures, their reports and awards brandished as advertisements or ridiculed and abused. Conflict was spectacular, sometimes venomous, for the stakes were high. Like international athletics and football for later generations, these exhibitions belied the myth of international amity which was their alleged *raison d'être*, but they were a potent force for the creation of an image.

The conquest of Europe

Steinway's first European appearance was at the 1862 London Exhibition. The musical instruments section was judged by Fétis, director of the Brussels conservatoire; Sterndale Bennett, a Cambridge professor and composer esteemed by his English contemporaries; Schiedmayer, the aged conservative Stuttgart piano maker; and William Pole. This hapless jury had to apply caucus-race rules which compelled the indiscriminate award of medals, but eight makers received special mention. Broadwood, showing four grands, was described as 'without controversy at the head', sustaining 'the mechanical pre-eminence of our own country'. Bechstein making his London debut with a grand, and Schiedmayer with an upright and a grand, were given medals 'for excellence of construction combined with cheapness'. The award to Streicher, Viennese descendant of Mozart's favourite Stein, was inspired, as Fétis later revealed, by sympathy for the firm's venerable past and the desire to avoid harming its reputation.[28] Hopkinson, Pleyel and Herz also received special mention; and finally Steinway joined this select list of eight. There were also numerous medals

awarded to makers ranging from the distinguished Viennese Bösendorfer
to various nondescript English and French makers. Chappell showed a
'student's pianoforte of four octaves, constructed at the suggestion of Mr
John Hullah', the class-singing enthusiast. It was cheap at eight guineas,
but Bord's pianette at twenty-one pounds was probably a better bargain.
The jury's published verdict was that there had been no significant improvement in manufacture or 'very important novelty' since 1851. Despite
this lack of enthusiasm, they could not ignore the American newcomer
for, as Fétis later recalled, William Steinway's 'incessant playing attracted
great crowds and demonstrated his instruments' power and charm,
delighting both public and jury'.[29] The report praised their 'powerful,
clear and brilliant tone, with excellent workmanship'. Cross stringing and
the whole iron frame were cited as a bold design deserving 'attention on
account of its cheapness, its strength, and the unity it gives to the system
of framing'. The crucial advantages of strength, better placing of the
bridges, unity, and potential cheapness, were all acknowledged. Yet the
jury apparently failed to grasp the revolutionary implications of the new
system, assuming that it was essentially the same as that 'shown in Russian
pianos exhibited in 1851'.[30]

The official report of the 1862 exhibition is thus, for all its information
and insight, a confused and equivocal document. More revealing are the
comments of a French visitor to the exhibition. Louis Adolphe le Doucet,
Marquis de Pontécoulant, was a prolific musical journalist whose unconventional background freed him from deference to established reputations
and entrenched ideas. Born in 1794 and educated at Saint Cyr, he had been
in the retreat from Moscow, fought at Waterloo and in Brazil, and finally
settled in Paris to study astronomy and acoustics, contributing to various
encyclopædias. In 1861 he published an important two-volume work
entitled *Organographie: essai sur la facture instrumentale, art, industrie et commerce*. The following year a visit to London resulted in the entertaining and
informative *Douze jours à Londres—Voyage d'un Mélomane à travers L'Exposition Universelle*. His account begins with a splendidly assured demonstration of Gallic verve and prejudice. Before looking at the exhibits Pontécoulant assumes that in France the art of piano construction has reached a
state of perfection. He then examines the German and Austrian instruments, trouncing them for their poor sound, 'formes lourdes, absence de
toute élégance'.[31] Elsewhere he finds little improvement since the 1855
Paris Exhibition. Belgian makers have made some progress and are now
better than the English, save for Broadwood and Collard. The former is
brilliant, like the French Erard; the latter charming, an English Pleyel;
though neither, of course, quite achieves Paris standards. Undoubtedly
the Pleyel surpasses all rivals, with its perfect blend of suave and brilliant

sound, its excellent repetition and damping. Returning to the attack on Germany he finds few instruments which sound well; all look hideous and many are cheap rubbish, destined to rapid disintegration.[32] Only the Bechstein is well made but it too lacks sonority: an opinion to which we must return. Despite their frankness and lively turn of phrase, these xenophobic views scarcely deserve particular attention. What distinguishes Pontécoulant's account, however, is his perception of incipient change in the industry's international balance of power, to which we shall return in Chapter 4, and his practical common-sense approach to the Steinway. All the experts on acoustics, he reports, had found the American system defective on theoretical grounds. Yet the fact remains that the pianos are very well constructed and their sound is remarkable: practice apparently confounds theory.[33]

Other visitors were less discerning. The *Musical Standard*'s correspondent felt unable to 'record the introduction of any very important novelty' since 1851. A long list of medal winners was duly noted, including awards to Greiner and Wornum for 'novelty of invention' and to Harrison for 'simplicity of action'. Welcoming cheaper and 'more humble instruments' the writer accepted the increased price of Broadwood grands, raised from 175 to 250 guineas, as justified by improved construction. His sole complaint was against the continued and unreasonable rise in pitch, dictated by opera and concert bands, which increased both string tension and cost.[34] No English evidence exists of an awareness of incipient revolution, even of interest in a new, potentially profitable technology. The prevailing complacency was well expressed in a book which purported to view the exhibition as a panorama of the 'Industry, Science and Art of the Age'. Its author remained convinced that 'England held its position as the first pianoforte manufacturing country of the world'.[35] Meanwhile, for William Steinway the exhibition had served its exploratory purpose, a preliminary bout before the grand heavyweight contest. He sold his stock to Cramer Beale and Co., and returned to New York. The purchasers were equally satisfied. Twenty-eight years later, Concert Grand 4607, the prize winner of 1862, was renovated and reported 'good as new'.[36]

The Paris Exhibition of 1867 was a magnificent affair, an invitation by Napoleon III to view a transformed France. Its cosmopolitan delights included a Chinese theatre, Indian dancing girls, a Krupps cannon, the orchestra of Johann Strauss, and the delectable Mlle Schneider, Offenbach's *Grande Duchesse*.[37] For business men, preferably without their wives, it was a superb market place, better organized than its London predecessors. For the pianoforte makers of Europe it was the turning point. Twenty-five years later E. J. Mangeot, a leading French authority, looked back and described this watershed.[38] It was, he argued, 'simplement un fait historique' that in 1867 European piano manufacture was transformed. Five years earlier in London, American innovations had passed almost unnoticed, but at the Paris Exhibition only the French were unimpressed. The rest of Europe, led by Germany, fell immediately into step. Mangeot exaggerates the suddenness of transformation—the outcome of industrial conflict is rarely so swift and conclusive—and the obtuseness of his countrymen. Not all French manufacturers were arch-conservatives, nor was such intransigence confined to France. But the thrust of his argument is correct, and much subsequent piano history concerns its ramifications.

At first glance the exhibition's jury for musical instruments might have been selected to favour tradition and oppose new trends. Several of its members, including the ubiquitous Fétis, were in their eighties. Julius Schiedmayer had trained with conservative makers and was head of one of the oldest German firms. In addition to a French general and two flowers of the English aristocracy, there were also Georges Kastner, a minor composer and writer of textbooks, and Ambroise Thomas, composer of *Mignon*, professor at the Paris Conservatoire and shortly to become its director. Finally there was Hanslick, the eminent critic, who in the following year was to be lampooned by Wagner as Beckmesser, the epitome of reaction. The age and background of these men are important. Most musicians judge the quality of sound by what is familiar to them, even in modern conditions when radio and recordings enormously widen experience and encourage catholicity. The Paris jury was accustomed to the sound of pre-Steinway pianos, yet its awards were a triumph for the new instruments. Of the four gold medals two were for American pianos, one for a copy, and only one for a traditional instrument. The latter, awarded to Broadwood, was described by Pontécoulant in a wounding and prophetic phrase as a 'souvenir des travaux passés'.[39] Streicher's award reflected a complex state of affairs. It owed something to Hanslick's advocacy,[40] but the instrument, far from being representative of traditional Viennese practice, was based upon Steinway's 1862 model. Streicher had been so impressed by this instrument at the London Exhibition that he had abandoned traditional methods and adopted iron frames and overstringing. 'The transformation is complete and the result a happy one', reported Fétis.[41] Equally spectacular were the gold medals awarded to Steinway and Chickering, and the ignominious absence of any French maker from the list.

The jury's report, written by Fétis, contained an enthusiastic description of the American pianos commending their powerful tone which resulted from more solid construction and heavier strings than were found in European instruments. This, however, required more energetic and therefore noisier 'attack' from the hammers; and here the Steinway gained over its rival by virtually eliminating hammer noise. Both manufacturers had achieved a sonority hitherto unknown, filling the largest concert halls, but Steinway had established an undoubted advantage over Chickering in expression, delicate shading and variety of tone. It was, concluded the report, the ideal piano for concert room and parlour.[42]

Reactions to this spectacular result were diverse, ranging from gloomy foreboding to bland indifference. Steinway and Chickering had gone to Paris fully realizing the commercial importance of success. Allegedly they had each spent some 80,000 dollars in a preliminary two months of promotion, hiring pianists, issuing brochures, providing entertainment and inspiring newspaper comment.[43] Fulsome eulogies of their products need to be read against this background, but cynicism should not be pressed too far. Against suspicions of palm greasing we must balance the distinction of many of the eulogists, the later success of both firms and the quality of surviving instruments. Having secured their medals they proceeded, of course, to extract from them the maximum of publicity, but in his eagerness Chickering precipitated an acrimonious, if slightly comic, internecine conflict. By influence or merit he had become a Chevalier of the Legion of Honour and claimed this as the exhibition's highest award, ranking above mere gold medals. This version of the result was transmitted by the new transatlantic cable, before publication of the official report, and celebrated by Chickering's workers with a holiday parade in Boston. Later pamphlets were issued claiming 'Chickering's American pianos triumphant over all the world. . . . The Legion of Honour is officially announced as the First Grand Prize. . . . Gold medals are rated as third prizes'. William Steinway retaliated by publishing a letter from Fétis which confirmed that his firm had secured 'la première médaille d'or pour les pianos Américains'. The row went on for several months in the Paris, Boston and New York papers, with errors of translation and misprints fanning the flames. In one memorable exchange the *Gazette Musicale* was confused with *Le Ménestral* and described as an 'obscene' instead of 'obscure' musical journal! A blow by blow account of the affair, with an amusing commentary by the musicologist Oscar Commetant, appeared in *Le Ménestral* between April and November 1867. In the nature of things such an imbroglio could have no simple resolution, but it did serve to imprint the names of Chickering and Steinway more firmly upon the public mind, and to deepen antagonism and distrust between the two leading American manufacturers.

Meanwhile, English and French makers remained disdainfully aloof. Only Auguste Wolff, director of Pleyel, entered an apologia. Stung by the suggestion that his pianos had been withdrawn from the exhibition because he feared defeat by Steinway, he retorted with *noblesse oblige*. As an official at the exhibition and representative of a house which had won every honour in the past, he had regarded it as his duty to remain *hors concours*, leaving the field to newcomers with a reputation to make.[44] The plea was unconvincing. Once again it was Pontécoulant, returning to his 1862 theme, who provided the most trenchant reply. In a series of articles for *L'Art musical*, later published as a book, he remonstrated with the European, and particularly the French, manufacturers for having produced nothing new in twenty years, and for failing to meet the American challenge. 'Oh! Pierre Erard, où es tu?' he lamented, invoking an image of the great craftsman shuddering in his winding sheet with shame at the weakness of Old World manufacturers who had accepted defeat without combat. Europe is tired; America has accepted the burden! And so forth for many pages.[45] The *Revue et Gazette Musicale de Paris* pronounced Steinway's instruments 'une véritable révélation', but preferred Chickering's grand (perhaps because it was straight-strung, though iron framed). So perfect an instrument had never left the workshop of a European manufacturer.[46]

It would be tedious to continue enumerating even a representative sample of the votaries who paid homage to American pianos in 1867. Two final examples must suffice. The first is unfortunately in the French rhetorical style of musical criticism, but is particularly interesting because the piece which was played, Liszt's *Legend of St Francis*, was ideally suited to display the new instrument's qualities. John Ogdon has said that it requires 'Busoni's monumental performance, with the theme sculpted in relief, the accompaniment a wash of sound'.[47] It also required a modern piano: its effect when played on the new Steinway was enthusiastically described by Commetant: 'Ces notes parlent comme la voix d'un chanteur, s'élèvent graduellement, se lient entre elles, prient, soupirent, s'éxaltent et s'éteignent ainsi que la pensée qui, après avoir aspiré vers l'infini de l'idéal, retombe accablée dans le néant de notre impuissance'.[48]

A plainer, more technical appreciation came from the greatest French composer of the age. Hector Berlioz's inability to play the piano was notorious—it had prevented him from securing employment at the Paris Conservatoire. But he had long experience as a critic, and many acquaintances among pianists, including Marie Pleyel, an eminent virtuoso and wife of the manufacturer. All this had made him familiar with the instrument's resources, and very critical of its defects.[49] For him the Steinway's chief attractions were its 'splendid and noble sonority' and the virtual elimination of the 'terrible resonance of the minor seventh' which afflicted the bottom eight or nine notes of other pianos, and made 'cacophoniques' the simplest and most beautiful chords.[50] Precisely the same point was made by Fétis who noted in his report that several instruments which were otherwise excellent suffered from this 'insupportable' fault.

English commentators were cooler and less well informed. Several reasons account for the paucity of informed comment. There were no English composers, pianists or academic musicians of sufficient eminence to carry much weight. There was as yet no trade press; only a few general musical journals with peripheral interest in the instrument. Nevertheless, the sheer ineptitude and ignorance of correspondents visiting the exhibition are striking, and were probably a serious barrier to the education of both industry and public. The general level of competence is represented by a report that 'musical amateurs seem greatly to admire Steinway's pianos, which by means of oblique chords [*sic*] and a curved arrangement possess a beautiful tone and powerful sound.' [51] The *Musical Standard*'s reporter found Blütner's [*sic*] grand piano fair but lacking equality, admired Bechtein's [*sic*] instrument for its external beauty, suggested that in Steinway's grand 'the frame *appears* to be of cast iron' and concluded that the Broadwood was 'undoubtedly the finest piano in the building . . . the grandest we have ever heard'. The English industry was otherwise poorly represented, he argued, because of the 'farce and evils of the prize system', the expense and risks of transport, and the fact that improvements could be copied by 'the intelligent foreigner'.[52]

More culpable than this innocent chauvinism was an official report on the exhibition prepared with the avowed object of directing attention to improvements in manufacture. The section on musical instruments was blind to the new trends. French pianos were admired for their facile touch and brilliance and condemned for their lack of power. The American pianos were admired, but Broadwood's concert grand was pronounced the finest on show. Most German instruments were judged deficient in 'strength and character'. Such makers as Bechstein, Blüthner, Duysen, Ibach and Irmler, destined shortly to conquer England's domestic and foreign markets, were ignored.[53] No hint of significant developments in the industry can be discerned in England during this crucial period. The prevailing mood of patriotic euphoria is well caught by the *Musical Standard*'s announcement that 'We have no reason to dread competition in the manufacture of music instruments.[54]

Adopting and rejecting the new technology—Vienna 1873 and Paris 1878

Six years later, at the Vienna International Exhibition, the 'American system' consolidated its victory decisively, but without significant representation from America itself. Only two American piano manufacturers took part: George Steck, who made high quality instruments,[55] and a Louisville firm exhibiting obsolete squares. Both received 'honourable mention' (*Anerkennungsdiplom*) but were dismissed in the official report as 'feeble imitators' of the Steinway system.[56] Although Chickering and Steinway were reluctant to undertake the risks and costs of participation, neither could afford to leave the other a clear field. They therefore signed a formal confidential agreement to abstain or to pay a forfeit of 50,000 dollars. The pact was short-lived: both firms kept to its letter but Steinway's extensive extra-mural activities incurred his rival's wrath, expressed in a pamphlet entitled: 'A plain statement of facts concerning the American pianos which were not to be exhibited at the International Exhibition of Vienna, 1873.' According to this document, four members of the musical instruments jury were invited to a private demonstration, liberally entertained, and persuaded to write into their report a glowing tribute to Steinway's pre-eminence, regretting the firm's absence from the exhibition. The official report did indeed contain these words, worth more than any prize for an official entry: 'It is very much to be regretted that the famous path-breaking firm of Steinway and Sons, New York, to which the whole art of piano making owes so much [so viel zu verdanken] was not represented'.[57] But this was more probably a genuine appreciation by expert practitioners than the obsequious testimony of hired lackeys. The four 'accused' were Hanslick and Schiedmayer, already met in these pages; Oscar Paul who had recently published a scholarly history of the piano, and Friedrich Ehrbar, one of the most distinguished of Viennese piano makers and lifelong friend of the Steinways. Chickering's understandable exasperation at his rival's astuteness should not be allowed to confuse the main issue: the Steinway *was* pre-eminent and anyone in Vienna with a genuine interest in the piano was naturally anxious to see new models and likely to praise them.

More significant than verbal appreciation, however, was the compliment of imitation, for a large proportion of the instruments exhibited in 1873 were modelled upon Steinways, some frankly acknowledging in the catalogue their adoption of the 'American system'. According to William his pianos at the London 1862 Exhibition had been 'immediately copied by all the German . . . and many other continental makers'; prize-winners in Paris (1867) had included numerous imitations, and at Vienna more than two thirds of the medals were awarded to direct copies.[58] Available evidence does not allow a precise assessment of this claim, but it is broadly corroborated by catalogues and jury reports.

Table II summarizes the main features of the piano section; there were also instruments from Belgium, Holland, Switzerland, Sweden, Norway, Denmark, Italy and Spain. Grand pianos were a prominent feature—a total of 164 were shown, in contrast to the sixty-seven exhibited in London in 1862 and seventy-six at the Paris 1867 Exhibition. Two influences

Table II Pianos at the Vienna Exhibition of 1873

	Firms	Grands *	Uprights	Squares	Total
Germany	66	35	92	2	129
Austria	48	86	13	—	99
France	11	11	23	—	34
England	2	4	8	—	12
Russia	10	10	—	—	10
United States	2	2	1	2	5

* including short grands, or 'Stutzflügel'. Austrian makers exhibited twenty-eight of these.

account for this: an increasing number of firms seeking prestige, and the traditional bias of the Austrian market where, in contrast to England, musicians were a significant group of consumers and uprights therefore were not yet popular. Nevertheless some Viennese makers, including the great Bösendorfer, showed overstrung instruments with iron frames, and there were a few similar examples of progress in a generally nondescript group of pianos from France. Even Pleyel exhibited two concert grands and a short grand which were overstrung. The ground had been prepared for this *volte face* at an elaborate demonstration in Paris where several pianists, including Saint-Saëns, played the new Pleyels which, a correspondent claimed, were equal to Steinways in every respect and better in the clarity of their bass. The same writer was convinced that overstringing was impracticable for uprights, a view which, despite its absurd wrongheadedness, was apparently shared by most French manufacturers.[59] The jury gave short shrift to these sentiments. One official report congratulated Pleyel on its successful adoption of the American system; the other mentioned the firm only in an historical introduction, and remarked that most prominent firms had taken Steinway's instruments as models.[60]

If American and French representation was inadequate, the English contingent was derisory. Kirkman, claiming origins in 1730 and by 1873 distinguished for little except antiquity, showed several grands and uprights. Henry Ivory, with an optimistic disregard for obsolescence, displayed three cheap, wooden-framed straight-strung uprights with primitive 'sticker' actions. The German display was infinitely better, not merely because of its size or the presence of such distinguished makers as Blüthner and Ibach (surprisingly not Bechstein), but because of the large numbers of modern upright pianos by hitherto obscure makers, many of them recently established. Moreover, most of them were moderately priced at between forty and sixty pounds. A trend which was perceptible at the Paris Exhibition had become an efflorescence: the German piano industry was poised for its conquest of world markets.

After these repeated American and German successes, some kind of reaction was inevitable. It came at the next Paris Exhibition in 1878. Since Germany did not compete and America sent no pianos of distinction competition was not severe in terms of quality, but was intensive because the commercial stakes were high. The proceedings were enlivened by a jury which emerged from internecine warfare to shower awards upon every French manufacturer in sight, and by an obtuse chauvinistic report. All this was extensively discussed in an expanded trade press which contributed to the general gossip and rancour.[61] The jury was to have included Liszt, who wisely declined (allegedly after seeing the names of his fellow jurors) and was replaced by Antoine Bord, the energetic successful French manufacturer of cheap mass-produced pianos. This appointment was greeted by the English trade as proof that the Exhibition authorities had no intention of even appearing to be impartial. Among the other members were Gustav Chouquet, curator of the Paris conservatoire museum; Hanslick; and Dr Stainer, organist at St Paul's, composer of *The Crucifixion*, and described by a sympathetic compatriot as wise and knowledgeable, but not about pianos.

The awards exceeded the critics' worst expectations. French musical instrument makers received seventeen gold medals, fifty-three silver, seventy bronze and thirty-six honourable mentions. England's share was, respectively, one, three, four and six. The ration for other countries was even more exiguous. Inevitably there was a storm of rebuke and rumour. Most of the jury were deemed 'utterly ignorant of piano construction' and alleged to have judged pianos without hearing them. It was thought that a prime source of trouble was the 'idiotic rule' that any firm which had won a gold medal in earlier Paris Exhibitions should not now be given a lesser award. Probably it was this which precipitated a split in the jury and the resignation of five of its members, leaving power in the hands of one 'inimical to British and American interests' (obviously Bord) against strong protests by two of the principal English exhibitors, Brinsmead and Challen. The outcome was that Hopkinson gained the sole English gold medal, presumably on grounds of past glory; Brinsmead's original gold was transmuted to silver, and Challen left with a bronze. All this was attributed to Bord's determination to use his position to depreciate his most successful competitors in English and colonial markets. Dr Stainer 'acted manfully . . . against the slippery Frenchman' but was hampered by being 'hopelessly ignorant of the technical details of pianoforte manufacture'. John Brinsmead, the rising star of English piano manufacture, was compensated by becoming a Chevalier of the Legion of Honour. The ensuing warfare by advertisement between Brinsmead and Hopkinson, each claiming a higher award, echoed the Steinway-Chickering row of the previous decade. 'The truth is that the Paris Exhibition has been a glorious muddle, and the sooner it is forgotten the better', concluded the *Music Trades Review*, adding hopefully that the forthcoming official report by M. Chouquet 'must redeem' Paris.

Far from bringing redemption, the report when it finally appeared in 1881 opened old wounds and inflicted a few new ones. Because Chouquet's report represents the high water mark, or dying gasp, of French conservatism, its main features deserve some attention. Since Steinway's brilliant success in 1867, he argued, too many piano manufacturers had allowed themselves to be deceived ('séduire') by iron and overstringing; some had even adopted the unnecessary third pedal. Most French and English makers, unlike the obsequious Germans, had fortunately shown more reserve in the use of metal and had merely experimented with crossed strings. Erard was thus to be congratulated for remaining faithful to the traditional disposition of strings, and Hopkinson and Brinsmead were also 'wisely progressive'. Pleyel's use of iron could be accepted since the metal was wrought, not cast. Herz had changed nothing, and 'we do not complain . . . why modify that which is good?' While M. Bord, placed *hors concours* by his membership, deserved applause for his modestly priced instruments of great solidity, M. Mangeot's 'servile imitations of Steinway' merited disapproval. Alfred Dolge, who sought to dethrone European manufacturers of felt, needed first to eradicate the 'insupportable odour' from an otherwise good material. In conclusion, Chouquet considered that the French piano, both upright and grand, had reached an ideal state of perfection but was in danger of losing its character. Created as a chamber instrument it lost its best qualities when forced to battle against an orchestra. Having thus dismissed a vast repertoire of music and a generation of technical progress, M. Chouquet concluded with the happy thought that the three greatest French houses retained their incontestable superiority, serving as patterns to imitators from all other countries.[62]

Piano makers outside France were so flabbergasted by this farrago that they responded either with incoherent fury, or with a point by point rebuttal of Chouquet's arguments which it would be tedious to enumerate. Two reactions are worth quoting. The *Music Trades Review* reported accurately that leading French makes, far from acting as 'patterns', had been copied by no one for many years, and published a letter from Dolge, who was by then the world's leading manufacturer of felt, denying that his products stank and offering them for test.[63] William Steinway, above these battles, scoffed at Chouquet's 'ridiculous attempts to talk away facts' and explained that such absurdities justified the determination of 'manufacturers of standing with a first class reputation to keep away from exhibitions if they can'.[64] From his viewpoint the argument was unassailable: once an international reputation had been attained it was probably wise to avoid international exhibitions. But how else could a 'first class reputation' be established, or regained, than through success at the maligned exhibitions? If the malfeasance of successive juries had tarnished their prestige it had neither quite demolished their *raison d'être* nor deterred future aspirants from their appraisal.

After a quarter century of business what had Steinway achieved? First, its name had been firmly imprinted upon the public mind as representing the *ne plus ultra* of piano making, a reputation challenged by few, even special pleaders within the trade, and only seriously by Bechstein. This victory was remarkable not least because it was in an area remote from the 'rough wares' or mere commercialism at which Americans were allowed to excel. Mechanical ingenuity had been demonstrated in farm machinery and small arms; but now an 'art-product' had overcome deep rooted prejudice against the New World. Moreover, Steinway's pacemaking had been followed and the 'American system' was now adopted by all progressive or—if the word offends—successful European manufacturers. Above all, a viable upright had been created, setting the pattern for all future development. It compared with its predecessors, ran an English advertisement in 1882, 'as a MODERN IRONCLAD to a CANOE'. Few advertisements have departed less from the plain truth.

The 1878 Exhibition requires a final footnote. Among the exhibits was a modest square piano, unrewarded and barely noticed. It came from Japan.

Chapter 4

The Emergence of Germany

The rise of the German piano was sudden and swift. In 1860 the industry was small and undistinguished; few makers were known or respected outside Germany. Even local needs would sometimes remain unsatisfied, for in addition to production deficiencies, marketing procedures and stock control were rudimentary and unable to cope with seasonal fluctuations. In 1873 Amy Fay complained: 'There isn't a piano to be had in Weimar for love or money, as there is no manufactory, and the few there were to be disposed of were snatched up before I got here. I . . . was obliged to go first to Erfurt and finally to Leipzig before I could find one —and even that was sent over as a favour after much coaxing and persuasion.'[1] A few years later she would have had no difficulty. By the mid eighties German instruments were to be found in concert halls, conservatoires and drawing rooms everywhere in Europe outside France, in Welsh mining villages, provincial parlours and the Australian outback. This efflorescence is difficult to measure. German statistics are little better than English, particularly for the early decades. They frequently refer, for example, to all musical instruments rather than to pianos alone, and are subject to errors and contradictions. Nevertheless it is possible, by sceptical manipulation, to piece together some quantitative evidence. In 1861 there were less than 8,000 workers making all kinds of musical instruments throughout Germany. By 1875 their numbers had doubled, and by 1882 trebled. In 1907 approximately 6,700 firms were employing 47,000 people, of whom sixty-three per cent were at work in piano manufacture.[2] Total production can only be roughly assessed. During the 1880s it was probably between sixty and seventy thousand pianos, lower than output in the USA but more than three times that of France. By 1913 it exceeded 100,000, probably greater than English production, four times that of France, but only one third the size of America's vast industry.

This rapid growth was firmly based upon a prosperous, protected but discriminating home market which never took less than half of total production. Exports, of course, played a vital role, but the industry's dependence upon them, which was later exaggerated by some English makers and their apologists who were worried by German competition in home

68

and colonial markets, could never be fairly described as 'dumping'. The real significance of German exports was the extraordinary speed with which they wrested markets from competitors, demolishing French competition and transforming, by their impact and example, the English trade and industry.

England was Germany's largest foreign market, taking by the mid eighties perhaps half of her exports (i.e. roughly one quarter of her total production) with Australia second, and Russia, Brazil and South Africa

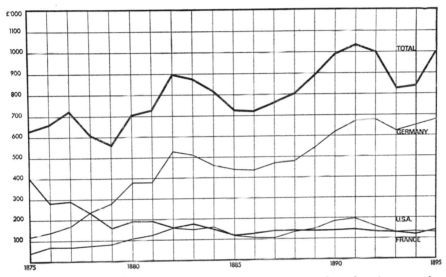

Figure 1 UK gross imports of musical instruments—totals and main countries of origin 1875–95 (values in thousands of pounds).

also significant outlets. Figure 1 illustrates Germany's achievement in the English market. British statistics for this period do not separate imports of pianos from those of other musical instruments, but they probably accounted for more than sixty per cent of the total. This estimate is confirmed by other scraps of information. In 1882, for example, £400,000 worth of German pianos were said to have been shipped to London.[3] Since others went directly to provincial ports our estimate of sixty per cent is very modest for that year. The slowly rising American line is partly explained by imports of Steinways up to the early eighties, after which England's supplies came from the new factory at Hamburg. Another influence was the increasing sales of American 'reed organs' or harmoniums which, with their improved 'sucking' action, virtually drove their French 'blowing' competitors from the market. It will be noted how rapidly French imports fell during the late seventies as German pianos took over, and continued to fall, never to recover in the aggregate, though

69

a few makers retained a peripheral market. Figure 1's principal feature, of course, is the continual rise of German imports,[4] dipping only slightly during the 'depression years' and asserting an unequivocal dominance over an expanding market which remained unchallenged until 1914. In calculating these figures we have added Dutch imports to the official estimates for Germany because, as was common knowledge in the trade, 'supposed imports from Holland' were 'nearly all pianos from Germany shipped for convenience from Rotterdam or Amsterdam'.[5] In fact the graph understates Germany's growing influence in the British market, for as her shipping and port facilities improved, more pianos were sent direct to such markets as Australia, rather than being routed through England. Net or 'retained' imports into England therefore rose faster than gross imports, and Germany's importance was proportionately greater.

Table III   Piano Imports into the Argentine and Brazil
(all figures represent values in £'000)

	Argentine				*Brazil*		
		Imports from				*Imports from*	
	Germany	*France*	*USA*	*England*	*Germany*	*France*	*England*
1900	33.5	1.4	1.5	1.8			
1901	28.8	3.9	5.0	0.4			
1902	21.9	1.9	1.8	1.0	40.2	12.8	1.8
1903	30.5	3.7	4.1	0.6			
1904					48.0	12.4	1.4

[*Source: Music Trades Review* June 1905 and July 1906.]

German success in 'colonial' markets was even more sweeping. In 1869 France exported 2,000 pianos to Australia; Germany a mere 200. By 1890 the situation was completely reversed, Germany sending 3,900 and France 92. Figure 2 (p. 86) illustrates the main trends in Australia. Statistical sources are again refractory, indicating, for example, ports of origin rather than countries of manufacture, so that English figures for earlier years are, for our purpose, overstated. Nevertheless the general trend of German dominance is unmistakable. No French figures are quoted because they rapidly dwindled to insignificance. A similar process is illustrated finally in Table III. The Brazilian case is a rare example of France retaining a sizable part of the market. The failure of English pianos was particularly remarkable in the Argentine where British capital and influence were substantial. Noting this fact, the *Music Trades Review* added a significant detail: 'again our higher class pianos are beaten and we are left with the cheap trade'.[6]

By what means were these extraordinary successes achieved? The essential cause, argues Loesser,[7] was economic rather than cultural, part of the general industrialization and thrusting external trade which followed German unification and the defeat of France. Before this, her craftsmen had perforce copied French and English models or, like Pape and Steinway, migrated to countries where their skills could be better exploited. Now the centre of gravity changed: in the modern piano industry, machine technology and commercial skills became more significant than craftsmanship and a great musical tradition. The argument is sensible and illuminating. It suggests an explanation for the decline of piano manufacture in France and Austria where, at least in the latter case, an unsurpassed musical environment was unmatched by industrial advance. Similarly the insignificance of Italy's industry was probably more a result of enonomic backwardness than of an operatic tradition which neglected instrumental music. Most piano makers everywhere could get by without undue musical sensitivity or awareness. Few 'garret makers' in Berlin or Camden Town were concert goers or pianists. Some highly successful manufacturers were no more cultivated. One American tycoon published an autobiography of 352 double-columned pages replete with personal reminiscence without betraying any interest, knowledge or liking for music.[8] He differed from several of his English contemporaries only in being more garrulous; yet cultural factors cannot be totally excluded, as Loesser implicitly concedes throughout his book. A George Payne Bent could not have captured Europe; a Bechstein does not emerge or survive in a climate of philistinism; a national music industry ignores music and musicians at its peril as will be demonstrated in later pages. Meanwhile, to understand how and why the industry's international balance of power underwent a sea change we must attempt to get beneath the surface of these impressionistic generalizations.

Germany's success was based upon a formidable amalgam of qualities, technical, commercial and cultural. First there was a willingness and ability to adopt the latest technology, backed by the best system of technical and commercial education in the world and a widespread respect for applied science. Secondly, the Germans exerted a commercial thrust of prodigious vitality through agents with initiative, linguistic ability and, not least, modern catalogues—again the product of modern technology. Finally there was, of course, the immense prestige of German music which attached itself to the country's pianos.

Substantial evidence of these achievements appeared at the Amsterdam Exhibition of 1883, where fifty-five German makers showed 143 pianos, more than two thirds of the total displayed. This eagerness to compete was in marked contrast to British attitudes which were well expressed by the *Music Trades Review*: it was folly to trust 'the jury of an outside exhibition of this sort with a decision which may affect the status of a valuable business'; firms staying out lose little; those competing *must* do well. German houses 'particularly of a lower rank' could rush freely in, but leading English and French makers knew it did not pay. The best Americans had learned the same lesson and even the leading Germans would probably follow suit.[9] In fact, some of the best German makers did take part, including Blüthner, Feurich, Lipp and both Schiedmayer firms. Outrage was expressed after the announcement of awards, despite the fact that Brinsmead, the sole English competitor, had taken a first prize. Some of the best firms were alleged to have received only minor awards because they had refused to incur the trouble 'and expense of an agent to work the racket' [*sic*]. Such comment is more useful as a reflection of contemporary opinion than a record of fact. Most of it was conveniently forgotten or even retracted a few months later when the same journal advised its readers that in reading the Exhibition's official report the opinions of the rapporteur, 'a gentleman so gifted with business experience and artistic knowledge and taste, should be received with becoming respect'.[10]

The jury was by no means undistinguished, including the heads of Pleyel and Kaps. Its perceptive report was written by Victor Mahillon, a Belgian manufacturer of brass instruments who was also an acknowledged authority on acoustics. It is so remarkable for its grasp of both the technical and the economic implications of Germany's success that it deserves careful scrutiny. Mahillon begins with an historical résumé of recent changes in the industry, unequivocally welcoming the contribution of American technology. At the 1862 London Exhibition Steinway's pianos had 'surpassed in quality and fullness of tone all that had hitherto been made' and, despite uninformed criticism, further progress and experience had established the absolute superiority of the American system. The German trade was the first to realize this and its present prosperity is the inevitable result. The system's advantage lies in its ability not merely to produce durable instruments but to economize in the use of skilled work, substituting machinery for manual labour and increasing 'the division of labour—the first source of cheapness and business perfection'. The necessities of the epoch demand two kinds of piano, 'the art and the industrial'. Mahillon does not elucidate these 'necessities', but he does suggest that three quarters of all buyers 'merely follow the fashion of the time', and his report is imbued with a practical sense of market realities. The Amsterdam Exhibition, he argues, demonstrates that England, France and Belgium (mandatory patriotism here) can still compete in 'art manufacture' but not in cheapness. Some German pianos are now exported at half the price of those manufactured 'under ordinary conditions'. Why are they so cheap? Despite much propaganda, cheap labour cannot be the explanation since wages in Berlin, from which most of the pianos come, are not significantly lower than in other capitals, and many of the instruments use actions (the most labour intensive part) made in France. The answer lies rather in the 'suppression of unnecessary work', economizing in all materials which do not directly contribute to tone, sensibly leaving 'unfinished' those parts which cannot be seen and, above all, in thoroughgoing specialization. Nor is the success of these methods confined to commercial instruments, for the finest German makers have demonstrated that 'pianos of the new school respond to all the most delicate exigencies of art'. At present buyers of art pianos are little influenced by price, and famous makers of the old school have not yet experienced much price competition from the Germans, but this will surely come. In both art and commercial manufacture, therefore, survival can only be achieved by a decision to 'break definitely with the old method, and to adopt, like our neighbours on the other side of the Rhine, the American system'.[11]

The Amsterdam Exhibition thus demonstrated, and its report explained, that Germany's success was firmly based upon the adoption of American technology. Yet, as in the history of Steinway's, technological superiority was a necessary but insufficient key to commercial success. Marketing skills were equally significant, and here German firms succeeded not merely in wresting existing markets from their competitors, but in tapping hitherto undeveloped sources of demand. To illustrate these processes we shall describe first the evolution of some representative firms, then the general structure of the industry and, finally, the conquest of Germany's two principal export markets, England and Australia.

Distinguished Firms—new and old

Undisputed leader of the German industry because of the quality of his instruments and the energy of his drive for exports was Carl Bechstein. Born at Gotha in 1826, he was already foreman of G. Perau, a prominent Berlin firm, by the time he was twenty two. Not content with this he left for Paris to join the group of ambitious young apprentices studying under the great craftsman Pape. Dolge's suggestion that he spent part of his *wanderjahren* in London is probably wrong: Bechstein's first visit appears to have been for the 1862 Exhibition. But at Kriegelstein's factory he acquired 'a thorough knowledge of Parisian commercial tactics' and, according to Dolge, 'an insight into modern business methods'.[12] It is likely, however, that the latter skills as practised in France at that time were to prove less useful than friendship with Jean Schwander, whose piano actions were soon to be used by first class makers throughout

Europe. In 1853 Bechstein commenced business in Berlin making a few uprights, and in the autumn of 1856 he scored a notable success when his first grand piano was inaugurated by von Bülow with a performance of the Liszt Sonata.

Thus began one of the most significant relationships between instrument maker and virtuoso in the history of music, each stimulating the other to higher achievement. Convinced that until then 'nothing really outstanding had been produced in Germany ' [13] Bülow did everything in his considerable power to help Bechstein establish an international reputation. It was because of his recommendation to Klindworth that Bechstein was encouraged to take part in the 1862 London Exhibition, and his loyalty to the firm probably accounts for Bülow's refusal to play Steinways in America. On his extensive concert tours he was constantly looking out for commercial opportunities: 'In Wurzburg there are many rich foreigners (Russians, English, etc., there to consult the famous doctors) and they can buy pianos. Why leave the field to Blüthner?' [14] From Florence he writes in January 1870, 'Bülow and Bechstein in Italy. It must come. Business here is good—people buy many grands—particularly new Erards, Pleyels, Herzs'.[15] From Amsterdam three years later, 'Quite an uproar here because I'm playing your pianos ... Pleyels have complained'. But Bülow was far from being an obsequious tout: his criticism was knowledgeable, trenchant and persistent. One letter, for example, complains in detail about a piano's poor repetition, and offers to demonstrate several passages which cannot be played on it, the failure lying not in Bülow's technique, but in the instrument—'an old weakness with your pianos as with those of your poor imitator [schlechten Nachahmer] Blüthner'.[16]

As a craftsman Bechstein combined the exalted standards inculcated by Pape with an eclectic awareness of new developments. Thus every one of his pianos after 1855 was fitted with a check action, and after 1870 all had iron frames. There can be little doubt that he scrutinized the Steinway exhibited in 1862, and subsequently borrowed many ideas from his greatest rival. Moreover, he was aware from the outset that the 'American system' was far more than a matter of design, but demanded a fundamental commitment to mass production and machine technology. Ten years after starting he was employing over one hundred workers and making three hundred instruments. In 1882, output passed the thousand a year mark and rose steadily thereafter, until 1913 when the firm was employing 1,200 men making 5,000 instruments, half of them exported to England. This apparently low physical productivity is offset by the high price of his pianos, and the fact that Bechstein's pianos were consistently among the most perfect ever made. It is a remarkable fact that Germany's finest manufacturer was also one of her largest, refuting a prevailing myth of the small craftsman's superiority.

Such levels of output would have been impossible without those 'Parisian commercial tactics' noted by Dolge, which were, of course, the same as those previously employed by William Steinway. In addition to Bülow, many leading European pianists played Bechsteins. In October 1892 Bechstein Hall, named as a tribute by its owner, the impresario Wolff, was opened in Berlin with recitals by Bülow, Brahms, Joachim and Anton Rubinstein. A catalogue of that year lists among the firm's patrons Queen Victoria (who purchased a Bechstein grand in 1881), and twelve other monarchs including the Kaiser and Czar, twenty-six Royal Highnesses and Serene Highnesses, 'etc. etc.'. Among the etceteras were many English stately homes. As Noël Coward accurately notes, it was a Bechstein grand that could be pawned. In London, another Bechstein Hall (later the Wigmore Hall) was opened, which until 1914 provided an important platform for visiting artists and a constant reminder of the instrument's excellence. Retail prices in England, which were firmly maintained, ranged during the 1890s from £60 for the smaller uprights to £300 for a concert grand, some fifteen per cent below the prices of comparable Steinway models.

Bechstein's most serious competitor was Julius Blüthner. Born at Falkenhain in 1826, the son of a village carpenter, he trained first as a cabinet maker and then, in 1840, joined the important Zeitz piano firm of Hölling and Spangenburg. In 1853 Blüthner started his own business in Leipzig, with three men and a boy, won a prize at a Munich industrial exhibition in 1854, patented a good repetition action, and then rapidly expanded his business. Between 1858 and 1863 his labour force increased from fourteen to a hundred. In 1881 there were five Blüthner factories producing a total of one thousand instruments a year, and by 1890 output had again doubled. Like Bechstein he soon became convinced—certainly, by 1867[17]— of the American system's superiority; but his instruments were subtly different. Lighter hammers and felts were in part responsible for a thinner more silvery tone than the 'velvety' Bechstein, a contrast particularly noticeable in the uprights of these two makers. Verbal descriptions of tonal quality are never adequate but the interested reader will appreciate the difference at a glance and touch.

Although all Blüthners had iron frames, some were still straight-strung long after that system had been abandoned by most good makers everywhere outside France. A representative upright of this design made in 1908 still (in 1975) has a clear bass and outstanding evenness of tone through all registers. A unique feature of many Blüthners was rather more controversial: the 'aliquot system', patented in 1873, by which upper notes had an extra string not struck by the hammer but allowed to vibrate sympathetically. This was said to enhance the instrument's tone, though some critics were unconvinced. A typically adverse opinion appears in Mahillon's report on the Amsterdam Exhibition: the system's tonal effect does not appear to offer a sufficient compensation for the complications which it necessitates. Nevertheless, Julius Blüthner's technical grasp was considerable despite the handicap of a limited formal education. This he demonstrated in a textbook of piano making [18] jointly written with Heinrich Gretschel which, unlike Edgar Brinsmead's *History of the Pianoforte*, is far more than an apologia for one firm. Blüthner's marketing followed the familiar German pattern: excellent catalogues, endorsements and performances by leading virtuosi, royal patronage—a 1902 advertisement announces that the firm has been 'honoured by HM Queen Alexandra's command to supply a grand pianoforte for her personal use at Windsor Castle'. He even tried to penetrate the American market, competing at the 1876 Philadelphia Exhibition and, typically, leaving his son to study for two years with Steinway, Chickering and Knabe 'as an assistant, and almost as a workman', exclaimed the *Music Trades Review*, unaccustomed at home to such humility among the scions of great houses.[19]

Bechstein and Blüthner were representative German firms in that they started late and, practically from the outset, embraced the new technology. A few good makers could claim earlier origins but their output had been small, their reputation and market provincial. Some of these, unlike their contemporaries in England and France, refused to live in the past. A remarkable example of a firm which retained sufficient thrust and initiative to carry it successfully from the eighteenth into the twentieth century unburdened by the legacy of past distinction was Rudolf Ibach of Barmen. Established in 1794, it had produced about 400 instruments by 1820 and 2,000 by 1850. In 1873 the founder's grandson Walter began ten years of extensive training in Brussels, Paris (with Gaveau), London (with Steck) and America (studying felt and hammer-making with Dolge). Two years after his return, Walter Ibach opened a new factory solely for the manufacture of modern uprights, with a success indicated in Table IV.[20] His 1886 catalogue was enthusiastically noticed by the *Musical Opinion*: a beautifully illustrated 'prospectus which German enterprise prints in 5 languages . . . some day, we suppose, our English firms will think it not unwise to do something similar'. The Queen had recently purchased a 'magnificent upright grand' by this maker.[21]

Another old but progressive firm was Irmler of Leipzig, which began in 1818 and slowly expanded production to about one hundred a year in 1861, when it became one of the first piano manufacturers to introduce steam machinery. Probably the most widely known of the old German firms was Schiedmayer of Stuttgart,[22] established in 1809 but with intricate earlier origins: two brothers started an independent business making harmoniums, but after this they began to compete with the old firm as piano makers, causing much family bitterness, and confusion among buyers. The firms were known and conventionally dated as Schiedmayer and Sons (1809) and the Schiedmayer Piano Manufacturing Co. (1853). Despite Schiedmayer's 1851 gold medal and the prominence of its director on the juries of later exhibitions, its two rival offspring were to attain greater fame and prosperity in later years. The existence of these older firms should not, however, obscure the fact that Germany's pianoforte industry, like that of America, was essentially a creation of the second half of the nineteenth century.

The general structure of the industry

In 1884 the *Zeitschrift für Instrumentenbau* estimated that there were 424 piano 'factories' in Germany, employing 7,834 workers dispersed as follows: [23]

Location	Number of Factories	Labour Force	Average number of workers per factory
Prussia	240	3471	7
Saxony	90	2301	25
Württemburg	44	998	22
Hamburg	19	735	38
Baden	16	169	10
Bavaria	15	170	11

Total annual production was estimated, perhaps liberally, at 73,000 pianos valued at thirty-five million marks (the mark was worth approximately one shilling), about half of which were exported. It will be noticed that, in contrast to England's London-based industry, German piano makers were widely dispersed, reflecting past political boundaries. Another contemporary writer surmised (a stronger verb would imply unmerited accuracy) that 112 were in Berlin, in addition to some 250 manufacturers of 'actions, parts, organs, etc.'; thirty-three firms were said to be in Hamburg, twenty-six in Stuttgart, twenty-three in Dresden, twenty in Leipzig, and a few in Hanover and Munich.[24] Clearly such figures can serve only as a rough guide to the industry's structure. The estimates of average numbers of workers per factory are particularly misleading since they do not indicate dispersion about the mean. The Prussian figure, for example, includes such large firms as Blüthner lumped together with tiny workshops.

According to Roos,[25] the German piano industry consisted by 1907 of 1,681 factories and workshops employing 26,828 workers, distributed as follows:

Size of firm	Number of firms
Self-employed individuals	823
2–5 workers	309
6–20 ,,	257
21–50 ,,	166
51–100 ,,	76
101–200 ,,	26
200+ ,,	24
1000 ,,	1

The predominance of very small firms is remarkable and will be discussed below. The solitary giant was established by Max Zimmerman at Leipzig in 1884 after he had worked at Steinway's New York factory. In 1895 the business became a limited company and was soon manufacturing 3,000 cheap uprights and grands a year. By 1912 it operated by far the largest factory in Europe, employing 1,400 men and making 12,000 instruments a year. No other firm outside America approached this size although, of course, many made much better pianos.

To supplement these incomplete and unsatisfactory contemporary estimates, Table IV presents information which has been reconstructed from our fairly accurate knowledge of piano serial numbers. Although incomplete, Table IV gives a reasonably comprehensive picture of the industry and its growth. Moreover, its lacunae can be broadly identified. Many very small firms will have escaped the net, particularly if they were short lived or their instruments were too poor to survive long enough for their serial numbers to interest later purchasers. Some makers may not have attached numbers, or may even have sold their instruments anonymously under a 'stencil' or a middleman's name. In this category we have several hundred names with, in many cases, dates of establishment, but inadequate further information to merit their inclusion in the table.

One business excluded from the table is Emil Ascherberg of Dresden, upon whose piano Number 6021 Queen Emma of Hawaii was said to have written 'Aloha-Oe'.[26] Ascherberg was a linen draper who established a quick reputation with a few acceptable instruments and then proceeded to buy meretricious objects in Thuringia and Silesia, to which

Table IV   Some Representative German Manufacturers

I. *Firms producing more than 2,000 pianos a year by 1910*

	Location	Year Estab.	Approximate Annual Production						
			1870	1880	1890	1900	1910	1920	1930
Bechstein	Berlin	1853	600	900	2500	3700	4600	1000	1400
Blüthner	Leipzig	1853	800	1000	1000	2500	3000	2000	1000
Grotrian-Steinweg	Braunschweig	1865	300	350	400	600	2000	1700	1100
Ibach	Barmen	1794	300	800	1700	1900	3200	900	700
Kaps	Dresden	1858	250	1000	1000	2000	2000	500	300
Mannborg	Leipzig	1889	—	—	300	900	2000	1100	1100
Neumeyer	Berlin	1861	500	1000	1500	2000	2000	—	—
Rönisch	Dresden	1845	500	900	900	1500	2000	800	600
Schiller	Berlin	1884	—	—	300	600	2000	500	100
Thürmer	Meissen	1835	?	400	1000	1700	2500	1200	1000

II. *Firms producing more than 1,000 but less than 2,000 pianos a year by 1910*

	Location	Year Estab.	1870	1880	1890	1900	1910	1920	1930
Feurich	Leipzig	1851	100	400	500	500	1200	1000	900
Förster	Lobau	1859	50	500	500	700	1000	1000	2000
Irmler	Leipzig	1818	100	100	500	150	1250	4000	1000
Niendorf	Luckenwalde	1896	—	—	—	350	1200	1000	3000
Perzina	Schwerin	1871	300	300	300	1000	1000	1000	100
Roth & Junius	Hagen	1889	—	—	200	400	1000	1000	400
J & P Schiedmayer	Stuttgart	1853	400	800	800	1000	1200	500	600
Seiler	Leignitz	1849	500	700	900	1300	1700	1000	1500
Uebel & Lechleitner	Heilbronn	1871	—	100	200	500	1300	800	600

III. *Smaller firms*

	Location	Year Estab.	1870	1880	1890	1900	1910	1920	1930
Adam	Wesel	1828	100	250	300	500	500	200	300
Dörner	Stuttgart	1830	120	140	300	350	400	200	300
Duysen	Berlin	1859	200	250	300	220	75	75	125
Ecke	Berlin	1843	100	300	300	500	500	300	300
Fahr	Zeitz	1887	—	—	300	500	800	300	400
Finger	Eisenberg	1887	—	—	50	150	200	200	100
Lipp	Stuttgart	1831	300	500	500	900	900	400	300
Mand	Koblenz	1835	400	400	500	500	100	600	—
Manthey	Berlin	1868	50	60	250	400	600	100	200
Pepper	Berlin	1863	200	200	300	500	600	500	300
Quandt	Berlin	1854	300	300	400	400	500	300	300
Rachele	Hamburg	1832	200	200	200	250	250	250	200
Rosenkrantz	Dresden	1797	300	300	?	?	?	—	—
Römhildt	Weimar	1845	200	200	500	500	500	400	400
Rösler	Dresden	1868	100	100	70	150	400	600	500
Schimmel	Leipzig	1885	—	—	200	500	500	600	500
Schwechten	Berlin	1853	600	600	1000	1000	500	400	800
Schiedmayer & Sons	Stuttgart	1809	300	400	500	800	800	400.	200
Steingraeber	Bayreuth	1852	200	150	300	900	800	100	250
Westermeyer	Berlin	1863	100	200	200	300	200	200	100
Zeiter & Winkelmann	Braunschweig	1837	200	300	300	500	700	500	1500

he attached his name. His attempt to enter the Melbourne Exhibition in 1880 was prevented by a German official ruling that he was a trader not a manufacturer. When the Ascherberg crash came in 1883, it was spectacular: liabilities of some £40,000 were backed by assets of £2,000.[27] The case is interesting for the light it sheds on murkier regions of distribution, which were not confined to Germany, of course: the principal trade paper sometimes published warnings against 'Englische Schwindelfirmen'.[28] Without further information it is impossible to measure Ascherberg's productive activities. His successor, the Apollo Piano Company, took the front page of the *Zeitschrift für Instrumentenbau* with an advertisement in German, French, Dutch and English seeking 'firms which are in a position to do justice to and to push the Apollo pianos'.[29] But again no later information is available.

Some reputable large firms are excluded from Table IV through lack of data. Zimmermann has already been discussed, and we have also met the young Julius Blüthner's mentors, Hölling and Spangenburg. Established in 1843, this firm's instruments began to appear in England in 1878 at prices upwards of forty guineas. An advertisement by the London agent, Barnett Samuel, is worth quoting because its technical inaccuracy and invocation of a magic name are typical of the period: 'in all makes over 60 guineas the action [*sic*] is overstrung after the Steinway system'.[30] By 1881 Hölling and Spangenburg were making 1,600 instruments a year, of which 1,200 were exported, mainly to England and Australia. In October 1883 their 20,000th piano was completed [31] but we have discovered no information about the firm's subsequent history. Cheaper but also reputable were the products of F. Hundt and Son, Stuttgart. An undated advertisement (*c.* 1890) [32] claims a history beginning in 1850, thirty years of imports into Britain, and offers a range from the 'vertical strung pianino' at twenty-five guineas to a concert grand for 150. A testimonial is attached from the Reverend F. Scotson Clark, composer of some 500 feeble and popular piano compositions, who recommends the Hundt as 'the cheapest reliable instrument in the trade'.

Apart from the omissions Table IV is fairly representative of the German piano industry in its golden age. By no means all the firms listed were first class makers but most produced substantial instruments; many examples, now septuagenarian, still command high prices today. The three sections represent size of firm not quality of instrument. While several top grade names are to be found in section I, this also contains humble makers such as Thürmer, who took a first class prize at the 1889 Melbourne Exhibition for 'good pianos at a low price'. Contrariwise, among the firms in section III are names like Lipp which were highly regarded by musicians. Output from all the listed manufacturers amounted in 1910 to some 46,000 instruments, about forty per cent of the country's total production.

A remarkable feature of this industrial structure was the fact that small firms were able to survive, even to flourish in good years, despite the rapid advance of a costly new technology and the fall of piano prices in an international market which, largely as a result of the German advance, rapidly became highly competitive. Two factors made this possible: the growth of a 'supplies' industry, and the ease with which pianos could be sold through a marketing system of great flexibility and resource. An almost unlimited variety of parts became available on credit and in any desired quantity; iron frames (used in virtually all German pianos after about 1870); soundboards; timber which had been seasoned, cut and shaped; veneers and a myriad of small parts and accessories, including the ubiquitous sconces for candles. Finally and most important, cheap actions came onto the market embodying the latest improvements and solving, at a stroke, the greatest problem which had tormented earlier piano makers. The advantages of 'buying out' will be readily appreciated if the reader recalls Broadwood's forty separate operations in 1851 (pp. 36–7). The growth of 'supplies' enabled a piano maker to avoid, if he so wished, most of these processes by buying parts which were cheaper and better than could have been produced in most workshops. He could then concentrate essentially upon the functions listed by Broadwood's as seventeen to thirty, although these could be further simplified by the purchase of soundboards, even of ready 'strung-backs'. The enormous simplification which followed a general adoption of pre-cast iron frames and standard mass-produced actions was of crucial importance. 'Supplies' made it possible for economies of scale and new advances in technology to be employed throughout the industry, without overwhelming advantages accruing to large firms. Of course the latter still enjoyed many benefits—bulk purchase of materials, access to the highest skills and, given intelligent supervision and costing, the familiar benefits which flow from specialization and the division of labour. Nevertheless the small man could still hold his own with a modicum of capital and skill, and the drift from established firms of men eager to try independence, which was as old as the industry itself, continued into this new era.

The pioneer in German action-making was J. C. L. Isermann who, after extensive journeyman travels throughout Europe, including the indispensable period of training in Paris, opened in 1842 an action factory in Hamburg and soon demonstrated that he could produce a better action more cheaply than even the larger piano manufacturers. Isermann's example was followed in 1854 by Adolf Lexow of Berlin, who installed steam-powered machinery in 1867 and was soon claiming sales of 250 actions a month. Fritz and Mayer of Stuttgart, with a similar output by the mid-eighties, and several other firms, entered an increasingly competitive international market offering efficient actions, 'ready made' but tailored to the specific sizes and designs of piano makers, at astonishingly low prices. Thus a Lexow catalogue of 1885 gives simple directions in German, French and English about the measurements required from piano makers to execute an order, and adds, 'All scales and models are given a special number—for repeat orders just quote'.[33] Another from Langer of Berlin in 1896 displays beautifully clear diagrams of thirty different models with similarly precise instructions. An excellent *underdamper* upright action was priced at 42*s*. Isermann's prices for upright actions in 1900 ranged from 38*s* to 51*s*.

This ready flow of supplies, all neatly and exhaustively catalogued, made it possible for small masters to assemble pianos with little capital outlay and a limited range of skills. If the results were not equal to those coming from the great houses they were sturdy and cheap—infinitely superior to their laboriously manufactured predecessors of earlier decades. During a depression, as in 1885, many small makers would come under pressure and some be forced out of business. Suppliers of parts would stop credit, agents offer lower prices for finished pianos, and a maker with insufficient capital to tide him over to better times would be forced to seek employment with one of the larger factories. At first signs of a trade recovery, and before 1914 this was never long delayed, he would return along with other eager aspirants to the freedom and risks of entrepreneurship.

The small master's access to 'suppliers' was matched in Germany by opportunities to enter, alongside the bigger firms, rapidly growing markets for his instruments. Manufacturers of every size were thus able to take part in the attack upon the two principal export markets, Australia and England.

Competing for the Australian market

In 1880 Australians were spending at least ten times as much on English as on German pianos. By 1900 the pattern of expenditure was exactly reversed in a vastly expanded market. Germany's success in Australia was based upon superior products and energetic marketing. Exhibitions were a beach-head for advance, their reports a promulgation of quality. In 1878, in one of its attacks upon the Paris fiasco, the *Music Trades Review* looked forward to a Sydney Exhibition which would be 'on British ground and impartial'.[34] Such optimism was misplaced. At first the jury awarded 'first prize with commendation' to Brinsmead and unadorned first prizes to Steinway, Chickering, Bechstein, Blüthner and Erard. This result was so patently absurd and elicited such a storm of protest that all were raised to the special category. In addition to the now customary complaints against the jury's incompetence and bias, a new form of grievance came from Steinway who explained that they had not entered at all. The instrument shown had been placed by a local Australian dealer and inadequately prepared; Steinway therefore denied all responsibility.

For the Germans, Sydney was merely a rehearsal for a more substantial exhibition at Melbourne in 1882 where they launched an overwhelming attack upon the Australian market. Forty-three makers took part, including Blüthner, Grotrian, Kaps and Schwechten, against a handful of English and French firms. German official scrutiny ensured that the image was not sullied by adventurers trading in shoddy goods. Only instruments coming 'from the workshop of the maker . . . not mere traders' were allowed to take part. It was on this occasion that Emil Ascherberg was rejected by the Imperial Commissioner.[35] The London correspondent of the *American Art Journal* noted that German and even French firms were making 'a heavy bid for colonial honours' while 'the habitual lethargy of our makers allows them the field practically to themselves'.[36] With brutal frankness the same reporter later revealed what had taken place at a 'very stormy meeting' of the jury, where it was ultimately decided to allow makers scoring thirty-four points to qualify for a first class award. Otherwise, he explained, no English firm would have earned such a prize. In the outcome, Challen and Brinsmead were placed in this category, along with five German, three French, and one Italian maker.[37]

The jury's report noted that 'while the German makers have adopted the American system, the French and English makers have, as a rule, kept to the old style of wooden construction using iron bars only as a support to counteract the tension of the strings. It is but lately that Broadwood and Pleyel have employed iron, and this reluctantly and more as an experiment than the result of conviction. The firms of Hopkinson and Erard have, on the contrary, retained the wood which, according to them, insures greater equality, distinction and evenness of tone and homogeneity of registers than the others'. With becoming modesty and caution it accepts the possibility that 'iron pianos like iron ships will entirely supersede wooden ones' but concludes that it is 'not for an exhibition jury to decide on principles'. It was regretted that 'such firms as Broadwood, Collard, Hopkinson and Kirkman have not exhibited'.[38]

German successes at the exhibition were followed by vigorous marketing through diverse outlets. A Melbourne dealer complained that pianos were sold through 'furniture dealers, sewing-machine vendors, and country storekeepers (a kind of superior chandler's shop)' and thought it 'most regrettable to see a trade diverted from its original and true artistic channels'.[39] There followed an enlightening correspondence, in which some robust letters from Australia enlivened an English trade press which hitherto had been prone to a rather prim avoidance of trade realities. Australian opinion was virtually unanimous on two points: that the German pianos were better and cheaper, and that they were sold energetically, without much deference to established procedures but with great attention to consumers' tastes and preferences. A big importer of Bechsteins, Schiedmayers and some cheaper grades challenged comparison with Broadwood, Collard, Erard, Challen and Brinsmead, and guaranteed to supply better German instruments at twenty per cent less cost. Their great superiority had been abundantly demonstrated in Australia for more than a decade, but was particularly evident since the exhibition, and was even acknowledged in England.[40] Another importer complained that 'Broadwood, Erard and Collard think it beneath their dignity to solicit business' although the latter made 'feeble attempts by means of an advertisement occasionally inserted in the Melbourne *Argus*'. In contrast, German firms 'holding positions quite equal to your three great makers do not think it derogatory to their interests . . . to canvass and make special lines to suit the Australian trade'. Moreover, while some English firms were beginning to move in the direction of new technology, the 'mere introduction of iron frames is not sufficient for us'.[41] The manager of the largest business in Queensland named names in embarrassing detail and swore that the English makers could not 'hold a candle to' the Germans on musical quality or price.[42]

There were a few letters from opponents of the German invasion. A Mr Mooney who refused to recognize Steinway as a great maker explained that the 'superior education of the French and English nations' led them to avoid exterior show, and therefore lose colonial custom.[43] This expressed a comforting view which became fairly common among the defeated: that commercial ineptitude was essentially virtuous, indicating, perhaps, a sense of higher values. Another vested interest was represented by a witness before the Melbourne Royal Commission on Tariffs who complained that he had manufactured pianos successfully in Victoria for twenty years, employing nearly thirty hands by the late seventies. Then in the autumn of 1882 German pianos came 'in such frightful shiploads', imported 'for £20 and hawked with sewing machines around the country for £40'. He therefore demanded a high tariff.[44]

One inevitable allegation was that support for German instruments was inspired by self-interested importers with German contracts. But as the *Music Trades Review* retorted, 'responsible houses do not enter into large contracts until they are convinced they cannot do better elsewhere'. Its editor then attempted a more elaborate defence of English failure: Australians would 'naturally prefer English pianos to German goods of unknown makers' but they are discouraged by dealers who ignore the new English models in order to avoid having German goods left on their hands. Cheap German instruments were bought in Germany for about £16, landed in Melbourne, after paying duty, for £23, and easily sold at forty-five guineas, or five pounds deposit and two pounds a month. This argument was based on evidence given before the Victoria Royal Commission in which costs are explained as follows: price in Melbourne £19 10s + £3 10s duty. Retail price in Melbourne £30. Up country price, 'hawked about the country with sewing machines in carts', £40–£45. The article goes on to poke fun at the 'style and manner in which the goods are pushed': the ten year warranty, the spelling mistakes—'rest' instead of 'wrest', 'effect' for 'affect'—and concludes that this 'preposterous rubbish' cannot be defeated by the modest efforts of independent Australian dealers. It needs the 'younger sons or trusted employees' of English firms, backed by adequate capital. Since 'the great English makers suffer rather from a surplus than a want of capital, there ought to be no great difficulty'.[45]

No such leadership was forthcoming, though Brinsmead conducted an advertising war in the sanctimonious bellicose style which was to become this company's principal claim to fame. Attacking the quality of German instruments, it accused the traders of Victoria of pushing their sales in a sordid quest for additional profit. The leading Melbourne house replied by reiterating its claim that German makers succeeded because they offered, at twenty per cent lower prices, a piano of 'imposing appearance . . . and full round tone against the plainer and less pretentious looking' English instruments.[46]

Meanwhile the German trade paper reported this controversy with evident satisfaction, and urged its readers to greater effort with practical advice: some small firms had done badly through 'want of taste and elegance', bad packing and failure to observe delivery dates. Ignorance of the market's requirements was the principal danger of small consignment business. After the Sydney and Melbourne Exhibitions there had been some unnecessarily speculative forays. It was inadvisable to send out a special 'traveller' unless the expenses could be shared. The best plan was to establish an agency with a good import house and to remember that Australians will not buy 'just anything'. Shipping direct rather than via England was preferable, though more expensive, because it saved trouble, delay, risk, and costs of transhipment.[47] The extent to which this advice was taken can be gauged from Figure 2, which also provides an effective comment upon the debate summarized in the above paragraphs.

For a few years after 1885 the English trade press appeared to lose interest in Australia, but there was a revival of comment on the eve of the next Melbourne Exhibition in 1888. The Germans again fielded a formidable team—seventy-one exhibitors of pianos against twelve from the United States and nine from England. Musical instruments made up one-third of the German exhibit whereas in past exhibitions they had never accounted for more than about one-thirtieth. The jury applied a suitably democratic 'colonial' set of rules, considering 'a cheap piano, constructed to meet the requirements of the majority of people, to be equally entitled

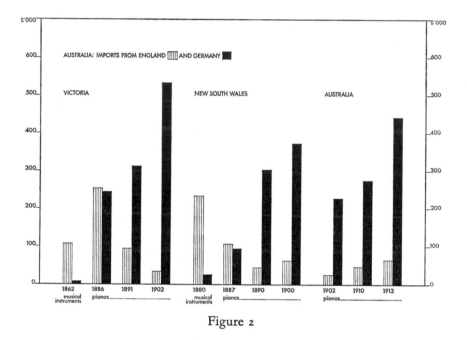

Figure 2

to award with an expensive instrument'. First prizes were therefore given to makers 'of leading reputation' including Blüthner, and of 'well-made but comparatively inexpensive instruments', such as Thürmer.[48] It was generally agreed that British participation had been inadequate in content and presentation. Whereas no German piano was shown without a local representative in attendance, some English instruments were untuned and thick with dust, in which visitors wrote 'shame' with their fingers.[49]

Between 1888 and 1915 English discussion of the Australian market was sporadic, alternating between calls for 'fair trade' and occasional short inquests on lost opportunities. In some quarters there was an undercurrent of thinly veiled contempt for antipodean philistinism. It was reported, for example, that an 'orchestral band' under Mr Cowen had given hour-long concerts of 'high class music (symphonies, etc.) at the

Melbourne Exhibition' but substituted 'lively military music' after protest by an unappreciative public.[50] Algernon Rose, a leading figure in the English trade, returned from a tour accompanying Sir Charles and Lady Hallé in an attempt to promote Broadwood sales, with views that were distinctly *de haut en bas*: Australians bought pianos from Germany which were 'very pretentious in appearance, very cheap in price, and uncommonly shoddy in quality'. 'Persuasive canvassers' touted them on time payment from carts in the bush. At Toowoomba he had seen an upright over which a bucket of boiling water had been poured in order to kill the cockroaches.[51] The implication was clear—this was no market for a reputable manufacturer.

Less exalted commentators tried to understand the new market and the reasons for England's failure to exploit it. Music had made great progress during the 1880s among people 'who had never had a piano before but wanted their children to learn'.[52] German manufacturers succeeded because they examined 'the particular wants of the uneducated masses who provide the giant markets of the future'.[53] Too many British firms were inefficient and indifferent to the customer's opinion. A 'Colonial dealer' wrote a careful detailed account of his attempts to trade patriotically. Having established a good business with an English firm he had ordered twenty-one instruments for delivery in October, received five in January without apology, and cancelled the rest of the order. He then wrote to forty English firms for catalogues and received only three replies, from 'firms not in the front rank'. After advertising in the *Musical Opinion* for catalogues he received two replies from England and twenty pounds' weight of mail from Germany, 'giving prices and every particular'. In 1898 all twenty-five pianos ordered from England had arrived several months late, 'thus losing the best part of the year'. Moreover this was obviously 'a general custom of the trade' for it happened every year, whether ordering direct or through an agent. He was therefore 'forced on to the German makers; they sell a good piano at a moderate price, are willing to make alterations whether they believe in them or not, are more artistic in their designs, and are prompt in delivery'. The Englishman's patriotism abroad could not survive such 'indifference and miffing'.[54] A supporting letter from another Australian dealer added that colonials wanted big pianos over four feet three inches high, without marquetry, and that, having been treated 'with silent contempt' by most English manufacturers, he dealt with Germans who listen and embody suggestions.[55] These representative complaints appear to have been unanswerable, for they were never answered.

Chapter 5

The British Market, 1880–1914

Germany's capture of the British market was similar in many respects to her success in Australia, but its implications were far more serious in a country which itself manufactured pianos. By the eve of the First World War, approximately one out of every six pianos bought in England was German. The proportion may appear too low to justify speaking of 'capture', but in terms of expenditure it was much higher because practically all the German imports were of good quality while many of the English pianos were very cheap. Moreover, the implications of such competition were more far-reaching than any figures can convey. Under its stimulus the whole concept of making and selling pianos was transformed. Old clogged channels of distribution were rejected and new outlets created: 'They came through general merchants and commission agents, not the legitimate trade' was a common complaint in England, as in Australia. For consumers there were enormous gains: entrenched monopolies were broken, inflated trading profits and prices cut, and a wide range of choice made available for the first time in the industry's history. Above all, the hitherto unbridgeable gap between expensive instruments and shoddy was filled, at first by German makers and later by new English firms adopting similar methods of manufacture and trade.

It took several years for English manufacturers and traders to realize that a revolution was taking place. Early reactions tended to alternate between bland indifference, prejudice and bewilderment. In 1878 the *Music Trades Review* expressed surprise at the arrival of pianos from Germany which were overstrung—'a system which nearly all the English makers have long abandoned'.[1] Early German successes were usually dismissed as transient: outwardly appealing and cheap, these newcomers would soon disintegrate, blacking their country's reputation and leaving the solid traditional domestic product in command. As German sales increased and the hollowness of such special-pleading became apparent, established manufacturers and traders naturally resented a threat to their prosperous quiescence, and the lines of defence began to change. There was much talk of German influence at Court and among musicians which was said to have bred an ignorant snobbery in consumers, directly influencing the sale of high quality pianos, and to have infected even the lower orders with a thirst for the spurious prestige of a German name. An alternative line of attack was that underpaid German workmen, subject to rigorous discipline, made it possible to 'dump' pianos at prices which by some mysterious economic process made 'fair' competition impossible yet brought vast profits to Hunnish employers. Along these lines it was inevitable that some English piano makers should become eager participants in the ill-fated 'fair trade' agitation for protection which will be discussed in a later chapter. Meanwhile it can be disclosed that self-interested appeals to patriotic sentiment had little general effect upon the general public, at least until the war.

From the outset of German competition it was the medium and upper class market that was principally under attack. Discussing the trade figures for 1877 the *Music Trades Review* explained that imports from Germany had increased since 1873 because of the establishment of several agencies for 'good overstrung uprights', which were assisted by the advertisements for the more expensive American overstrung instruments.[2] This revealing comment meant that the best German makers, led by Bechstein, were offering acceptable and cheaper alternatives to Steinways. There was undoubtedly a large market for foreign pianos of quality which enterprising traders were eager to exploit. In 1878, for example, Ramsden, a dealer from Leeds, brought back from the Paris Exhibition the entire stock of Brodrene Hals, the leading Norwegian maker.[3] Kaps instruments were advertised by Sims and Sons of Bath, 'Pianoforte Sellers to Her Majesty, sole provincial agent for the United Kingdom'. Uprights were priced from forty-five guineas, and it was claimed that 9,000 short grands (six feet) had been sold by 1884.[4] A trade circular of 1885 offers instruments by several German makers, including: W. Hilse, a prize-winner at Amsterdam—uprights from twenty-eight guineas; August Förster, at forty-four guineas; and Ritmuller, listing a concert grand, 'system, Steinway and Son' at a hundred guineas.[5] Neumeyer claimed to have the most extended German sales in England—5,000 instruments between 1876 and 1882—and offered to show doubters his books. Replying to demands for a tariff, Neumeyer argued that it would simply allow British makers to raise their prices, and why 'should Broadwood and Collard enrich themselves still more?' A tariff of say £2 on an upright would lower his profits but not keep him out. Even these English makers who claimed to be foremost in the world could not compete with the leading Germans—and in most ungentlemanly fashion he named names on both sides. Finally he countered complaints against German tariffs by offering to refund duty to any English firm that could sell 300 instruments in Germany during the year, and thanked English 'dealers in nearly every town for their support, despite old connections'.[6] Such verbal pugnacity was rare among German firms; the majority were content with silent conquest.

Our emphasis upon the high quality of most imports is intended to correct later claims that the *typical* German instrument was a meretricious product of the 'Berlin garret' dumped upon a gullible public. A few deserved this abuse, particularly during the early years of German exports, as dealers and public learned to discriminate among the proliferation of new names. 'Stencils' were rife, some adopting a posture of humble innocence, like the 'Sunbeam' and 'My Cottage' made by Wolframm, one of Aschenberg's successors. Others, like Steinmayer, were reminiscent of, or even deliberately masquerading under an approximation to, a famous name—an ancient practice, rampant in England long before German pianos became popular. The trade press carried endless reports of 'Brechstein' pianos sold at public auctions, and warned dealers (could *they* have honestly been deluded?) against 'Brachsteins'.[7] Bechstein made repeated attempts to stop this abuse. One culprit was successfully traced back to Hamburg and sentenced to a £50 fine and two months' imprisonment for labelling instruments 'C. H. Bechstein, Court Piano Maker' which were exported to England for £25 and retailed at £45.[8] But such practices were never completely stamped out.

Such was the power of a German name that the most absurd stencils were apparently effective: an advertisement in a Worcester paper announced the sale by auction of 'Six excellent cottage pianofortes, all of superior make and finish by the following makers—viz., Kraus, Limmerman, Händel, Beethoven, Schubert and Mozart'.[9] It is by no means certain that these were actually German instruments, for in the nether reaches of the market only the sound of the name mattered, and dealers attached teutonic stencils indiscriminately to rubbish from Berlin or Camden Town. Evidence that some were coming from Germany is provided by such occasional advertisements in the German trade press as the following: an English 'Engros-Händler' seeks 'cheap pianettes' between £8 and £15 with the chance of eventual contracts for one hundred instruments a month with one or more firms. Replies c/o Queens Hotel, Leeds.[10] Probably the advertiser was most interested in tenders at the lower price, and for this he could hardly have expected reputable instruments. It is unlikely, however, that shoddy pianos remained a significant proportion of German exports for long. They were discouraged by the German government, as we have seen in the case of the Melbourne Exhibition; by pressure from within the trade—blatant advertisements ceased to appear—and by market forces. Freight charges to England were an additional though minor barrier to the cheapest instruments, and abundant supplies of highly competitive trash were available from London sweat-shops.

The bulk of German imports were neither Bechsteins nor rubbish but moderately priced pianos solidly constructed on the new system. An unprejudiced outsider's view was expressed by the Hanover correspondent of the (American) *Musical Courier* who reported that numerous small German houses were manufacturing wholesale for the English market and were 'really crowding in upon the standard London £15 upright'. He was referring to the wholesale price, about half that paid by the ultimate buyer. Most of these pianos were cased in 'that German Renaissance style which is now everywhere cropping up in the houses of the refined, with its profusion of massive but still graceful and harmonious forms, its quaint carvings, its honest big wrought brass ornaments, its deep rich tints'.[11]

After 1883 there is mounting evidence of the German industry's growing ability to produce well constructed 'medium class' pianos. It was spoken of as a 'movement', fathered and led by Ibach (see page 76). In 1885 the Leipzig correspondent of the *Musical Opinion* reported that an advertisement for the supply of £20 overstrung uprights had been answered by twenty-five makers, including several of high repute. New firms were constantly being launched: two of Bechstein's former workmen had just begun manufacture 'on the Bechstein system' and the great maker's former London representative, with experience at Steinway, had also started on his own account. Where were the markets coming from, asked the *Musical Opinion*?[12] The question can easily be answered in superficial terms of geographical distribution: Britain and Australia remained the largest markets for German pianos, continuing the pattern described in Chapter 4. But this does not explain the extraordinary piano mania of late Victorian society. By the early twentieth century perhaps one Englishman in 360 purchased a new piano every year, a proportion at least three times higher than in 1851 and exceeded only in the United States where it was 1:260. In Germany the ratio was 1:1000, and in France 1:1600. The late nineteenth-century piano had a high expectation of life. Those that were discarded for new models were not destroyed, but generally moved to a humbler milieu. It is therefore reasonable to cumulate production figures over thirty to forty years in order to arrive at an estimate of the national 'stock' of instruments. This calculation suggests that by 1910 there were some two to four million pianos in Britain—say one instrument for every ten to twenty people. Since few households contained more than one piano even the lowest estimates imply that ownership was by no means confined to the middle classes.

Piano mania, respectability and social emulation

It is a commonplace that pianos were popular in Victorian England, but the extent and intensity of piano mania have been forgotten. By 1899 even the *British Medical Journal* was expressing concern: 'All—except perhaps teachers of music—will agree that at the present day the piano is too much with us.' The 'torture' of professional performance, 'the ineffective strumming of the amateur, and the damnable iterations of the learner' have 'sundered ancient friendships . . . wrecked many enterprises of great pith and moment . . . disturbed the cerebral machinery in many literary and scientific workers . . . driven studious men from their books to the bottle . . . and stimulated peaceable citizens to the commission of violent assaults'. Nor had players escaped unscathed: 'the chloroses and neuroses from which so many young girls suffer' were largely attributable to practising the piano.[13] A more common complaint was against the 'scandalous waste of time, money and labour' expended in lessons for the unmusical: 'an ordinary intelligent girl will learn half the languages of Europe in the time given to her abortive struggles with an art she really does not care for and cannot understand'.[14] Amateurs were a common butt. Even the quintessentially decorous Cassell's *Household Guide*—'On no (account may ladies say "bravo" to a lady performer'—was forced to confess that 'amateur musicians at a party are frequently principally attractive to each other'.[15]

But the piano did not lack supporters. The Reverend H. R. Haweis, who guessed in 1871 that there were about 400,000 pianos and one million pianists in the British Isles, stressed the instrument's importance in a girl's musical and social education: as Latin grammar strengthens a boy's memory, so 'the piano makes a girl sit upright and pay attention to details'. It also provided an essential outlet: 'A good play of the piano has not infrequently taken the place of a good cry upstairs; and this was important at a time when a woman's life was 'often a life of feeling rather than of action . . . and society, whilst it limits her sphere of action, frequently calls upon her to repress her feelings'.[16] Nor were men denied its benefits: the Irish Society of Musicians were assured, in 1895, admittedly by a piano maker, that 'for an educated man to seat himself at the piano is no longer thought effeminate'.[17]

Indoctrination started young—a *Child's Guide To Knowledge* dating from the 1870s asks: 'Q. What musical instrument is now seen in almost every household? A. The pianoforte.' It continues, with typical mid-Victorian confidence in unequivocal progress: 'Q. Pray, what musical instrument was used by our ancestors before the introduction of the piano? A. The harpsichord, an instrument somewhat similar, but very inferior in tone.'[18] Middle class girls could hardly escape the piano, for mothers were insistent on the social graces, and teachers were backed by incessant propaganda. Even the *Girls Own Paper* (price 6*d*) included Lady Benedict on piano playing, and in the *Girls Own Annual* (1881, price 8*s* 6*d*) the same aristocratic mentor was joined by 'a professor of music of sixty years' standing' who advised 'how to purchase a piano and keep it in order'.

Since every well brought up young lady was expected to be capable of entertaining company at the piano there was a great demand for appropriate music, but the increasing technical difficulty of genuine compositions presented a new problem. Professional virtuosity and amateur fumbling were both growing apace, with increasing divergence. There were exceptions of course in both camps. Schumann's *Kinderscenen* and some of the Mendelssohn *Songs Without Words* were within easy reach; and later in the century Grieg's 'pink sweets filled with snow' earned him in 1906 an Oxford degree as 'the most popular musician in the home life of England since Mendelssohn'. Only two years later Bartók's *Music for Children* recaptured an eighteenth-century ability to combine musical quality and technical simplicity. Moreover, if few good composers wrote simple music, many amateur pianists took their hobby seriously. George Eliot, who foolishly bought a Kirkman grand in 1861 and soon found it 'a piano on which it is impossible to play delicately', played Mozart and Beethoven symphonies *quatre mains*, and accompanied Schubert songs and Mozart violin sonatas, delighting in a 'fresh kind of muscular exercise as well as a nervous stimulus'.[19] She was representative of a great body of amateur musicians who, without gramophones, radio, or even, outside a few metropolitan centres, frequent public concerts, experienced music with great thoroughness. The extent of their interest is indicated by the common nineteenth-century practice of publishing most operas, symphonies, and even chamber music in 'reductions' for piano solo or duet, presumably for amateurs incapable of reading a full score but determined to explore the repertoire. Few of these editions are available today when, as Benjamin Britten has argued in a memorable lecture, music is 'free for all', but true musical experience less common.[20]

Nostalgia for the best amateur music making, of which the 'household orchestra' was a true centre, should not blind one to the fact that its functions were usually less elevated. If young ladies were to demonstrate that money had been well spent on instrument and lessons, it was imperative that they be provided with 'effective' pieces. Here was a steady market for a special product, heir to the emasculated classics described on page 17 but now mass produced for the ungifted and semi-trained to perform to the unmusical and half-listening. A new generation of non-composers emerged to construct this non-music: Charles d'Albert with 300 such items in print; Joseph Ascher whose 'Alice where art thou?', and Sydney Smith whose 'Jet d'Eau' and 'Golden Bells' were inescapable at 'musical evenings'. Saddest of all, perhaps, was George Alexander Osborne who left Limerick to study with Pixis, Fétis and Kalkbrenner, who knew Chopin and Berlioz, and then descended to teach at the Royal Academy of Music and wrote 'La pluie des perles'. It was such stuff as this which drove serious musicians to denounce the piano as 'an evil influence upon home music' and even to rejoice that, in the sixties, it had not yet 'driven far away the madrigal and the glee' from lower class homes. Redemption could be achieved only by dragging 'down the piano from its place of pride and power'.[21]

Such aspirations were short-lived for, in the language of modern commerce, the piano was a prestigious consumer durable. When Hardy's Gabriel Oak woos Bathsheba, it is with the promise of a piano, which 'farmers' wives are getting to have now'; and when she acquires one she is accused of getting ideas above her station.[22] Even Sam Weller perceived a certain idiosyncratic utility, planning Mr Pickwick's escape by means of 'a pianner forty as von't play, and with no vorks in it; but as will hold him easy, vith his hat and shoes on, and breathe through the legs, vich is holler'. The demand for pianos was highly elastic in terms of both income and price. In other words, as people's incomes rose pianos ranked high in their list of desirable possessions, and as the price of instruments fell demand rose more than proportionately. These buoyant market conditions were determined by economic, cultural and social factors. Living standards were rising, not merely among a growing middle class but, particularly after the 1870s, for the mass of people who benefited from lower prices for food and many necessities. In the second half of the nineteenth century real national income per head more than doubled and real wages increased by more than eighty per cent. This left some disposable cash to be spent on leisure which became increasingly commercialized during this period. Professional sport, the music hall and working class seaside resorts began to flourish. The new popular press, *Tit-Bits*, *Answers* and the *Daily Mail*, which had one million readers by 1900, were a response to rising incomes and belated public education. A growing demand for music had similar roots which were nourished by a variety of activities— popular concerts and a wider appreciation of music, cheap sheet-music and dirt-cheap piano lessons—and these in turn influenced the market for pianos.

In the concert world, more meant, on balance, worse. As Nettel writes in this context: 'There is always a good deal of drivel in anything that commands the attention of the multitude',[23] and we can record the piano's role in such events. Thus in 1868 Londoners were entertained by a Batavian lady who played 'two different arias with each hand at the same time and likewise sang a fifth'.[24] Piano playing marathons were another measurable achievement: in 1887 a Mr N. Bird played for twenty-five hours in Stockport, advertising a particular instrument with such ill effect that we have no record of its name. Perhaps the ultimate spectacle was presented by Sandow the strong man, who carried a piano and its player off stage (the stool was attached to the piano). For this the historian has ample documentation since, on one occasion, Sandow dropped both and was successfully sued for damages.[25]

There were more solemn events. In 1864 Master Willie Pape from Alabama undertook an arduous series of forty-two piano recitals, which began in Hastings and ended, via Devon, Cornwall, Wales, Yorkshire and Lancashire, in Dundee. Such extensive tours were probably rare, though little is known about the activities of the concert agents Beale and Mitchell, or precisely why Clara Schumann despised 'Oxford Street business'.[26] Certainly there was nothing resembling the American circuit, and recitals were never used to promote pianos on the scale of the Rubinstein and Paderewski sorties for Steinway. The working class were mainly confined to choral music and brass bands,[27] but working men's concerts began in Manchester during the late seventies, with the cheapest tickets costing only fourpence, and average attendances of over 3,000. Similar opportunities arose elsewhere in the provinces where, as Nettel observes, the keynote was respectability, a concept to which we will shortly return. In London music reached a wider public at the Crystal Palace (starting in 1855), the South Place People's Concert Society (1878) and at Toynbee Hall (1886) where the moving spirit was J. M. Dent the publisher.[28]

Ticket prices are a treacherous guide to the social structure of audiences. When the *Star*'s music critic descended upon the Bow and Bromley Institute one Saturday evening in 1889 he encountered 'a sixpenny and threepenny audience of discouragingly middle class aspect'.[29] Nor should the intensity of concert life be confused with its quality, as Shaw found earlier that same evening on a dispiriting visit to the People's Palace. Joachim, describing the Crystal Palace to Clara Schumann, respected 'the English people for maintaining such a costly marvel at their own expense and without the help of the state', but considered it 'monstrous' as a place for music.[30] It is impossible to resist the conclusion that, without civic or state support, public music making remained pitifully inadequate by the end of the century, but it had certainly been extended.

The price of sheet music fell rapidly and sales greatly increased. In 1837 a piano score of *Messiah* cost twenty-one shillings; fifty years later the price was one shilling, and much music was available in sixpenny editions. Several factors contributed to this. The abolition of the paper tax in 1861 substantially lowered all publishing costs.[31] A great expansion of distributive outlets through 'the stores', newsagents and stationers, lowered prices and stimulated sales of cheap editions, to the despair of 'legitimate' traders. It was said that in London and large provincial towns retail prices were cut to a third, while publishers' terms remained the same; a typical letter from a Putney dealer claimed in 1887 that he had halved his stock of music and was 'working pianos instead'.[32] Far more serious, because it threatened the lifeblood of popular music publishing, was an enormous increase in 'piracy'. Within a few days of original publication, copies of successful numbers were prepared by backroom pirates and sold for a few pence. The racket was far simpler and more profitable for music than for books, and the law, since it failed to provide summary penalties, gave no real protection. Some indication of the resulting loss to composers is provided by the meagre earnings of Leslie Stuart, composer of 'Soldiers of the Queen', 'Little Dolly Daydream' and 'Lily of Laguna'.[33] In the first six months of 1905, when these songs were at the height of their popularity, they earned Stuart £2 2s 3d. After a long campaign the situation was remedied in 1906 by changes in the law, allowing summary procedure against illegal copying and distribution.[34]

But even without allowing for piracy there was evidently a great increase in the market for printed music during the last quarter of the nineteenth century. The amateur repertoire was occasionally reviewed with confidence and acerbity in the musical press: '"Wild Winds" (4s) is the odd title of a commonplace air with variations in rapid and unmeaning arpeggios. The piece has nothing to recommend it. "Not for Me" (4s) is a song on the advantages of bachelorhood; the music superior to the words which are rather silly. "Florence Waltz" (2s) is brief, unpretentious, and of infantine simplicity. These may be negative attributes, but no others can be named.' [35] Nevertheless sentimental ballads and comic songs achieved unprecedented sales and were profitable despite piracy. 'The Lost Chord' sold 500,000 copies between 1877 and 1902; 'In the Gloaming' 140,000 during the eighties; 'The Holy City' 50,000 *a year* by the nineties. At a sale of Mascheroni's copyrights in November 1898, 'For All Eternity' fetched £2,240 and several more of his ballads were purchased at prices upwards of £200. Some instrumental pieces had equal success—the Myosotis ('Forget-me-not') Waltz sold more than 250,000 copies. Attractive by-products of this flourishing trade were the covers which were commissioned from such artists as Alfred Concanen and George Cruikshank. More than 80,000 were produced, many of which, apart from their intrinsic excellence, offer an illuminating commentary on Victorian society.[36]

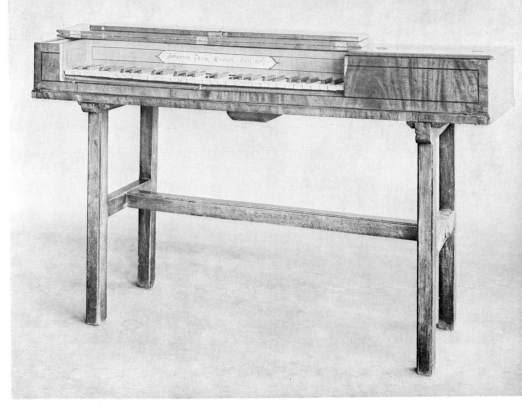

Zumpe square piano 1767.

Style I.—7¼ OCTAVES. SQUARE GRAND, EBONIZED, or ROSE-WOOD CASE, ... **$850**

With Overstrung Patent Duplex Scale, full Cupola Steel Frame (cast in Steinway & Sons' Foundry and possessing double the resisting power of ordinary Cast Iron), Double Dampers, Beveled Top, Fancy Fretwork Desk, carved legs and lyre. The outside casing consists of two thicknesses of wood crossed obliquely and then veneered lengthwise with Ebonized, or Rosewood veneers.

Large front round corners; ogee moulding; richly carved legs and lyre; three-stringed like our Grand Pianos; patent agraffe arrangement throughout the entire scale.

Length, 6 feet 11½ inches; width, 3 feet 6 inches.

Steinway square piano 1888.

The 'Action' or Internal Mechanism of a Cabinet Pianoforte.

Inside Broadwood's factory about 1840 (see pages 35 to 37).

Key-cutter at work.

By Her Majesty's Royal Letters Patent.

RÜST'S TUBULAR PIANOFORTES,

Piccolos and Cottages equal in Volume and Quality of Tone to Horizontal Grands.

For Novelty and Elegance of Design, Material, and Workmanship, cannot be Surpassed.

MESSRS. RÜST & Co. (from 320 and 309, Regent St.), beg to call special attention to their NEWLY INVENTED PATENT TUBULAR PIANOFORTES, to which they now intend devoting their sole energies, thus enabling them to offer these unique Instruments at a much lower tariff than they have hitherto done. When they say that the TUBULAR PIANOFORTES are unrivalled in volume and quality of tone—novelty and elegance of design, they are only expressing the opinions of the most eminent Professors and distinguished Amateurs in London; and Messsrs. Rüst & Co. will guarantee that the material and workmanship cannot be surpassed. Their terms will be strictly moderate compatible with a first-class Instrument, commencing from *Thirty Guineas*, which will not only include Mr. RÜST's new Inventions, but all the modern Improvements. ——o——

Testimonial from G. A. MACFARREN, ESQ.

MY DEAR SIR,—I have the highest opinion of your TUBULAR PIANOFORTES—the hollow bars and sound holes have a decided effect upon the tone, as has been proved to me by the repeated experiments I have witnessed.

R. A. RÜST.

I am, DEAR SIR, yours truly,
G. A. MACFARREN.

——o——

DEPÔT—207 & 209, REGENT STREET.

Manufactory—1, John Street, Oxford Street, London.

The Evolution of the Modern Upright I: a typical pre-Steinway English piano.

R. EXTRA FANCY STYLE.—7¼ OCTAVES. EBONIZED CASE, . $1,100

UPRIGHT GRAND, same size and interior construction as regular style **L,** with extra engraved case, designed and executed in the highest style of art. The three upper and the lower front panels are closed, beautifully engraved, and are set in handsome mouldings. Patent Tone sustaining Pedal.

Height, 4 feet 5½ inches; width, 5 feet 1½ inches; depth, 2 feet 4 inches.

The Evolution of the Modern Upright II: a Steinway upright of 1888.

The Evolution of the Modern Upright III: a post-Steinway German upright of the early twentieth century.

FERD. MANTHEY

Pianoforte-Factory (founded 1868).

Berlin S.O., Reichenberger Strasse 125.

Best Isermann Underdamper Action
(System STEINWAY).

Mod. C. 4 foot 6 inches Height.   Model D f. 4 foot 3 inches Height.

Trying over new music.

A modern Steinway—Model K, about 1955.

A Bösendorfer *Imperial* concert grand piano 1975.

The proliferation of cheap lessons and learning manuals is further evidence of the piano's descent to the lower orders. In a fruitless battle for professional standards and recognition, the *Musical Standard* scornfully reprinted advertisements by unqualified teachers. A 'Gilder and Piano-forte Tuner' offered piano, violin and dancing at sixpence a lesson; [37] another included 'use of piano for practice' at the same fee.[38] 'Why not learn to play the piano by Christmas?' asked a rapid-results specialist in November 1887,[39] and autodidacts were inundated with 'How to' books, and such persuasive offers as 'The Art of Playing at Sight, by One who has taught Himself'.[40] Although the Associated Board of the Royal Academy and Royal College of Music began in 1889 to improve standards and impose some uniformity, the majority of teachers were poorly trained and ill paid. Their meagre earnings made them greedy for trade discounts on pianos for their pupils, a practice which incurred much odium from dealers who never ceased to complain about 'the mongrel individuals who describe themselves as professors of music'.[41] Their numbers greatly increased. In 1881 there were less than 26,000 'Musicians and Music Masters'; by 1911 the census recorded over 47,000. In 1901 the 'Teachers of Music Registration Bill' was introduced 'to enable the public to guard itself against incompetence and imposture'. It never received a Second Reading.[42]

Neither a growth in purchasing power, nor the exploitation of musical needs would have been sufficient to elevate the piano to its extraordinary place in Victorian society. A more fundamental social need was at work—and this was respectability. It was, as Professor Best has argued, 'the great Victorian shibboleth and criterion'; it marked 'the sharpest of all lines of social division'. Inevitably it entailed 'the emulation of superior styles', and in such emulation the piano was a potent instrument. The importance of social emulation has frequently been stressed. 'If consumer demand . . . was the key to the Industrial Revolution, social emulation was the key to consumer demand.' [43] For Thorstein Veblen it was, apart from self-preservation, 'probably the strongest and most alert and persistent of the economic motives'.[44] To the Victorians a piano symbolized respectability, achievement and status. A South Yorkshire miners' leader, giving evidence to the 1873 Select Committee on Coal, describes recent progress in his district: 'We have got more pianos and perambulators', but the piano is 'a cut above the perambulator'.[45] In 1885 colliers at Pontypridd were 'beginning to devote their Saturday evenings to the study of the pianoforte under a competent teacher'. The *Musical Times* rejoiced at this substitute for the 'public house . . . the eloquence of music is far beyond that of the most earnest lecturer on temperance'.[46] Even Charles Booth's social survey, so frequently quoted as evidence of dire urban poverty, contains the following passage: 'A rather higher standard of home involving accumulations of some kind, is suggested by the . . . purveyor of musical instruments on the hire system who advertises on every wall "What is home without a piano?"' [47]

The Three Year System

A study of hire purchase is particularly revealing because it illustrates both the extent of social emulation and the genesis of its most powerful agent. The large potential demand for pianos was made effective by the evolution of the 'three year system' which by the end of the nineteenth century pervaded all but the upper class trade. This development has been curiously neglected or misunderstood by historians, who tend to assume that it did not become common until the 1930s.[48] Thus it is misleading to describe the ambitious Edwardian poor as scrimping and saving 'to amass the necessary £20 or so' to buy a piano, since only a down payment was required.[49] The evolution of consumer credit can be traced through a tangled mass of changing custom, developing financial institutions, legislation and legal opinions. During the second half of the nineteenth century the credit available in shops for middle class customers gradually assumed its modern form of the weekly or monthly bill, with far more shopping done for cash. Shops specializing in luxury goods for the rich, however, including vendors of high class pianos, tended to maintain the old practice of extending lengthy credit. This costly and inefficient tradition in the old retail trades—hatters, tailors and jewellers were accustomed to waiting up to two years for payment—was first successfully challenged by the Civil Service and Army and Navy Stores during the late sixties and early seventies, but it persisted into the twentieth century.

Since the piano was downgraded socially during our period, its precise status and therefore its appropriate form of payment was frequently a source of dispute which was tinged with acerbity for at least three reasons. First there was the problem of depreciation: some hire purchased instruments were so shoddy that they became worthless before payment was completed. Secondly there was the vexed problem of the transaction's legal status, with abundant opportunities for cheating by both traders and consumers. A final source of rancour lay in the elusive but undoubted influence of snobbery: many a patrician voice was raised against the mill-hand's or miner's piano.

These matters are discussed in F. J. Crowest's significant *Phases of Musical England*, published in 1881 before good cheap pianos had made their mark. He devotes a highly critical chapter to 'Pianofortes on the three year system' which are attacked as typical of the age: 'cheap and nasty . . . veneered modesty . . . artificial sanctity'. The progress of musical taste in England, he argued, had made it 'well nigh imperative upon a section of the community to provide themselves with music in the home', and had even attracted 'the poorer classes to a sense of the virtues of a household orchestra', driving them 'to a spirit of emulation for the possession of . . . that highly respectablising piece of furniture'. Nothing could approach its usefulness as a family instrument and for social gatherings, so the growth of the piano trade was hardly surprising. Hence changing musical taste had been 'no less remarkable in its effect upon the instrument-manufacturing interest than upon our social status'. But what and how to buy? For rich people the answer was simple, but 'the middle class purchaser . . . without a long purse', wanting an instrument for say twenty-five to fifty pounds, faced many hazards. Crowest then lists the rackets already described in Chapter 2, which still menaced 'a too eager and clamorous public': fake advertisements by ladies in distress or families going to India; disreputable auction rooms trying to 'dispose of their double-braced, iron-strung, seven octave, trichord, truss legged, check-repeating, cottage pianoforte at half its original cost'. But his harshest words are reserved for hire purchase traders, who console themselves 'with the flattering unction that they are doing humanity and the state a service in furnishing means whereby the working classes may provide themselves with pianofortes, just as the pioneers of cheap literature have rendered invaluable aid in educating the masses'. To achieve this 'the literature must be good and wholesome, and so must the pianofortes'. Until then he must attack 'so baneful and so reprehensible—yet unfortunately not illegal—a system of trading'.[50]

'Good and wholesome' pianos were becoming available as Crowest wrote, but the legality and social acceptability of hire purchase had yet to be established. Its history can be depicted in terms once used to describe the evolution of joint stock enterprise in Britain: 'the story of an economic necessity forcing its way very slowly and painfully to legal recognition against strong commercial prejudice . . . and in the face of determined attempts of both the legislature and the courts to deny it'.[51] Slowly emerging during the early decades of the nineteenth century, it had to overcome formidable legal and social obstacles, the former arising from failure to identify and clarify its status, the latter from society's bewildered reactions of apprehension, prejudice and need. Nor were these obstacles finally overcome, though some progress was made. 'The law on consumer credit is outdated, confused and irrational', announced *The Times* in 1970, welcoming the Crowther Committee's attempts to unravel a tortuous maze facing 'lender and borrower alike'.[52] Obsolescence, confusion and irrationality are as old as hire purchase itself.

The three year system was widespread by the 1860s. A typical advertisement of 1864 offered pianos 'Let on Hire for 3 Years, after which the
instrument becomes the hirer's property'. A '28 guinea pianette' cost
ten guineas a year; a '40 guinea cottage' fifteen, and a '60 guinea semi-
oblique' twenty. The alleged values were, of course, greatly inflated.
Local newspapers carried many such advertisements. In the *Bethnal Green
Times* Moore & Moore, who were alleged to have pioneered this trade,
offered 'Let on hire. 3 years system. Pianettes 2½ guineas per quarter.
Piccolos 3 guineas. Cottage pianos £3.10.0. Drawing-room model cottage
£3.18.0'.[53] The pretentious nomenclature merely served to obscure the
identity of various sizes of unprepossessing uprights. 'It is through the
modern system of "hire with option to purchase" that an incalculable
number of wretchedly inferior instruments are sent into the market',
lamented the *Musical Standard* in 1868.[54] A year later it was explaining that
consumers were ignorant and defenceless: 'Not one in twenty piano purchasers have the slightest notion of what is good and what is defective in
the instrument.' There was 'a great demand for pianofortes among even
the working classes' and they were supplied mainly by unscrupulous
auctioneers and the three year system 'now adopted . . . to get rid of second
and third rate pianos'.[55] Hire purchase had obvious attractions. For dealers
it was an easy way of extending trade in goods which were sufficiently
immobile to discourage, though not prevent, 'moonlight flits' (as indicated by frequent advertisements for 'wandering pianos'). For consumers
it offered access to a coveted possession which was cheap enough to be
within reach of the respectable artisan, and sufficiently durable to encourage a belief, sometimes correct, that it would last beyond the period of
payment. Cheapness and durability were attainable by the 1890s, but, meanwhile, economic advantages were seriously offset by legal and financial
hazards. In 1878 the *Music Trades Review* reviewed a booklet entitled
'*Organs and Organists* . . . with a chapter on the Law of the Hiring of
pianos and the Three Years System', and complained that the law of hire
was in a 'delightfully tangled state', particularly in relation to landlord and
tenant, and bankruptcy.[56] Its ensuing history illustrates three interrelated
themes: 1. The growing extent and scope of hire purchase. 2. The recognition, which advocates naturally exaggerated and opponents decried,
that hire purchase was a potent force for *embourgeoisement*, as well as an
indispensable instrument of trade. 3. The complexity of legal procedures
which resulted from cases decided in the courts, with occasional attempts
at codification.

Case law was contradictory and confusing. Over the long period one
can discern a general trend from a brutal and anarchic *caveat emptor* towards
consumer protection, but it was by no means a process of steady improve-

ment. Under common law a landlord was entitled to seize any property found on his premises up to the value of rent owing to him. A few categories, such as a man's tools of trade, were apparently exempt, but there was an obvious threat to hire-traders, and a series of conflicting legal decisions kept them in a constant state of apprehension and uncertainty for several decades. Thus an initial decision in one such case (Hattersly v. Blanchard) made it appear that a trader's only adequate safeguard would be to obtain the landlord's agreement that he would not seize a hired instrument for rent. Apart from being extremely inconvenient this would have been socially unacceptable to many people unwilling to admit that their instrument had not been bought for cash. The dealer won this case on appeal, producing affadavits from a number of piano manufacturers which proved that hire purchase was available in 'practically every shop where pianos are sold'. But euphoria in the trade was short-lived, for the new Bankruptcy Act of 1883 was expected to threaten the credit-worthiness of 'the honest poor'. There were many attempts to explain the legal situation to the trade. A typical example was a series of four articles published by the *Musical Opinion* in 1888 which, to judge by the ensuing correspondence, explained little and confused many of its readers. [57] A prominent feature of such journalism was the claim that a particular form of contract, available from the publisher, would alone safeguard the trader's interest. Thus the *Music Trades Review* tempted its readers with a document drawn up by an 'eminent counsel who is now one of the most celebrated of judges',[58] and the *Musical Opinion* claimed that its form was more suitable than those of its competitors or home-made documents.[59] Such inducements doubtless extended the readership of the trade press. In 1888 the Directory of the Provincial Music Trades' Association contained a guide to hire purchase which implied great confidence in its legal status, quoting the Hattersly-Blanchard case and listing a number of satisfactory convictions for infringement.[60] Yet one year later the system was again under attack.

Widespread public disapproval of hire purchase was an amalgam of snobbery, ignorance and genuine concern at its misuse. Vociferous criticism came from the Bench. Thus a judge in the Bolton County Court denounced piano dealers who perpetrated 'a descreditable, mischievous and pernicious trade' and pitied its victims, 'the ignorant silly working classes'. A formidable attack upon high interest rates and seizure on default came from William Booth in an influential book.[61] Even the trade press admitted that some contracts permitted the hirer to break open doors and seize possession. One judge denounced such a clause as 'the most monstrous he had ever seen in any document'.[62] The trade's response to pervasive criticism was a confusing alternation between defensive praise of a system which assisted 'the working classes in procuring home enjoyments',[63] and firm assurance that it preferred a cash transaction: 'the emblem of melodic honesty and self denial embodied in wood, ivory, and metal'.[64] Some argued that hire purchase was not really suitable for the lower orders: it was absurd and untypical that a housemaid earning £13 a year should be allowed to contract for a £28 piano—thus 'socialism is advancing by leaps and bounds'.[65] The allegation that many dealers deliberately allowed the accumulation of arrears in order to foreclose was bitterly denied: a piano 'used on hire for six or nine months would not be worth anything like its original value'.[66] The implication here that profit margins were high and depreciation rapid is worthy of note. The seizure of instruments frequently led to ugly incidents which induced more public disapproval. Several dealers incurred damages for trespass, and a 'piano inquiry agent' who seized about 300 instruments a year admitted in court that one attempt had developed into a pitched battle lasting an hour.[67] Manchester's Official Receiver in Bankruptcy voiced another common complaint in asserting that hire purchase encouraged 'improvident marriages and reckless trading'.[68]

In 1892 it appeared that the government might attempt to regulate hire purchase contracts, compelling their registration, by attaching a clause to a Bills of Sale Amending Act then before Parliament. Alarm at this attempt to subject a 'reputable normal business activity' to the same law regulating the 'abnormal desperate device of bills of sale' enforced an unprecedented unity upon the various interests concerned. Representatives of the carriage-building, furniture, billiard table, sewing machine, cycle and piano trades assembled to organize resistance. A survey of 378 piano dealers revealed that over seventy per cent of their trade was in hire purchase, and it was generally agreed that between one and two thirds of all piano sales were so arranged. If hire agreements were registered it would 'virtually prohibit the use of musical instruments by the working classes'.[69] Among respectable people bills of sale were regarded as a prelude to bankruptcy, and publication of lists would therefore be a supreme deterrent. A 'vigilance committee' of the London Chamber of Commerce, including representatives of Broadwood and the Musical Instruments Trades' Protection Association, threatened to petition the Lords, and the offending clause was withdrawn.[70]

A final legal battle waged around two leading cases, Lee v. Butler (1893) and Helby v. Matthews (1895). In the first, a Mrs Lloyd took some furniture on hire purchase and sold it before completing payments. The Court of Appeal held that she had 'agreed to buy' and therefore, under section 9 of the Factors Act, the person buying from her had acquired a good title. 'The possibilities of collusion and fraud are thus unbounded', concluded the *Music Trades Review*.[71] Traders hastened to amend their forms of contract, and it was one of these forms, issued by the *Musical Opinion*, which centred in the Helby-Matthews case, by far the most important in the history of hire purchase.[72] Matthews, a pawnbroker, took as a pledge a piano which had been hired from Helby and not yet fully paid for. When Helby sued Matthews for the piano's return he was successful in the county court and, on appeal, in the divisional court. But the latter decision was reversed by the court of appeal and the case then went to the Lords. Matthews invoked the Lee-Butler decision and the protection of the Factors Act, but the challenge to his form of contract, extensively used throughout the trade, created a wave of apprehension. As the case took its slow and expensive course through the courts, the very existence of hire purchase appeared to be at stake. 'Does the hire system come under the Factors Act?' pleaded the *MTR*. 'One case decides yes, the next no. Apparently a contract must not indicate a sale, therefore we must not use the word "instalments". Therefore we have temporarily withdrawn our hire contract.' [73] Two months later they announced a new form— 'simply and absolutely a contract for hire only' but including a clause allowing the hirer credit should he ultimately decide to purchase.[74] Then in June, when the Court of Appeal found against Helby, the *MTR* remarked with evident *schadenfreude* that the transaction had been based on one of its rival's forms: 'there cannot be much doubt that . . . the appeal [to the House of Lords] will fail'.[75] In fact the Lords decided in favour of Helby, though he was dead by the time of final decision.

Thus ended the most important case in the history of hire purchase, leaving its legal status reasonably assured—which is not to say that it was as yet socially acceptable. The manager of the Army and Navy Stores voiced a representative middle class opinion when he explained that officers would make use of it only so long as it remained discreet and confidential.[75] At lower levels there was still occasional malfeasance and frequent condemnation. Particularly unpopular was the 'penny frightener', a spurious but imposing pseudo-legal document, got up by unscrupulous traders to bully the meek into prompt payment. In 1898 a prominent piano dealer in Leeds with over 3,000 instruments out on hire purchase came under attack from Labouchère, the editor of *Truth*. Ramsden had brought an action in Durham county court to recover a £20 piano on which all but £2 11s had been paid. Labouchère accused the firm of unfair and dishonourable dealing, was sued for libel, and won the case although his counsel called no evidence. *Truth* celebrated with a vigorous attack on the 'gross abuses' of 'pound of flesh trading' which 'must be curbed by legislation'.[76] There were faint hearts among the embattled legions. The *MTR* doubted the wisdom of pushing pianos 'into the houses of working men earning less than 30*s* a week' [77] but even the 'facetious ignorance and animosity of judges' [78] could not deter what was obviously an extensive and profitable trade.

Retailing revolution: the consumer's golden age

So much success was only possible because, despite many deficiencies, hire purchase met a deep-felt need. Originally it had been available only to 'civil servants, bank clerks, and men in permanent official employment'. During the 1870s it was extended 'to all with respectable references, able to pay a quarter's hire in advance', say three out of a total price of thirty-six guineas, which few working men could afford. By the eighties a few large firms began to accept monthly payments, and this practice was soon generally adopted.[79] Thereafter competition between dealers led to such an improvement in credit terms that by 1910 payments of less than 10*s* a month, without deposit, were common, spread over a far longer period than three years.

Moreover, the pianos were better and cheaper. Crowest had attacked hire purchase in 1881 because it was responsible for 'flooding the market with inferior instruments, the vamping up of this stuff of our musical life, the glueing together of unseasoned woods and common materials ... the carrying of false harmonies and untrue chords and intervals into the houses of hundreds of thousands of families'.[80] Twenty years later, industrial progress, hastened by German competition, had transformed supplies to satisfy a greatly extended demand initiated by social emulation and made effective by hire purchase. The process of assembling pre-manufactured parts had so diffused the new technology and raised standards that cheap uprights were recognizably distant cousins of the Steinway; below the salt, to be sure, but superior in most respects to the expensive domestic instruments shown at the 1851 Exhibition.

It would be convenient at this point to give a list of prices, showing their falling trend after the mid-eighties, and neatly summarizing what was available at different prices—but it would also be misleading, for several reasons. Trade prices (the word 'wholesale' is rarely appropriate) were a jealously guarded secret, never to be shown to the public, who were charged what the market would bear in different localities and situations. A representative example of coy reticence is the following statement: 'This paper is read largely by the trade, yet, as it may fall into lay hands, there is no need to refer to the exact trade prices in print.' [81] A large number of 'trade tallies' are preserved in the British Museum's invaluable Stephen Collection. German makers in 1903 list suggested retail prices which range from forty guineas for the cheapest upright to 122 guineas for a six foot boudoir grand. Trade prices for the same instruments were £18 to £64, delivered free to London or Hull, with an additional discount of 'five per cent cash in 30 days or 6 months net bill'.[82] Many British firms offered similar terms.[83] Dealers could therefore attempt to get double the trade price. But in practice, a bewildering range of discounts could be procured, not merely for cash as against various periods of credit, but for 'professors' acting as intermediaries, for associates in other trades, fellow members of friendly societies, unseasonable purchase and so forth. The situation was described with uncommon frankness by the *MTR* in 1885: 'We look upon the retail list as a little piece of pleasantry which is perfectly well understood alike by manufacturers, dealers and the public. Nobody would dream of paying the price mentioned in the retail list, which has come to be considered as merely the basis upon which discounts, further discounts and extra discounts are reckoned.'[84]

Despite a natural tendency to inflate nominal prices in preparation for subsequent deflationary enticements, and the confusion which always arises when prices are not fixed, this state of affairs was clearly better for consumers than the conditions of the 1850s described in Chapter 2 (pp. 43–4). Improvements were a result of intense competition and publicity in an open market, despite frequent attempts to impose old rigidities. Competition came from manufacturers who sold directly to the public, from dealers with agencies for German pianos or the new English makers, from furniture shops in the lowest reaches of the trade, from the much maligned Army and Navy and Civil Service Stores, and increasingly from the department stores—Whiteleys, Selfridges and Harrods. Operating with low profit margins and unprecedented turnover, these large attractive shops were inevitably popular with the general public. Outraged traders protested in vain, and sometimes with truth, that they offered a superior specialized service which justified higher prices. Obsessive attempts to maintain secrecy were similarly unsuccessful: tedious reiteration of complaints in the trade press over a quarter of a century are merely evidence of a losing battle.

In 1886 a Provincial Music Traders' Association was formed, initially to challenge Broadwood's alleged 'monopoly of provincial tunings' (see Chapter 8) but with wider aspirations.[85] 'Black lists' were prepared of firms giving tallies to 'professors and others not entitled to have them'.[86] Manufacturers were urged to send these precious documents in sealed envelopes, and not by the halfpenny post.[87] It was even hoped that supplies of pianos could be restricted to 'bona fide' dealers, defined as those showing instruments in front windows on the ground floor.[88] United by little else than a vested interest in old trading patterns, the Association had small chance of success in an era of free trade and healthy publicity. The latter was particularly significant because a vigilant press seized upon examples of high profits which were revealed in occasional court cases and by comparison shopping. In one such case a manufacturer was not allowed to prevent, by injunction, a dealer from selling at low prices. The *MTR* sadly published the prices 'contrary to our rule' because they had already appeared in 'general newspapers'.[89]

It was in the home counties, of course, that traders felt the full brunt and consumers the full benefits of such competition. Suburban trade, wrote a disillusioned correspondent in 1911, was 'hopeless, particularly at the posh end . . . much better go to a Northern manufacturing town where you can sell seven or eight pianos a week, unless there are labour troubles'. [90] So great was the thirst for pianos, however, that most provincial traders managed to survive while the more efficient thrived by cutting price margins, carefully selecting good pianos, and establishing goodwill based on genuine knowledge of their merchandise. Such a firm was James Vincent of Belfast, whose stock books from its beginning in 1891 until 1938 are an invaluable source. Remote enough to deter people from shopping in London, Vincent was nevertheless able to import pianos from the metropolis or the Continent at little additional cost—between one and two pounds, depending on size and weight. There was sufficient technical knowledge and education in the family—one son gained a Cambridge music degree—to handle good instruments and even attempt, not very successfully, their manufacture. Beginning modestly with a few second-hand and cheap English pianos, the firm experimented with different makers and rapidly established a few good lines, including the excellent Schmidt-Flohr instruments from Switzerland (for which transport cost £4), several minor German makes, and eventually Bechsteins. Gross profit margins were rarely more than thirty per cent of selling price, much less on cheap instruments. Unpopular instruments were never re-ordered or, if bought in part exchange, were ruthlessly dumped into auction rooms. These stock books provide an objective commentary upon such controversial matters as the comparative competitiveness of different makers, and the rejection of obsolete technology by the public.

English pianos, mainly by Cons, Hicks and Wright, were the cheapest sold, at prices around £20. A few English firms, including Rogers, retained a hold in the £40 class which was dominated by minor German makers. Above this the best Germans were supreme. Some pianos by famous English makers were returned unsold, while purchasers of Bechsteins had their choice vindicated in later years. One example must serve to illustrate a common experience. In 1909 a Bechstein model B grand which cost Vincent £80 was sold for £110. In 1935 he bought it back (the serial number is listed in the stock book) and resold it for £117. The same instrument in 1975 would fetch at least £1,000, after a modicum of renovation. The absence of certain names from this list, such as Chappell's, which he later sold, reflects the activities of other Belfast dealers rather than Vincent's preference. But the general pattern is clear and representative. Since Belfast was hardly the most competitive of markets it can safely be assumed that consumers elsewhere enjoyed at least as wide a choice, and all the evidence suggests that they responded in similar ways.

For buyers at all levels, the years before the First World War were a golden age. A Bechstein model 9, perhaps the best small piano ever made, could be purchased for little more than £50. Excellent German overstrung instruments cost about £30 and good English pianos upwards of £20. The Army and Navy Stores offered a five feet two inches German grand 'manufactured for the society' for £63, pianettes for £24 and a good overstrung upright for £37. Gamage's prices started at £15 for a cottage instrument. With artisan wages averaging between forty and fifty shillings a week the 'piano purchasing power' of working class incomes had approximately doubled since 1850, and the instruments were much improved (see page 41). When effective demand is widespread, consumer satisfaction is probably the best indicator we have of economic progress. To go further is to question the basis of that satisfaction. Was social emulation 'a good thing'? As Professor Best has argued, it 'had a refining and civilizing influence in a hierarchical but mobile society'.[91] An alternative view is best expressed by D. H. Lawrence: '"Don't you think the collier's pianoforte . . . is a symbol for something very real, a real desire for something higher, in the collier's life?" . . . "Yes. Amazing heights of upright grandeur. It makes him so much higher in his neighbouring collier's eyes. He sees himself reflected in the neighbouring opinion . . . several feet taller on the strength of the pianoforte, and he is satisfied."'[92]

Chapter 6

France

The history of the modern piano in France and America presents an extreme contrast, a polarity against which the experience of other countries can be measured. In France the story is one of stagnant production and parochial conservatism in an industry which consisted of a few old firms determined to preserve an outmoded technology, and a number of small makers, proud of their traditional skill and seemingly indifferent to new techniques or commercial opportunities. In the United States, a large and rapidly growing market stimulated the growth of a dynamic industry, with many new large firms wholly committed to modern technology and machine production, alert to the values of the market place, and sceptical, even brashly dismissive, of past tradition. There were exceptions of course: Antoine Bord was a pioneer in the manufacture of cheap mass-produced uprights, and another French business, Herrburger-Schwander, became the world's leading manufacturer of actions. In America some firms were small or inefficient, while a few retained or acquired conservative traits which would have earned the plaudits of Great Pulteney Street or the Rue de Mail. Moreover both countries were superficially alike in being virtually 'closed', excluding foreign competition at home and failing to develop an export trade which was quantitatively significant. But this apparent similarity is misleading and the contrasts are far more important. In a period which witnessed an enormous expansion in world output, from some 50,000 pianos a year during the 1860s to about 650,000 by 1910, American production increased from 10,000 to 350,000 while that of France barely changed, from perhaps 20,000 to 25,000.

The French industry's poor record during the second half of the nineteenth century has generally been unnoticed, or misrepresented, by historians unaware of the statistics or bemused by the past glory of a few famous names. Thus Closson notes a decline in the number of makers but attributes it to industrial concentration 'in conformity with the general law of industrial evolution', and is apparently impressed by the fact that total production did not actually fall.[1] In fact the record is a remarkable example of entrepreneurial decline, which is interesting both as a chapter in piano history, and as a contribution to the more general debate among economic historians about French entrepreneurship.[2]

The leading makers

In 1850 France was producing fewer pianos than England, but the value of her exports was not markedly less and was growing vigorously. Between 1848 and 1857 it increased more than threefold, with flourishing markets throughout the world and particular concentration upon Belgium, the United States, Italy and Latin America. This success arose largely from the great prestige of five leading makers, Erard, Pleyel, Pape, Kriegelstein and Herz, whose instruments sold at prices similar to their English rivals—from about 1,000 francs for the smallest pianette to 4,000 for a concert grand.[3] (Twenty-five francs were equivalent to £1.) Subsequent failures at international exhibitions and in world markets have already been briefly described. For more detailed understanding we can again make use of serial numbers, on which Table V is based.

A comparison with the analysis of German firms in Table IV shows marked contrasts. Whereas virtually every known German business expanded continuously and exported vigorously throughout the period, not one French firm enjoyed a comparable success, while many stagnated and some regressed. Despite Closson's remarks no really large manufacturer emerged by the standards of Germany, still less of the United States. The record of makers not represented in the Table—and we have some information about fifty—reinforces these impressions. The typical French piano-making business remained small and restricted in scope and outlook. Even the once renowned house of Herz falls into this category. We have already met Heinrich (later Henri) Herz on tour in America (p. 49). As a prolific composer and exponent of feeble profitable music, darling of the less cerebral salons and professor of the ladies' piano class at the Conservatoire, he could afford to sink the profits of his 'insipid virtuosity' (Robert Schumann's phrase) in a piano business which steadily declined.[4] After his death, at the age of eighty-six in 1888, his widow ran the firm for a time, but in 1891 it was taken over by Thibout.[5] The latter had started humbly in 1840, and by 1868 was employing 150 men making 500 pianos a year [6] but appears to have left no further record.

Until 1855 the house of Erard was pre-eminent, not only in France, but throughout the musical world.[7] Its founder, Sebastien Erard, was a craftsman of genius who transformed both the concert harp, with a 'double action' copied by all subsequent makers, and the grand piano, with the 'double escapement' action (described on p. 23). Erard's pianos were models of consistently high craftsmanship and elegance. A

Table V   Some Representative French Manufacturers

I. *Firms producing at least 800 pianos a year by 1860*

	Year Estab.	Approximate Annual Production								
		1850	1860	1870	1880	1890	1900	1910	1920	1910
Bord	1840	500	1000	2400	3000	1300	2100	2000	200	600
Erard	1785	900*	900*	1000*	1000*	2000	1700	1900	500	1000
Herz	1825	600	800	700	300	300	200	200	100	200
Pleyel	1807	800	1200	2500	2500	2500	1500†	3000	800	2400

II. *Other firms*

	Year Estab.	1850	1860	1870	1880	1890	1900	1910	1920	1910
Burgasser	1846				100	300	500	500	400	300
Elcké	1846	150	400	500	600	600	500	500	400	1000
Gaveau	1847		400	300	1000	1000	1600	1900	1500	1600
Hansen	1873	—	—	—	100	300	300	400	200	700
Klein	c. 1874	—	—	—	400	1000	1300	800	600	600
Kriegelstein	1831			300	400	400	400	400	300	300
Labrousse	1876	—	—	—	60	400	300	300	500	500
Léguerinais	1856	—		300	300	800	500	600		800
Mussard	1822			300	300	400	700	400	500	200
Oury	1860	—	100	300	300	400	400	800	600	600

* Excluding output of the London factory. See Text.

† A bad year, not typical of the period. 2700 would be more representative of the triennium.

remarkable and little known example made in Paris is the huge and ingenious *pedalier*, Number 24598 (with extra notes to be played with the feet) now in the Conservatoire's museum. Built in the early 1850s for the eccentric composer Alkan,[8] whose quirkish compositions have recently enjoyed a revival which would have astonished Schumann and his contemporaries, it is a veritable showpiece of the old technology. More orthodox but equally impressive is a London Erard, made about 1855, which is now in the Colt Collection, and can be heard on a gramophone record [9] in performances of pieces by Alkan. A rather misleading sleeve-note implies that this is virtually a modern instrument, but its thin clean bass and feeble treble betray its composite (as distinct from integrally cast) iron frame, its parallel, low tension strings and small, lightly clad hammers.

Sebastien, his brother Jean Baptiste, and his nephew and heir Pierre, cultivated an impeccable and profitable circle of social acquaintance on both sides of the Channel, beginning in 1777 with the patronage of the Duchesse de Villeroi, who allowed the establishment of a workshop at her castle. They delighted Marie Antoinette with a transposing keyboard (which could play in a higher or lower key than that fingered by the pianist), flattering a limited voice and musicianship. Attempts to limit their resourcefulness by the jealous guild of Luthiers were thwarted by the personal intervention of Louis XVI—an ironical episode in the history of a firm which was to become the most conservative in Europe. After the Revolution the Erards fled to London, but returned to Paris in 1796 and thereafter made pianos in both cities. The extent and influence of the firm's contracts in England were amply demonstrated in 1835 when Pierre successfully petitioned the Privy Council for an unprecedented extension of the 1821 patent on double escapement. The opportunity was seized for a formidable parade of aristocratic support and artistic endorsement which, in addition to securing the patent's extension, provided great publicity through an impressive pamphlet which reproduced evidence to the Committee.[10] Even George IV acquired an Erard for Windsor, whence it was removed only to follow the court to Brighton.

Pierre's death in 1855 coincided with the Paris Exhibition where the highest award was won, and for which another self-glorifying brochure was published.[11] Complacence was pardonable, for this bi-national enterprise was *sui generis*. Claiming, probably with some exaggeration, to manufacture annually 1,500 pianos in Paris and another 1,000 in London, with respective labour forces of 425 and 300 workers and wage bills of 755,000 and 560,000 francs, it could also reasonably boast of rivalling Broadwood's in technology, craftsmanship and organization. Nor was it lacking in commercial acumen and profitability, for though no detailed accounts appear to have survived, ample evidence exists of great wealth. Sebastien was said to have paid 800,000 francs in 1803 for the domaine of Muette near the Bois de Boulogne: a good investment since in 1895 his descendant, the Marquis de Franquerilla, allegedly refused an offer of thirty million francs, by which time the total Erard estate was thought to amount to at least seventy-five million francs.[12]

If the firm's owners continued to prosper in the later nineteenth century —chiefly, one suspects, through judicious investment in real estate as was then customary among the rich in France—[13] its record in piano manufacture after 1855 was less successful. In terms of sales (at least outside France) and technical leadership, the decline was precipitous and indisputable; the artistic record is more tenuous and controverisal. Sales are concealed by the figures in Table V which only show the output of Erard's Paris factory. Until 1890 Erard's London production increased these totals by between one half and two thirds. Aggregate output therefore hardly increased at all over the whole period, a deplorable record during a time of enormous expansion in world markets for a firm which in 1850 was one of the greatest in Europe. Between 1870 and 1914 Erard sold, at most, 78,000 pianos. During the same years Bechstein sold about 106,000 and Blüthner 85,000, both firms starting the period with modest reputations.

With lofty antecedents and a fashionable clientele, the home of Erard could scarcely be expected to tout for custom in the luxury market, less still to explore its lower or middle reaches. But survival outside France required that the challenge from America and Germany be met. There is no evidence that this was ever seriously contemplated. In England it was not until 1881 that a travelling representative was appointed 'to drum up the country trade' by 'the last of the old houses who deemed it *infra dig*'.[14] Advertising was avoided, of course, although on occasion the antics of vulgar newcomers would elicit a dignified rebuke. Thus in 1885 the Belgian press was enlivened by an announcement that, despite American and German intrusions, Erard still led the world. A reply came from Antwerp's biggest dealer, a relative of the distinguished pianists Franz and Walter Rummell, who explained that since Erard had not changed a model for thirty years, he preferred to sell pianos by Steinway, Blüthner and Ibach, and would gladly prove their superiority by public demonstration. Erards failed to silence him by threatened legal proceedings, refused the challenge and retreated.[15] In 1890 retreat turned to rout with the closing of their London factory. Blom sees this as mere business routine, 'concentration being essential to modern wholesale manufacture',[16] but a less euphemistic interpretation would probably be nearer the truth. Within the trade it was common gossip that German competition, particularly from Bechstein, had bitten deep into the upper class market, and that Erard's London factory was too inefficient to sustain the comparatively high level of English wages.[17] In 1896 a final outpost was abandoned when the Sheffield branch was closed, leaving no salesrooms outside London.[18]

The decline of a great business resulted not merely from apathy and failure in marketing, but from an inability to adapt its product to new technological opportunities and changing demand. In the fundamental design of its instruments Erard pushed conservatism to the point of caricature. This tendency, ineradicably entrenched after half a century of public adulation, was probably reinforced by abandoning manufacture in London, where an open market encouraged exposure to new ideas and techniques, and concentrating production in Paris, where political, cultural and economic nationalism provided an impenetrable shield for self esteem.

We have already noted (p. 61) Pontécoulant's fear that in 1862, only seven years after Pierre's death, the firm was resting on its laurels. It is difficult to illustrate with specific examples the process by which a pacemaker of technology became a guardian of obsolescence, but hammer making may be taken as a representative example. The old method was tedious and costly, wasteful of material and highly skilled labour. Material was cut separately for each hammer and glued in several layers on to the wooden head. There was no simple guide to requisite thickness and hardness but a good craftsman could ensure correct textures for the desired tone. The invention of various hammer-covering machines, notably by Dolge in America, simplified, cheapened and standardized the process: an entire set of hammers could now be covered from one continuous sheet of felt which had already been graded to appropriate thicknesses. The last fine adjustment could then be left, as it still is in the best factories, to the skilled needle of the tone regulator. Machine covering was common in America by the 1860s, and in Europe by the 'seventies. At the Paris 1867 Exhibition a French manufacturer, A. Kneip, displayed machine-covered hammers, but had to wait twenty years for local patronage.[19] When the editor of the *Musical Courier* visited Erard's factory in 1894 he was astonished to find that each hammer was still being individually covered three times by hand before the outer cover was applied. It was absurdly wasteful of material—cut and thrown away—and of labour, but 'the care and circumspection and the final finish are worthy of a watch factory'.[20] The firm's general attitude towards the 'new' technology, by then at least thirty years old, was that pianos had reached a peak of perfection by the 1840s and that, apart from superficial improvements, no further change was desirable.[21]

In 1901 all precedents were broken with the introduction of an over-strung instrument, in response to acknowledged demand but with unconcealed disapproval of the public's lack of discrimination, and a continuing belief that 'the best method to produce a pure tone is from a straight or obliquely strung piano'.[22] So persistent was this conviction that in 1925 M. A. Blondel, director of Erard, was still attacking iron frames and over-stringing in a standard work of reference and claiming support 'parmi les artistes que dans le monde des dilettantes'.[23] If the latter world eludes documentation it can be said of the former, with some confidence, that few concert pianists in 1925 were performing on straight-strung pianos. Erard's loss of the concert platform outside France was of little direct commercial significance—the great piano makers tended to lose rather than gain immediate profit from such transactions. What mattered, of course, was the publicity from a mention in the programme, and the firm's name displayed in prominent letters on the side of the instrument facing the audience.

It was generally accepted that prestige for a high grade piano could only be maintained in the concert hall, which the *American Art Journal* described as 'the battle ground for opposing piano manufacturers', condemning talk of 'subsidized musicians' for they 'must have their tools'.[24] This was overstating the case since a variety of inducements was offered:

free hire and tuning, purchase of blocks of seats (£15 to £30 worth, according to the artist's standing) and, most important, the simple guarantee of an adequate instrument in outlandish places.[25] Such ties could be cut by national frontiers or loosened by idiosyncrasy. An important example was Paderewski whose insistence upon playing a Steinway in America was sufficiently rigid to cause a major confrontation at the 1893 Chicago Fair,[26] but who continued to play an Erard in Europe, despite frequent criticisms. Arthur Rubinstein recalls an incident which illustrates the intensity of feelings once aroused by these controversies. On a visit to Paderewski, Charles Steinway asked him to name his second preference of piano, expecting the answer to be Bechstein. Instead the pianist chose Erard, and when Steinway described it as an 'antique' instrument sounding like a harpsichord, he was loftily informed that Paderewski could get from it a 'fine sonority'. Further expressions of disbelief earned an outraged rebuke from Madame Paderewska, and Steinway left the house! [27] He was not alone in his opinion of the Erard's tone. G. A. Briggs, an expert on sound, remembers Paderewski's 'French piano which sounded as though the iron had entered its soul'.[28] G. B. Shaw, whose self-confessed ignorance of piano technique was matched by a total unacquaintance with the instrument's technology, nevertheless devoted several paragraphs to the alarming sound of Paderewski's piano.[29] The pianist himself later explained everything with characteristic *hauteur* and ambivalence: Erard had ma le the world's finest pianos until the Steinway came along. While it had precision, clarity, elegance and technical perfection, only 'a real master of the Erard' could 'make it sing', but 'a Steinway is always singing, no matter who plays it'.[30]

The number of real masters appears to have diminished rapidly. Some openly confessed defeat. When the American composer MacDowell rehearsed his Second Piano Concerto for a concert at the Paris 1889 Exhibition, he found the Erard concert grand hopelessly lacking in tone and volume, 'like a combination of wood and glass' in solo passages and totally obscured in the *tutti*. No German manufacturers were exhibiting and Weber was the only American, from whom he took a baby grand. Despite bureaucratic opposition and the need to tune down to the low French pitch of the Opéra-Comique orchestra, '20 stalwart men' carried the little instrument half a mile up hill—no waggons were allowed in the grounds—and 'pushed Erard to the wall'.[31] The incident smacks of preparation and ballyhoo—MacDowell was a notorious Francophobe—but cannot wholly be dismissed.[32] MacDowell's concert took place in a hall seating 6,000 people, larger than New York's Carnegie Hall (built in 1891 with a seating capacity of 3,000) or Queen's Hall (1893; 2,500) and exceeded only by the monstrous Albert Hall (1871; 10,000). Large audiences required powerful instruments to withstand pianists with enough muscle to be heard above large orchestras. A new repertoire made similar demands —the first three Rachmaninov concerti (1891, 1901, 1909) are obvious examples.

Most solo recitals continued to take place in smaller concert rooms, several of which were built by piano makers. London had Steinway Hall, opened in 1878 and seating 400; Bechstein (Wigmore) Hall (1901; 600), the small Queen's Hall (1893; 500) and the Aeolian Hall (1904; 500). These were easier to fill with people and sound, but they were merely smaller arenas for the same new generation of athletic players. Erard's pianos were designed for drawing rooms and gentler pianists.[33] In 1897 August Hyllested, an excellent Danish pupil of Liszt, explained the situation with brash simplicity: French pianos generally, and Erard's in particular, 'living on a reputation made long ago', were no longer acceptable as concert instruments—'a vigorous player finds them totally inadequate'. 'Most great pianists would agree', added *Presto*, the Chicago trade paper, gleefully.[34] The age of subdued playing, or broken strings and hammers, was long past.

As they steadily lost the custom of professional musicians, Erards cultivated an image of luxury and elegance for those amateurs who could afford nothing but the most expensive furniture. Thus at the Paris 1878 Exhibition their show-piece, said to have cost £3,000 to build, was priced at £4,000.[35] A 1904 catalogue advertised 'far and away the best piano and the most perfect in touch, tone and durability'. Great stress was laid upon ornate cabinet work, 'Style Louis Quinze', and so forth. Prices ranged from 100 guineas for an oblique upright to £2,500 for a concert grand,[36] more expensive than the best German and American instruments. A contemporary Steinway 'Vertegrand', probably the finest large upright ever made, cost eighty guineas. Bechsteins ranged from £60 to £300. Such instruments are coveted today for regular use, but Erards of the period are rarely seen and excite only an antiquarian interest.

The record of Erard's technological innovation after 1865 is a blank except for a curious device, the 'Resonator', which was introduced in 1895 with a blaze of publicity, breaking completely with the staid traditions of the past. This gadget should not be confused with a similarly named device used by the American firm, Mason and Hamlin, which imparted pressure to the soundboard.[37] Erard's resonator consisted simply of a thin sheet of steel in which were cut slits with raised edges 'giving them the form and character of gongs'.[38] By attaching it to the back of an upright or below a grand, the tone of old or inferior pianos, it was alleged, would be enormously enriched for a mere ten to forty guineas: any instrument's life would thus be doubled, because players could produce the marvellous new effects without strenuous effort. A long list of tributes backed these claims, headed inevitably by Paderewski, but including such distinguished musicians as Nikisch and David Popper, the great cellist.[39] *The Lady's Pictorial* exclaimed 'it inspires the improviser, encourages the moderate performer, cultivates the student and does justice to the artist'. *The Sunday Times* was equally impressed, adding the information that each 'gong' was attached to the piano's soundboard by a piece of cat-gut.[40] Other piano makers ignored these provocative claims, except for Bechstein who warned against the gadget's use on his instruments. D. Mayer, Erard's London representative, responded with a challenge: the Resonator would be attached to any Bechstein piano, left for four days (what magic was there in this?) and then judged by ten experts. The challenge was ignored, as was the Resonator, apparently, for no more was heard of it and no surviving specimen has been traced.[41] There is a mystery attached to this episode. The contraption was patented as the Mayer Resonator in 1894 (Pat. 20,764) and 1896 (Pat. 24,366), and as the Schreiber Resonator in 1897 (Pat. 5,884). The Schreiber Piano and Resonator Co. Ltd was established in 1895 and advertised in the 1903 *Weltadressbuch* as aspiring 'to become the Bechstein of England'. An 1897 prospectus claimed that the French and Belgian patents had been sold for £25,000, and invited subscriptions for 50,000 one pound shares. Apart from a derogatory reference to a 'kipper box' no further record has been found.[42]

No piano business has been established upon a firmer musical base than Pleyel. Its founder Ignaz (1757–1831), after a thorough training in music, including lessons in composition from Haydn and posts in Strasburg and London, became a prolific composer and a publisher whose list included the master's quartets. His son Camille (1788–1855) studied with Dussek, was a talented composer,[43] and married one of the most distinguished pianists of the period: the beautiful, promiscuous, cigar-smoking Marie, de Quincey's 'celestial pianofortist', whose playing delighted Liszt, Mendelssohn and Schumann.[44] Also associated with the firm was Kalkbrenner, whom the young Chopin described as 'the leading European pianist . . . he is the only one whose shoelaces I am not fit to untie'.[45] Later critics were less complimentary: both Heine and Clara Schumann joked at Kalkbrenner's posturing,[46] but his close association continued to be valuable to the firm until his death in 1849.

Pleyel began making pianos in 1807, operating on a small scale—about one hundred instruments a year—for several decades. His highly skilled workers, supervised until 1818 by Pape, rapidly established a reputation for excellence. Chopin used one of these instruments whenever possible, rather than the 'too insistent' Erard. He is even said to have preferred a Pleyel upright for demonstrating to his students, a truly remarkable testimony to its quality when we remember the primitive nature of upright actions at that time. It is therefore not surprising that, by the time of Camille Pleyel's death, the firm had risen to a place in France second only to Erard in prestige and output.

The year 1855 was significant in the history of the French piano industry, when its two leading firms came under the third generation of management. For most family businesses this tends to be a dangerous time, for the founders' enterprise and ability have gone, and their successors inherit a tradition without necessarily having the ability or interest to adapt to changing circumstances. Since the technology and economic environment of the piano industry underwent a 'sea change' during the 1860s, the challenge to established firms was peculiarly severe and the quality of succession paramount. Camille Pleyel's marriage had been a disaster—after five years he publicly repudiated Marie—but his personal misfortune may well have been the firm's salvation. Instead of staying in the family it was taken over, and renamed Pleyel, Wolff & Co., by a young pianist sufficiently talented to have been engaged by the Conservatoire as a *répétiteur*, who had joined Pleyel in 1850. Continuing the firm's tradition of direction by a musician, Auguste Wolff (1821–87) also renewed its enthusiasm for technical developments, devoting 'all his attention to increasing the volume of tone without losing sweetness'.[47] The results of his experiments with stringing and the position of hammers were embodied in new overstrung concert grands which were introduced in 1870 at an elaborate demonstration recital by several pianists, including Saint-Saëns. Another countryman claimed that the new Pleyels were equal to Steinways in every respect, and better in the clarity of their bass, but weakened his credibility by asserting that overstringing was quite unsuitable for upright pianos.[48] The new instruments were also shown at the 1873 Vienna Exhibition and praised by the jury for their successful adoption of the American system.[49] This was misleading, for the adoption was by no means complete: wrought-iron reinforcement being employed rather than an overall cast-iron frame. But the prejudice against overstringing had been overcome, and the Pleyel factory, as described by Turgan in 1866, already contained some modern features, including machine planes and saws which were prominently illustrated.[50]

Wolff was succeeded in 1887 by his son-in-law, Gustav Lyon [51] (1857–1936), who contributed an enquiring spirit and openness of mind which was practically unique among French piano makers of his period. His friends included Edison and Rudolph Koenig, an expert on tuning forks, and much of his time was devoted to careful study of his rivals' pianos. Blumenberg, the editor of the *New York Musical Courier*, who rarely found much to admire in France, was impressed to find at Pleyels 'a laboratory . . . that would make an experimental mind wild with delight', and pianos by Bechstein, Schroeder, Broadwood, Chickering, Knabe, Steinway and Weber, all being subjected to minute investigation.[52] In 1894 Lyon even visited the leading German makers, Bechstein, Grotrian, Schiedmayer and Blüthner. At the latter establishment he took note of a 'giant planing machine' and ordered one. Such activities, which might be thought sensible but commonplace, were sufficiently rare in the French piano industry to excite much comment.[53]

Pleyel therefore succeeded in avoiding a blinkered conservatism, but differed from the best American and German firms in two vital respects: a restricted use of machinery, and an extraordinary neglect of overstrung uprights. By the 1890s saws and planes driven by steam power were in use, at least for rough work; and in contrast to Erard's practice there was a hammer covering machine. But the extent of mechanization was severely limited. Blumenberg noted several typical examples of inefficient hand processing: the covering of bass strings by using a simple wheel; and numerous gratuitous 'finishing' activities, even on the backs of instruments. Most costly of all, timber was still seasoned by the natural process which took nine years and tied up vast resources of capital. Among the stocks proudly listed by Turgan in 1866 there were 23,000 wrest planks, sufficient for more than eight years' production. Thirty years later the American dry kiln process was still not used in Pleyel's factory.

Neither Wolff nor Lyon appears to have been much concerned with the development of the upright: it is notable that all the foreign instruments seen by Blumenberg at the factory were grands. Bizet's little cottage piano, displayed in the museum of the Paris Conservatoire, is a typical Pleyel upright of the 1860s, vertically strung with overdampers. Few changes were made in this design until long after the firm had modernized its grands—an overstrung boudoir grand with metal frame was advertised in 1885. By neglecting to design a modern overstrung upright Pleyel greatly restricted its foreign markets; 'cottages' from fifty-two guineas and 'obliques' from sixty-eight guineas found few customers in England or Australia. But in France the firm's place was assured. By 1910 it had doubled the production levels of the 1860s and surpassed Erard in output and, arguably, in quality.

Erard, Pleyel, even Herz, are familiar names in musical history. Antoine Bord is not, yet for several decades his instruments were commercially the most successful made in France and were familiar in many parts of the world. He has already appeared briefly in these pages, as the manufacturer of the cheap little 'pianettes' which were popular in mid-Victorian England, and as a controversial juror at international exhibitions. The history of his business can be pieced together from fragmentary reports in the trade journals, although it would merit more detailed treatment if archives became accessible. However, Bord's taste for publicity, which was rare among his contemporary countrymen, provides information, mostly sycophantic, from which the sceptical reader can gain some insight into the evolution of one of the more successful, if less distinguished, French piano makers. Born in 1814, Antoine Bord started business in 1840 and rapidly expanded it to take advantage of the market for a small cheap instrument. Adroitly concentrating upon the mass production of one basic model, with resulting economies of scale, he rapidly succeeded in home and foreign markets without any radical changes in technology.

For several decades this was a sufficient formula for success. In 1879 the *Music Trades Review* noted with grudging admiration that Bord's pianettes were flooding the country and no English maker could compete in price.[45] Replies that they were 'so small as to be little more than toys' could not alter the fact that until the mid-eighties they remained virtually unchallenged as the first cheap instruments to offer some musical satisfaction. Their thin tone and primitive action were serious limitations, but in addition to being half the price of a better alternative they were light and transportable yet surprisingly rugged. These qualities were particularly attractive to the hire, as distinct from hire-purchase, trade which always accounted for a high proportion of the French market, and in centres such as English university towns where the ability to stand up to rough treatment was of primary importance. The firm's advertising lay great stress upon ruggedness. Thus the saga of Number 56221 found its way into the trade press: sentenced to transportation to the Orange Free State in 1883, it was hired first to a travelling circus, hauled over mountainous roads by ox cart, then to a 'low music hall' where it was lubricated with tallow, cigar ends and 'various brands of inferior liquors'. After serving five years it was released for sandpapering and tuning, and still managed to fetch twenty-five pounds.[55] The tone of this publicity, remote from the French manufacturer's traditional invocations of luxury and culture, marks a significant change in approach to the public. It was to become common in some sections of the American and, notably, the English trade, but remained unusual in France.

The precise level of Bord's output was a matter of controversy even among contemporaries. In 1885 he protested to the *Musical Courier* that his claim to be the only European manufacturing twelve pianos a day was true, that he had recently sold 3,722 instruments in a year and regularly held stocks of three hundred.[56] In 1894 his successors made a similar complaint: the *Courier*'s editor was denigrating their achievement without having visited them on his recent European trip—production was running at eleven pianos a day.[57] Our own estimates suggest that such claims were exaggerated. Moreover the value of Bord's output was considerably below that of Erard and Pleyel whose instruments sold at prices three or four times higher. Nevertheless, there was some truth in Bord's claim to be the only French piano maker of the 1870s and eighties to compete success-fully with foreign firms. The scale of his activities permitted, and the cheapness of his product required, division of labour, and even the use of 'machine tools driven by a powerful steam engine', methods which were sufficiently unusual in France to excite notice.

A puff on the occasion of his golden wedding and production of Number 50,000 claimed that mass production did not exclude quality control by the boss: 'a fact which seems incredible and even impossible, but which is not the less real and certain. M. Bord has never permitted a single instrument to leave his premises without having carefully examined and retouched it himself . . . if he breaks an arm he does not give up for a day nor an hour that daily control which will end only with his life.' These heroic virtues were accompanied by a paternal solicitude for his workers, offering sickness benefits, a doctor in attendance, and annual bonuses which varied from two to ten pounds per man for several decades. In his original will he intended to leave £20,000 to be divided among them according to years of service, but revoked this clause when they took part in a five months' strike which began in October 1881 and was later judged to have marked a watershed in the French piano industry. The strike began when several makers lowered wages in an attempt to meet the German competition which was biting deep into their export markets. Fifty-nine employers, led by the four principal firms, retaliated by locking out their workers, whose demand for a fifteen per cent increase in wages was nevertheless broadly successful.[58] Weekly earnings remained lower than in England, but in an industry which was highly labour intensive, i.e. technologically backward, the increase in costs was damaging, particularly to small businesses. Among larger makers Bord was mainly affected because two-thirds of his sales were normally overseas, and he was supplying the lower end of the market where demand was sensitive to price. In the luxury market increased costs could be passed on to the customer or, if competition or custom prevented this, could be absorbed by manufacturer or retailer out of high profit margins. At the lower end of the market margins were perforce narrower and, by the 1880s, were being eroded by the revolution in technology and distribution.

These pressures took several years to exert themselves. During the 1880s Bord's cheapest models retained a hold in England where he continued to sell one-third of his output. At a cash price of twenty guineas, or fifteen shillings a month on the three-year system, they were less than half the price of good German instruments, and superior to Ascherberg's rubbish or to the cobbled products from English sweatshops which were, for the moment, their only rivals. But their inherent limitations were becoming apparent. A feeble result at the 1880 Sydney Exhibition, which contributed to the decline of sales in Australia, was followed by a luke-warm reception at Amsterdam, where the jury politely refused 'to confirm by a high mark of distinction the success obtained by this important firm in preceding exhibitions'. By 1886 Bord's price advantage was narrowing dangerously. The more expensive models were difficult to sell outside France. Even at the reduced price of fifty-eight guineas the 'model 6', previously eighty guineas,[59] was no match for Germany's medium class instruments, while the attractions of iron frames, overstringing and impressive appearance were becoming available at lower prices each season.

Isolation and self-esteem

Antoine Bord died in 1888. An estate of £160,000 and a spectacular funeral, with music by stars of the Opéra and Opéra Comique, accompanied by Pugno at the organ, marked a fitting end to a highly successful career, probably the last in the history of piano manufacturing in France. It could not conceal a deepening crisis for both firm and industry. French exports of musical instruments to England were a little over £140,000—less than half the totals of a decade before—and were never again to approach the levels of the early seventies. America had long ceased to be a profitable outlet, even in the southern states which had remained loyal to French instruments for many years. Other old markets had also disappeared. The Paris correspondent of the *Music Trades Review* lamented the loss of a large trade, 'especially in cheap instruments with Holland, England, your colonies, South American ports, Russia and even with Germany itself. . . . We make our pianos in the old style and, to the national disgrace, are being cut out by the Germans, even in our own French colonies'.[60]

Bord's successors attempted to meet the crisis by diversifying their production with a motley of instruments embracing the old and essaying the new technology. At the Paris Exhibition of 1889, they showed two overstrung iron-framed grands and eight uprights of widely varying types: overstrung, oblique, vertical, with iron and wood frames. In 1893 they even had the temerity to enter a grand piano, allegedly much improved, for the Chicago Exhibition, but were laughed at for their pains. Despite the obligatory medals awarded at French exhibitions, and frequent laudatory puffs, the Bord instruments never regained considerable sales or prestige abroad, although they continued to flourish at home.

Section 11 of Table V illustrates the predicament of a representative group of smaller French makers. Without leadership into foreign markets —indeed the leading firms were the most conservative—all were restricted to a home demand which was securely protected by tariffs and national sentiment, but dormant. Only Gaveau achieved a measure of sustained growth, but this was based upon commercial acumen rather than intrinsic quality, and was therefore confined to the uncritical French market. Arthur Rubinstein, recalling his Paris début in 1904, is again a reliable witness. It was to be financed by Etienne Gaveau whom the pianist describes as ambitious, resourceful and alive to modern publicity methods. Accustomed to Bechsteins, Rubinstein was apprehensive, but assured that a foreign piano was improcurable in Paris. Gaveau agreed with him that Erard's good action was offset by tinny sound, while the Pleyel's tone was lovely but inadequate for a modern concert hall. His own instruments, however, were quite as good as Bechstein's. Reluctantly the pianist acquiesced and had his début all but ruined. In a Chopin concerto 'the delicate filigree of the Larghetto was hardly audible', and in the Saint-Saëns Second Concerto he was 'again cruelly handicapped' by the piano's inadequate power and lack of sparkle.[61]

Adverse criticism by visiting artists and rejection by foreign buyers had little effect upon the industry's self-esteem, which was sustained by a continuous stream of nationalistic musicology and journalism, and periodically boosted by predictable but vaunted successes at the Paris international exhibitions. Thus in 1889 the Weber piano chosen by Mac-Dowell was criticized for its 'confused, woolly tone' and bad 'break', and awarded a mere silver medal, along with Brinsmead and twenty undistinguished firms. 'Grands Prix' were taken, of course, by Erard and Pleyel, and gold medals by five French makers, including Bord and Gaveau. The official report was less absurdly biased than Chouquet's of the previous decade (p. 66), but it reiterated a national preference for a quieter, more 'pure and distinguished' tone, appropriate, it argued, for the smaller apartments of Parisians.[62]

The 1900 Paris Exhibition was a very grand affair: 'Never at any time or in any place in the world's history has a more colossal or grand demonstration of human genius been seen,' exclaimed one publication.[63] But its musical instrument section was of more political than technical interest. There were no German pianos, of course, and 'England's indifference was greater than that of the United States'.[64] Diedrichs of St Petersburg exhibited an upright with ornamented figures symbolizing the Franco-Russian alliance. The jury's deliberations were enlivened by Krehbiel, the American musicologist, removing his coat and offering to fight.[65] Its report paid the customary obeisance to Gallic virtues—'un caractère

d'élégance, de bon goût, de sobriété devant lequel il faut bien s'incliner' [66]
—and announced a list of awards reminiscent of 'a school prize giving'.[67]
Most French manufacturers remained opposed to overstringing, and one
notable assured *Monde Musicale* that a good instrument must contain as
little metal as possible.[68]

A similar chauvinism prevailed among French musicologists. In 1885
Marmontel paid tribute to a 'supériorité incontestable' in the manufacture
of both uprights and grands, arising from innate qualities 'spéciales à la
race française', and even discerned, in a singularly inappropriate phrase,
a 'conquête pacifique' of world markets.[69] A few years later Constant
Pierre expressed the same faith in French superiority: where prizes were
not won it was because his compatriots were, deservedly, the judges and
therefore *hors concours*.[70] Such pieties were typical of musical opinion in
Paris, where the Conservatoire under its octogenarian director, the distinguished composer Ambroise Thomas, exercised a formidable influence,
continuing to train pianists and favour pianos in the old tradition. Pugno
(1852–1914) and the great artist Cortot (1877–1962) have left evidence
of this style on gramophone records. The *Musical Courier* went so far as
to blame the Conservatoire for retarding French piano manufacture,
provoking furious denials in the Paris press.[71]

It is impossible for the historian to be entirely objective about these
matters, for aesthetic, commercial and nationalistic judgments were in-
extricably interlaced. French pianos like French singers cultivated a distinctive sound in which elegance, refinement and clarity were esteemed,
even at the expense of fullness and warmth.[72] Unfortunately for France
the former qualities were undervalued in world markets after 1870. The
dilemma is well illustrated by controversy at the Chicago Exhibition of
1893 where some French manufacturers made an attempt to compete. M.
Thibouville-Lamy, their leader, found the American pianos lacking in
'finesse de touche et égalité tonale', but admired their greater sonority
and urged his compatriots to emulate their solidity and finish.[73] The
Musical Courier described the French pianos as well made, and approved
their 'delicacy and regularity of touch' but deplored their weak tone.[74]
Clearly there was common ground and willingness to differ, but these
courtesies were submerged by the customary nationalistic abuse ('rep-
tilian prose' was one of the politer epithets) which was exacerbated, said
the French, by Americo-German Francophobia.[75] In the warfare of international commerce no holds were barred. It would be naïve to accept
every American and reject every French judgment of intrinsic merit, but
the verdict of the market place cannot be gainsaid. If French manufacturers wished to export their pianos they needed to adapt to changing
circumstances, and this they failed to do. Everything appeared to conspire

to maintain French insularity. As the industry grew to believe its own propaganda, its assurance of innate superiority and indifference to competition merged imperceptibly into a dangerous self-delusion. Even the government lent a hand through tariff policy, but more significantly by a general encouragement of insularity through such measures as the prohibition of foreign pianos at the Colonne and Lamoureux concerts.[76]

There were two exceptions to this national paralysis of self-esteem: a failed manufacturer turned crusading journalist, and a firm which became the world's leading manufacturer of pianoforte actions. Edouard Mangeot (1835–98) was born in Nancy and took over his father's small piano-making business in 1859. His instruments were successfully shown at the 1862 London Exhibition, where it can be assumed that he was impressed by the new American pianos, for he visited the USA in 1866 and returned as an enthusiastic advocate of the new technology. Tentative proposals that he should become Steinway's European representative never materialized, but by 1877 he was advertising 'pianos Franco-Américaines' with iron frames (apparently the first to be made in France), some overstrung.[77] In 1878 he won a gold medal at the Paris Exhibition, became a Chevalier of the Legion of Honour and moved to Paris, after which his business rapidly disintegrated.

The reasons for this sudden reversal can only be guessed, but there are clear hints in Mangeot's obituaries. *Monde Musicale* suggests that he was more concerned with the artistic than the commercial aspects of piano manufacture.[78] An American tribute is more explicit: the cost of reorganizing his factory, discarding 'the plans and models of half a century, and adopting the sound theory of a new world . . . coupled with a polite refusal of the French people to listen to a larger, firmer, fuller and more musical tone, destroyed the house'.[79] In 1889 Mangeot founded a journal, *Le Monde Musicale*, to crusade against French conservatism and 'insouciance'.[80] For a decade he patiently advocated the 'American system', explaining its technical, artistic and economic advantages to 'ce pays, hostile à toutes les innovations'.[81] Before 1867 the leading virtuosi had everywhere played French pianos; now they had all switched to American or German instruments.[82] But recovery was possible, and neither workmen nor employers need fear the new system: high wages and low prices could both be achieved through specialization and machine production.[83] Too many small makers and too great a diversity of models prevented this.[84] Future success, argued Mangeot, lay through an extension of Bord's methods against the conservatism of Erard and the national predilection for 'petits propriétaires'.[85] 'The idea that every workman should know the piano from A to z is a dream . . . anyway foreign competition leaves us no choice.'[86]

In fact there was an alternative: to ignore foreign developments and remain content with the protected home market. Here demand was highly inelastic for several reasons. Population and incomes were growing very slowly: whereas Britain doubled her population between 1850 and 1910, the population of France increased by less than fourteen per cent, and there was a similar gap between income rates of growth. Moreover, these limitations upon demand were reinforced by prevailing social attitudes and structure. In marked contrast to England and America there was no working class market. One result of this was that the French, unlike the English, made little trash. Another was that hire purchase never became popular, although there were attempts to introduce it as early as 1877.[87] Renting was popular and profitable. An American trade journalist who was enraged by 'sybaritic workmen' and 'rotten erotic songs' was nevertheless impressed by rental charges of ten to twenty francs on instruments costing 350 francs! He concluded that France offered an easy but small market.[88]

In France the piano remained a bourgeois instrument, part of the 'salon, furnished with a piano, paintings, candelabras, clocks and bibelots, in which to receive visitors and to show . . . a surplus of wealth, dedicated to cultured living'.[89] Confined to France the industry could ignore change. Given these mutually reinforcing constraints of economy, society and culture, it is hardly surprising that Mangeot's evangelism died with him. After 1898 *Le Monde Musicale* soon fell in line with the general unquestioning approval of all things French. By 1904 it had apparently lost all interest in trade and become a journal of music criticism. The change was symbolic, reflecting the nation's abandonment of world markets. By the second decade of the twentieth century, France was exporting a mere 4,000 pianos a year, less than half the English level, and about one-twentieth that of Germany.

An exceptional success

The most successful and respected French business during this period made no pianos. Jean Schwander (1812–82) was born in Lauterbach, Alsace, studied action-making under Kriegelstein [90] in Paris—thus continuing Pape's extraordinary lineage—and opened his own workshop there in 1844. Ten years later he was joined by Joseph Herrburger (1832–1915), also from Alsace, who became his son-in-law and partner in 1865. The firm rapidly established a world-wide reputation by a long series of technical improvements to actions which it would be confusing to enumerate, but whose cumulative importance can scarcely be exaggerated.[91] The Herrburger-Schwander models, like those of their German competitors (pp. 81–2) were based, of course, upon earlier inventions, notably Sebastien Erard's 1821 design for grand actions and Wornum's 1826 patent for uprights. But the gulf that separates them from their ancestors is the fundamental difference between custom-built specimens of inventive genius and mass-produced products of precision engineering. It is true, for example, that Wornum's design was a prototype for modern upright actions, and ironic that its adoption and modification by such Paris makers as Pleyel, Pape and Kriegelstein, led to its becoming universally known as the 'French' action. But it is misleading to suggest that Wornum 'made the upright piano a practical instrument',[92] both because so great a revolution demanded the radical improvements in framing and stringing which we have already described, and because Wornum's original design was fit only for the puny cottage pianos of his period.

The most substantial achievement of Herrburger-Schwander was the mass production of sensitive but sturdy upright actions which functioned almost as efficiently (without needing constant adjustment and repair) as the intrinsically simpler, and traditionally far superior, action of the concert grand. The need for improvement was paramount by the early 1880s. It was 'the greatest simplification required in an (upright) piano . . . the other component parts of the instrument being plain enough'.[83] An improved mechanism, it was argued in 1883, would remove 'the various annoyances of sticking and irresponsive keys and sluggishness of touch' that were then inescapable.[94] Nor were grand actions yet satisfactory. In America the best firms used an Erard model but it was 'too expensive, too complicated, and goes wrong too easily'. The cost was about £22 and makers 'never knew when they were through with the work . . . there was always something more to do until the instrument was finally shipped out'. German manufacturers commonly used a cheaper, simpler action which could be repaired by an ordinary mechanic, but it was 'inferior to the Erard in meeting professional requirements'.[95] Great progress was made during the following decade by several firms specializing in this field, but Herrburger-Schwander were the acknowledged leaders.

Given satisfactory designs, action-making was peculiarly adaptable to large-scale machine production for both technical and economic reasons. Each action is assembled from a large number of small parts which must be precisely cut, drilled, shaped, fraised and trimmed or bushed with cloth or leather. By standardizing these parts and making them interchangeable between units, mass production became possible with specially designed machine tools and jigs, at greatly reduced cost. Such methods depended for their success upon the existence of large, clearly defined, homogeneous markets which permitted a scale of operation far larger than that of any individual piano manufacturer. By the late 1880s Herrburger-Schwander were making some 35,000 actions a year, over half of which were exported, mainly to England but even to Germany. So successful were they in the United States that American competitors, invoking the familiar complaints of protectionists against allegedly cheap and female labour, demanded an increase in the tariff from twenty-five per cent to fifty per cent, and got forty-five per cent.[96] The use of a Schwander action became an important selling-point, indicating an instrument's quality. At the 1900 Paris Exhibition several French manufacturers placed them conspicuously on top of their pianos in glass cases, but were ordered to remove them because the firm was not itself exhibiting.[97] By this time annual production was about 70,000 and Schwander actions were proudly or surreptitiously used by many leading German and English manufacturers, including Broadwood. In 1902 German imports of pianos and parts from France were valued at 355,000 marks, more than ten times her purchases from England, which came second in the list. Although separate figures are not available, it is certain that piano actions largely accounted for this trade, and that Herrburger-Schwander were the principal suppliers.[98] By 1913 the business was employing 1,000 workers and making nearly 100,000 actions a year. Thus, one French firm escaped the narrow confines of France by exploiting her ancient traditions of woodworking and mechanical ingenuity to enter the vast expanding world market.

Chapter 7

The United States

The expansion of American piano manufacture after the Civil War was without parallel in any other country. By 1900 more than half of the world's instruments were made in the United States, the industry employed six times as many men as in 1860 and the value of production had increased sevenfold. The number of firms increased more slowly, but this was indicative of a remarkable expansion in the average size of business unit and scale of production; in 1896 the five largest piano manufacturers in the world were all American. This efflorescence has been variously attributed to the quality of American iron and wood, or 'the general atmosphere of freedom and enthusiastic encouragement of individual initiative and industry'.[1] But such explanations neglect the fundamental economic determinants: an enormous and continuous increase in effective demand within a highly protected market which was amply satisfied by ideally elastic conditions of supply. In the century after 1840, the population grew, through natural increase and massive immigration, from seventeen to 132 millions, and real income per head doubled every forty-three years. An index of manufacturing output (1899=100) rose from sixteen in 1860 to 172 by 1910.[2] Waxing prosperity and a desire for home music and social emulation which was at least as powerful as in Victorian England, ensured a thriving market for pianos. The industry, consisting largely of new firms which enjoyed the immediate advantages of the new technology without commitment to traditional methods and conservative workers, grew rapidly in response and gave further impetus to this buoyant market.

In contrast to the paucity of European official statistics, American census material allows more detailed analysis than would be appropriate in the present book, but a few general indicators are outlined in Table VI.

Imports soon ceased to be important. To what extent this was due to the protective tariff of 1861, or to the innate superiority of American pianos, was debated by contemporaries, and the general significance of protection for industrial growth during this period continues to be discussed.[3] The complexities of this argument need not detain us, but a few points deserve

Table VI   Growth of American Piano Manufacture

	Firms	*Labour Force* ('000)	*Pianos* ('000)	*Value* ($ million)
1860	110	3	(20)	5
1870	156	4	24	8
1880	174	8	(30)	12
1890	236	12	72	26
1900	263	18	171	35
1909	294	25	374	67

Note. Bracketed figures are estimates. All others are from us censuses.

notice. The level of protection was far higher than in any other country. Even France, where non-tariff barriers were a greater deterrent, imposed only a ten per cent duty. Other countries levied tariffs of bewildering complexity—*ad valorem*, specific or by weight—but, with the possible exception of Russia, their protective effect was much lighter.

Extremes of climate and domestic heating were an additional barrier to imports. Today the ravages of central heating are generally acknowledged, and pianos are kept away from radiators and protected by humidifiers. But a century ago this was primarily an American problem and there was much scoffing, particularly in the English trade papers, at those who advocated special methods of construction and the use of watered plants, or a wet sponge under the piano.[4] The argument was heated and prolonged, tending to polarize between American patriots who maintained that all European pianos were made of 'green' wood, disintegrating on arrival, and those Englishmen who pooh-poohed the unknown. Intelligent European entrepreneurs studied the problem and attempted to deal with it. Herrburger-Schwander used selected American timber (a practice later adopted by Japanese manufacturers) in actions destined for the American market. Blüthner and Schiedmayer also made vigorous attempts to breach the tariff wall with the typically German paraphernalia of catalogues, attractive trade terms and excellent English which excited much comment; but neither attained much success.[5]

None of this proves that the American manufacturer's dominance of his home market was due primarily to the protection of climate and tariffs. Even German manufacturers were in no position to mount a sustained challenge to an industry of such vigour and resource. American trade statistics do not distinguish pianos from other musical instruments, but between 1870 and 1900 general imports remained stable at about one million dollars, while the value of indigenous products increased from fourteen to forty-four million dollars.

Patterns of demand

If immunity from foreign competition at home was a benefit which American manufacturers shared with the French, in other respects their market had more in common with England. Even the rackets were similar: 'stencils' were rife, and Americans were warned against advertisements by 'bereaved widows' and sellers 'just going to Europe'. Hire purchase was common and demand socially widespread. The tone was set from above: 'Today the piano is an indispensable part of a well regulated household; its social position is unquestionable and impregnable . . . how would society go on without it?' argued a leading article in the *American Art Journal*.[6] On another occasion the same paper summarized the factors determining a piano's market value: its standard of manufacture, approval by musicians, advertising and, not least, 'the social standing of the manufacturer'.[7] As in Europe, both leading makers and their clients sought an interdependent dignity, and some firms tended to adopt the airs and graces of their loftier customers. Morris Steinart, the musician, piano-maker and collector of instruments, writes amusingly of his attempts to get an audience at the court of a prominent New York manufacturer. A similar experience in London was reported by Christopher le Fleming a century later.[8]

Respectability was the great shibboleth, though it was never carried to quite the excess suggested by latter day commentators. A curiously persistent myth is the frequently reiterated belief that Victorians were so repressed as to cover even their piano's legs.[9] Years of diligent research have produced not a shred of evidence for this allegation, save for two American jests. In 1894 a '*Handy Music Lexicon* based upon Professor Kalaner's very humorous and famous work' reported that 'some people are so modest that they put pantlets on the legs of their pianos'; and in 1897 a Philadelphian family was alleged to have made 'little petticoats' for the same purpose.[10] The facts reflect taste in furnishing rather than repressed sexuality. In Europe and America the shape of pianos was generally regarded as ugly and needing camouflage. The *Ladies Home Journal* suggested 'dainty draperies or other elegantly devised decorations with needle or brush'; the *Queen* recommended five yards of lemon coloured muslin, draped prettily and nailed down. Manufacturers were incensed but the ladies persisted in hiding good wood. Draperies embroidered on silk plush were popular in England and 'piano scarves' were extensively advertised in America.[11] Another trivial but illuminating example of clashes between design and social practice was the public's refusal to accept mechanical page-turners. Many attempts to market such devices failed, it was generally agreed, because they would impede courtship. Englishmen threatened to 'kick the precious apparatus out of the window', while American girls exclaimed, 'What can such an attachment to a piano be in comparison with John's attachment for me!'[12]

A distinctive feature of the piano's widening market in America was the extent to which it was preceded by the harmonium, particularly in regions of recent settlement. Annual production of these cheap reed instruments exceeded 15,000 by the mid-sixties and reached 107,000 by the end of the century. 'As trade goes west,' predicted the *American Art Journal* in 1881, 'the emigrants who are settling there today will be ready for the organ canvasser five years hence, and for the piano drummer in five more.'[13] The accuracy of this forecast is proved by the following statistics of production in the two leading states which show both the rise of western manufacture and the shift from harmoniums to pianos (all figures represent values in million dollars):

	New York Pianos	Illinois Pianos	Illinois Harmoniums
1880	6.6	0.04	0.6
1890	14.5	0.75	2.7
1900	14.4	6.9	1.2
1904	16.7	9.7	1.7
1909	23.8	14.7	0.9

A British visitor to Chicago in 1893 was astonished at the extent and quality of manufacture. Some factories even had 'their own railway connection for shipping goods direct' and even the cheapest instruments were 'worthy of the name piano', though at higher prices than reigned in Hoxton and Hackney.[14] The great entrepreneur in this region was William Kimball. Neither musician nor craftsman, but with respect for both, he grasped 'the true principle by which great fortunes are gained . . . small profits from a large and constantly growing number of customers'. His ideal salesman was 'fresh from the farm himself with the manure still on his heels'.[15] But the product was substantial and well made—farmers accustomed to machinery and good timber would not buy shoddy.

Musical influences on the demand for pianos were similar to those affecting England, though again there were differences. The importance of concert tours by famous pianists has already been noted. They were generally agreed to be indispensable if a manufacturer desired prestige for his piano, and some observers thought they had a much wider influence: 'the demand for the pianoforte in the United States is largely due to performances by eminent virtuosi . . . if concert performances stopped for a year output would be halved'.[16] While none were as expensive and spectacular as the marathons undertaken by Anton Rubinstein and Paderewski (p. 54), many such circuits were arranged. In 1898 Rosenthal, the incredible pupil of Liszt, was touring for Steinway, the more austere Bauer for Knabe, and Carreno, 'the *Walküre* of the piano', for Chickering. Of more lasting influence was the great extension and improvement in education and instruction. As in England many teachers were ill-equipped, but a more substantial pedagogy made itself felt here, assisted by the return of musically literate Americans from training in Europe and the pervasive influence of German immigrant culture. Although the great American music schools, Eastman, Curtis and Juilliard, were not established until the 1920s, reputable standards were cultivated during the 1860s at such institutions as Oberlin, Peabody and the Boston New England Conservatory. It would be parochial to regard these colleges as inferior to anything available in England, even if they did not yet achieve the levels of Paris or Leipzig.

The pressure of higher standards of playing on the general level of manufacture was noticeable by the late eighties. The *Musical Courier* remarked that 'old school' makers had attempted to excuse poor quality by saying, 'Vell, vat's de difference, de peoples don't know'. But now many customers did know, because teachers insisted upon their buying instruments which responded to a proper technique.[17]

Serious students probably bought most of their music from such publishers as Schirmer, Schroeder and Gunther, and Pond, but sales of cheap music expanded at an even faster rate than in England. By the 1890s there were hundreds of publishers scattered across the country in every city. Between 1890 and 1900 their numbers increased in New York from fourteen to twenty-two, and in Illinois from ten to twenty-two, while the combined value of their publications more than doubled. Their products were much the same as in England: 'effective' piano pieces, in some of which the player had to cross hands; humorous and sentimental ballads. Indeed many popular 'English' songs, including 'Daisy Bell' and 'Ta-ra-ra-boom-de-ay', were of American origin. The market was much larger and the selling harder—the musically illiterate Chas. K. Harris sold ten million copies of 'After the Ball' in twenty years; the age of pop had begun.[18] Prevailing sentiments were similar if less reticent. Loesser detects a significant change in domestic piano music after 1890, from the *adagio* religiosity of 'The Dying Poet' towards the flirtatious amiability of Nevin and Moskowski.[19] Ian Whitcomb identifies 1892 as the turning point in popular song, when gaiety replaced moral uplift.[20] But tear-jerkers continued to fill the piano stools, and in 1893 'Hearts and Flowers' was published, the *ne plus ultra* of sentimentality whose *tremolando* strains epitomize an age.

In quite a different class aesthetically and technically was a new, blithely decorous art, the first black music to be extensively written and published. Classical ragtime flourished for about twenty years after 1896, achieving wide commercial success and musical influence (in Debussy, Stravinsky and Ives). Originating in Missouri it first reached a wider public when it was played by itinerant pianists at the world's fairs in Chicago, Omaha, Buffalo and St Louis. Although it was neither the first rag to be published nor the best of Scott Joplin's works, 'Maple Leaf', which appeared in 1899, was the genre's first great success, eventually selling more than a million copies. Its difficulties provided opportunities for specialist teachers and instruction books. In 1903 Axel Christensen, 'the Ragtime Czar', advertised 'ragtime taught in ten lessons', was besieged by pupils and, by 1913, supervised four schools in Chicago and branches in twelve other cities. Joplin himself published a set of six exercises 'to assist players in giving the "Joplin Rags" that weird and intoxicating effect intended by the composer'.[21] Despised by the contemporary musical establishment, which confused respectability with quality and failed to distinguish classical ragtime from its commercial derivatives, this music has received belated recognition, not merely in the passing revivalist craze of the early 1970s, but in scholarly publication and exegesis. At its best, in the later rags of Joplin and Joseph Lamb, its only important white practitioner, ragtime was a serious if minor addition to the piano's repertoire. The tragedy of Joplin's life—'a personal and an American tragedy' which symbolizes a great deal of black social history—lies precisely in his failure to gain that acceptance as a serious composer which he desired and so richly deserved.[22] But to the piano historian ragtime has another significance: captured and trivialized by Tin Pan Alley it became 'an indestructible part of the American musical scene, associated in the popular mind with the mechanical sound of the player piano'.[23]

The rise and fall of the automatic piano

If commercial ragtime gave a boost to piano sales, the instruments with which it was associated provoked so much interest that, for a time, they threatened to supplant conventional pianos. Manufacturers welcomed the automatic piano because it was a distinctively new product which could appeal to both new and 'replacement' customers. As potential buyers the latter were rapidly growing in importance, but they were difficult to tempt because, unlike most modern 'consumer durables', American pianos of that period had a long expectation of life. Few genuine improvements in design could be expected and therefore practically the only rational excuse for changing one's instrument was to buy a better, more

expensive one. This limited the replacement market to consumers sufficiently musical and affluent to care if their existing pianos were inadequate.
Consumer resistance was particularly damaging in times of business
depression. Between 1892 and 1894 the output of all durable goods,
including furniture, china and jewellery, fell by twenty per cent, and
production of musical instruments fell twice as fast. This of course was
partly due to a general avoidance of luxury spending in hard times, but
for an increasing number of people it simply meant delaying the replacement of an article which was still giving service.[24] Table VII shows the
extent to which this potentially dangerous market situation was transformed by automatic pianos, whose sales steadily grew to exceed those
of conventional instruments during the war and immediate post-war
years.

Table VII   Production of Conventional and Automatic Pianos

	Quantity (thousand instruments)		*Value (million dollars)*	
	Pianos	*Automatics*	*Pianos*	*Automatics*
1900	171	6	27	0.7
1909	330	34	49	9
1914	238	98	41	21
1919	156	180	39	56
1925	136	169	39	55
1929	94	37	25	13

The pianola's two basic principles, pneumatic leverage for the keys and
a mechanism driven by perforated paper, were both invented before 1850.
Various attempts to combine these ideas led to the construction of a
cumbersome device which could be wheeled up to a piano and made to
manipulate part of its keyboard. The next step was to place the mechanism
inside a piano and extend its range to the full eighty-eight notes. In 1898
the Aeolian Company, which had been making self-playing organs for a
decade, produced their first 'pianola', and by 1904 there were more than
forty different kinds of automatic piano on the American market.[25]

Their remarkable success was very much an American phenomenon,
despite considerable invention and some popularity in Europe, and can
be explained in various ways. Pianolas were new and highly mechanical,
welcome qualities in a society which embraced novelty and where it could
be seriously argued that even violins might be machine-made 'more
perfectly than is possible by hand'.[26] Conventional pianos were coveted
for solidity and prestige, but they were bought for women: in America,
even more than in England, playing the piano was a pastime for females
and foreigners. The pianola appealed directly to men, in addition to

embodying all the attributes of its predecessor. The advertisements have a clear persuasive message: a successful business man is seated at the pianola performing to a lady in evening dress—'Check up the successful people you know. Invariably you will find that they have music in their homes, generally a player piano'. There would be no more voiceless pianos. Amateur playing would be 'entirely done away with'. The new machine would economize in the time and expense of learning to play, and excite admiration, with due humility, for 'you can talk while it plays or play it if talk ends'. It offered 'Technique hitherto only obtainable by unlimited application by the great musicians; Touch almost identical with that of the human fingers; Expression, which alone crystallizes musical emotion, entirely subject to the will of the performer'.[27]

In truth the pianola required no operative skill save a steady foot on the bellows, and even this was soon usurped by an electric motor, but it conveyed, like elaborate 'High Fi' equipment in a later age, a spurious sense of artistic achievement. Enthusiasts will deny or vindicate this judgment—the reader can decide: 'a talented player-pianist might produce music as good as, if not better than, that played by a top pianist' because the notes are struck for him and he can concentrate on 'the subtle nuances of phrasing, tempi and accentuation attainable from his controls'.[28]

So great was the pianola's victory that it even inspired trade jokes: a small boy begged his mother to witness the rare sight of a piano being played by hand. It also inspired foreboding. In 1920 the *Musical Quarterly* published an article curiously entitled 'The rise of the musical proletariat'. Its author regarded the pianola as marking 'the extremist limit of the anti-musical which humanity has witnessed', but hoped that 'the machine which has slain music perhaps in the near future may become the means of its redemption'. A few electrical instruments would replace the orchestra, driven 'with absolute exactness by paper rolls' (the principle of the Duo-Art, Ampico, etc.). [29] The final approving reference is to the *reproducing piano*, quite distinct from the pianola in that it played back not a machine-made 'roll' but the actual performance of a specified artist. Among many competing systems three emerged as leaders, the 'Welte-Mignon', Aeolian's 'Duo-Art' and the American Piano Company's 'Ampico'. By 1920 practically every leading pianist was recording on these instruments and attesting their 'minute fidelity' to the original performance.[30] Public concerts were a triumph, in concertos with orchestra, accompaniments to singers, even duets for two unmanned pianos. All the best piano manufacturers embodied these mechanisms into expensive instruments.

In recent years several reproducing pianos have been carefully recon-
ditioned and demonstrated, purporting to represent accurately great
pianists of the past.[31] The present writer is not entirely convinced. Few
of them sound natural and none, in his experience, adequately conveys the
playing of artists heard in the flesh. When direct comparison can be made
with the same player on disc the difference is again apparent. Smudged
or missing notes and arbitrary phrasing can presumably be blamed
upon damaged rolls or faulty mechanism, but a lack of firm articulation
is a more serious fault—the player appears to be skimming over the notes.
Some performances sound too perfect, betraying the ease with which
recordings could be corrected: as Percy Grainger once said, his rolls
represented how he would like to have played. Admittedly the same can
be said of many modern disc recordings which have been pieced together
from innumerable 'takes', but if few responsible critics would judge an
artist from such discs, the basic elements of touch, phrasing and control
are never in question.

Why then were contemporary pianists, audiences and critics apparently
convinced by the reproducing piano? It was an amazingly complex and
subtle machine, far superior to any of its predecessors and kind to pianists.
Early gramophones were utterly incapable of capturing piano tone, and
primitive recording conditions imposed restraints which many artists
found insupportable, notably Busoni who was adamant on this subject.[32]
Audiences came to marvel and were not disappointed. Even the demon-
strably inferior pianola, attached to a Weber concert grand, had a great
success when it appeared with the London Symphony Orchestra conducted by Arthur Nikisch. Operated by Easthope Martin, it performed
the Grieg Concerto and Liszt's *Hungarian Fantasia*. Press comments were
extremely favourable and Nikisch expressed his satisfaction.[33] We who
are inured to the wonders of technology can listen more objectively, and
with a sense of the evanescent standards of 'fidelity'. Practically since
recording began critics have extolled the acoustical perfections of records
which, a few years later, sound inadequate. Advocates of the reproducing
piano will keep their faith, but its validity as an absolute record of past
performance remains equivocal.

The commercial significance of these luxury instruments was never very
great. Even at the height of their popularity in 1923 they never accounted
for more than ten per cent of total piano sales in America, and were far
outweighed by the cheaper pianola. But the entire market for automatic
pianos of every kind collapsed almost as quickly as it had risen, as Table VII
shows. By the mid thirties dealers were reported to be offering 600 dollar
instruments for twenty-five dollars,[34] and a decade later when good pianos
were scarce it became common practice to remove player mechanisms

and 'slim' the case in order to rehabilitate a conventional instrument. The reasons for this decline were much discussed. It was attributed to the cinema, the 'craze for dancing and athletics', and the motor car, 'the one big thing to be had at all costs'. But on purely musical grounds it was defeated by the cheaper and infinitely more resourceful gramophone and radio.

The American system of manufacture

The 'American system' has been met frequently enough in these pages for its essential features to be familiar. Mahillon had stressed the importance of specialization, labour-saving machinery and scientific management as 'the sole means by which cheapness and perfection are attained' (see pp. 72–3). The scale of enterprise on which all this depended is illustrated in Table VIII. Thirty-seven firms are listed, with a total production of approximately 150,000 instruments by 1910. This should be compared with an aggregate national output in that year of some 350,000 pianos valued at over 50 million dollars, by about 300 firms. The table excludes all makers producing less than 1,000 instruments a year by 1910, a rule which, if it were applied to France, would exclude all but four firms.

Several large businesses are missing from Table VIII because their instruments' serial numbers, if any existed, have escaped listing in the 'atlases'. An important example is the controversial J. P. Hale, a pioneer of mass production who 'manufactured pianos as he would have manufactured bedsteads'.[35] Assembling them at minimal, closely calculated cost with low stocks and high turnover, he ignored the prevailing 'agency system' of distribution and sold to all comers who were free to attach any 'stencil' they chose. By the late seventies Hale was allegedly selling over 5,000 pianos a year, more than any of his competitors, who attacked him with a virulence which stemmed both from his undercutting of prices and a genuine belief that his products were 'bogus pianos'. So fierce was this disdain that Hale is totally ignored in an exhaustive contemporary book on the American piano.[36] Yet, as Loesser suggests, his products were arguably better than most of the players and music for which they were destined, and they would lead some buyers to the later purchase of a good instrument.[37] Nor was there anything intrinsically wrong with Hale's approach which, as later firms were to demonstrate, could achieve higher standards while exploiting economies of scale. Several Chicago makers prospered by these methods. Kimball, whose output was unexampled in pre-war years and never surpassed, has already been mentioned (p. 131). Cable, operating on a similar scale, claimed that by combining division of labour, machinery, uniformity and high quality it had 'done for piano manufacture what the Waltham company did for watches'.[38]

A few distinguished makers were operating on too small a scale in 1910 to be included in the table. Mason and Hamlin made 500 splendid instruments that year, and Baldwin, who had taken a prize at the Paris 1900 Exhibition and was later to be renowned for concert grands, made about 900. It would be unwise, however, to attempt to be too precise about scales of production, for both firms were involved in the process of consolidation which was so marked a feature of American business during these years. Mason and Hamlin became part of the vast American Piano Company, and Baldwin controlled Ellington, Hamilton and Valley Gem (see Appendix I). We touch here upon another leading theme in economic history,[39] but the main point, for our purpose, is that Table VIII understates the extent to which large firms came to dominate the American piano industry.

Neither mergers nor the scale of enterprise precluded vigorous competition and a continuous improvement in quality. All observers agreed that there was a general levelling up of standards during the 1890s, particularly in the production of medium grade uprights which were soon practically as good as expensive instruments of the previous decade. Of course there were still some meretricious successors to the Hale legacy, repeatedly condemned in the trade press and various consumer guides which, if they were not wholly objective, nevertheless carried useful warnings against 'stencils': any label beginning with 'Stein' was suspect; even 'Baldner' was assumed to imply Baldwin.[40] As the new century began dealers reported a piano mania. Square pianos were completely replaced—many were publicly burnt—and mail order houses entered the market: Sears Roebuck advertised 'The New American Home Piano' for $98.50. *Presto*, the Chicago trade journal, devoted most of its weekly pages to pianos—gramophones were not yet important. There were various attempts to profit from a national predilection for gadgetry. Bent offered the 'Crown Piano with orchestral attachment' which imitated the 'harp, zither, guitar, mandoline, banjo, autoharp, music box, chime of bells, fife and drum corps, bagpipes, bugle, Bach's clavichord, Mozart's spinet, Handel's harpsichord' and was 'a perfect practice clavier' (i.e. it was a silent keyboard).[41] Any possibility of the market's flagging was prevented by the great boom in automatic pianos, which in turn maintained standards of construction because expensive player mechanisms would have been wasted on gimcrack instruments.

The next phase in the continuous upgrading of the market was a remarkable swing towards grand pianos, illustrated by the following figures

Table VIII   Some Representative American Manufacturers

I. *Firms producing at least 3000 pianos a year by 1910*

	Year Estab.	Approximate Annual Production					
		1880	1890	1900	1910	1920	1930
Behr	1881	—	1000	1000	6000	4000	2000
Brewster				4000	3500	3000	400
Cable	1880	2400	2400	5000	15000	8000	1000
Cable-Nelson	1903				5000	7000	2400
Davenport-Treacy	1873	—	—	1000	9000	11000	2000
Hamilton	1889			4000	4000	4000	700
Harrington	1886	—		1400	7000	2000	1000
Kimball	1885		7500	7200	22000	6000	5000
Kohler & Campbell	1894	—	—	4000	11000	4000	2000
Monarch				3000	5000	9000	6000
Steinway	1853	2000	2500	5000	5000	5000	5000
Sterling	1885		1200	2000	4300	2000	4000
Story & Clark	1869			1700	3000	6000	1000
Zellman-Socol					4300	4000	

II. *Firms producing at least 2000 but less than 3000 pianos a year by 1910*

Bjur	1887			2000	2000	2000	1000
Chickering	1823	2900	1300	1500	2200	900	700
Cunningham	1891			2800	2200	3000	1000
Ellington	1890			2000	2000	2000	—
Emerson	1849	1600	2400	2300	2200	2000	2000
Gabler	1854	1000	1000	800	2000	2000	2000
Hazelton	1849	800	1100	1600	2000	3000	1000
Knabe	1854	1400	2000	2000	2000	2000	900
Kroeger	1879	1400	1300	2000	2000	2000	1000
Laffargue	1895	—	—	2500	2500	3000	1500
Miller	1863	800	700	2500	2600	400	200
Steck	1857	400	600	1600	2100	1700	2000
Weber	1852	2300	3000	3100	2500	1200	1000

III. *Firms producing at least 1000 but less than 2000 pianos a year by 1910*

Behning	1861	600	500	300	1000	1100	1000
Estey	1885		600	1200	1000	2900	4000
Fischer	1840	1900	3300	2300	1100	1400	1500
Hardman-Peck	1842	1000	1000	2000	1900	2000	4000
Krakauer	1878	600	600	1500	1500	1300	200
Kranich & Bach	1864	1200	1000	1500	1000	1000	700
Lindeman	1887	750	600	1000	1400	1500	800
Marshall & Wendell	1836	600	1400	1800	1300	3000	1000
Mehlin	1888		800	1000	1000	600	1100
Sohmer	1872	800	900	1200	1100	1300	3000

of annual production, which include automatic and conventional instruments:

	Quantity (thousand pianos)		Value (million dollars)	
	Uprights	Grands	Uprights	Grands
1900	167	4	25	2
1909	356	9	54	4
1914	316	10	52	5
1919	311	22	81	13
1925	236	65	57	34
1929	68	52	12	26

While fewer uprights were made in 1925 than in 1919 the number of grands increased threefold. One historian deduces from this trend that science 'supersedes a product with a better one'.[42] Since a large proportion of the instruments were 'baby grands', which were by no means superior to good uprights, the impression is misleading. Nevertheless the continual exploitation of new market opportunities was remarkable, and the fact that by 1929 the value of grands sold more than doubled the value of uprights is astonishing.

International influences

We have argued that after 1860 the American market was virtually closed to foreign competition. While this is broadly true so far as pianos were concerned, the question of components, particularly actions, is more complex. As upright pianos began to replace squares there was a natural tendency to import actions from France and Germany, but the size and growth-rate of the market inevitably stimulated local manufacture. The long standing practice of importing actions for grand pianos also continued, although Steinways and a few other high quality manufacturers made their own. The relative merits and costs of foreign and American actions were hotly debated, controversy reaching a peak at the time of the McKinley tariff of 1890.[43] Although this ended in a victory for the protectionists (see p. 127), preventing even Schwander from getting a substantial footing, it is nevertheless true that American products were already abundant and broadly satisfactory. The largest of many firms was Wessel, Nichel and Gross: since all three partners were trained at Steinway's and the firm was established in 1875, neither timing nor the quality of product suggest that success was simply a matter of tariff protection.

Several branches of the 'piano supplies' industry developed rapidly, embodying Mahillon's precepts—Davenport Treacy made iron frames for 16,000 instruments in 1889—but one manufacturer who has appeared at various points in this narrative deserves special mention. The career of Alfred Dolge is a caricature of the American entrepreneurial experience. Addressing his workers in 1887 on the evils of political agitation, he described how, at the age of eighteen, he had 'stood in New York City penniless and friendless . . . did not understand the language . . . but had two strong arms'.[44] After serving an apprenticeship in pianomaking he began to specialize in manufacturing felt and covering hammers by machine. Since both processes were crucial for the new, heavily strung pianos, Dolge soon established a world-wide reputation, also mass-producing soundboards very efficiently. Starting in 1871 he made and lost a fortune and, in retirement, wrote an excellent book on the piano industry. The village where he built his factory grew from fifty to 3,000 inhabitants and was renamed Dolgeville. He was invited to address the American Social Science Association on profit sharing, and his essays on social and political economy were praised by the German emperor.[45]

If imports were at best of only passing significance, American exports of pianos were negligible before the war. The essential reason is that the home market was large enough to tax any manufacturer's resources, though the availability of cheaper German instruments built on the American system was also an important deterrent (cf. p. 89). The bulk of Steinway's exports after 1881 came from their Hamburg factory and therefore do not figure as American. During the 1890s depression when many Americans feared overproduction, the possibility of an export drive was inevitably invoked, but enthusiasm did not survive the ensuing boom. *Presto*'s changing views reflected common attitudes. In 1896 the appeal was vociferous: 'American sewing machines do the hemming and stitching for the world. American organs play its sacred music . . . American pianos are destined to supplant all others abroad, as they long have done at home . . . the whole world must have them.' [46] To be sure, existing designs were too large, heavy and expensive for export, but Cable announced a 'Kingsbury European Model', with the indispensable sconces, weighing 390 pounds and only four feet high. Another manufacturer attempted both to gain an export market and to impress his countrymen by assuming a 'royal warrant' through the agency of an obscure Aberdeen dealer entitled to that usage (p. 34). The *American Art Journal* was very upset, complaining that only Steinway was entitled to the honour, 'worthy of respect . . . even though it is suggestive of imperialism'.[47] The *Musical Courier* pictured Victoria herself at the 'celluloid-keyed piano', and employed heavy sarcasm to describe Her Majesty's saving for the next instalment and her plans for a matrimonial alliance between the two houses.[48]

As the home market recovered, enthusiasm for exports waned. By 1905 *Presto* had decided that Australians and Englishmen were content with 'a small, cheap, old-style piano of some sort or another, and the busy manufacturer in the United States . . . making full-sized, high-priced instruments to a roaring home trade will not bother to go backward'.[49] In 1913 American exports were less than those of France and about one thirtieth the level of Germany's.

The international significance of the American piano industry lay not in trade, but in its role as a pacemaker of technology and business organization. Its influence through the great exhibitions has already been discussed. Enterprising European manufacturers were quick to appreciate the advantage of visiting the leading American factories and sending their sons or younger brothers to learn the new techniques. In 1881, for example, Sigurd Hals arrived from Norway,[50] and the German trade press reported that Bechstein's son and a young Ibach were undertaking a 'studiums wegen' which included a long stay with Dolge.[51] A period of work and study in America became an accepted part of the training of the best German manufacturers.[52] These visits continued the fine old craftsman tradition of the *wanderjahre*, but they were also based upon firm national and cultural links. Nearly half of the 2,535 'pianoforte makers' listed in the 1870 American occupational census were German-born. No other country of origin approached this figure, and in no other industry was there such dominance by one national group.

Links were not confined to Germany, however, with an occasional Scandinavian visitor. In 1879 the Japanese government asked Knabe to supply pianos for its schools.[53] In 1895 it was reported that harmoniums identical to those made by Mason and Hamlin to sell at $40 were being manufactured in Osaka and sold for $17.[54] By 1907 *Presto* was warning piano manufacturers against Japanese workers who become 'insidious graduates'.[55] Apparently only French and British piano manufacturers lacked interest in the American system.

Chapter 8

The English Industry, 1870–1914

The piano industry in late Victorian and Edwardian England consisted of three disparate and unrelated groups of firms. First there were three old-established, high quality manufacturers, self-conscious guardians of a fine but obsolete technology who tended to live in the past and faced dwindling sales with varying degrees of equanimity. They are listed in Section 1 of Table IX. Poles asunder were some two to three hundred garret masters who do not appear in Table IX. Each produced alone, or with a handful of men, a supply of cheap and mostly shoddy pianos and 'dovetailed' their highly seasonal activities with summer work in cabinet making, hop picking or even professional cricket.[1] Although every year brought its crop of failures, and the slightest recession could be disastrous, this pool of small makers was constantly replenished by workers from the larger factories tempted by independence, ease of entry into the industry and a pervasive system of subcontracting by larger masters.

Between these two incongruent sectors a third set of middle-sized, 'medium class' manufacturers, as they were called in the trade, grew to increasing importance. Unhampered and unassisted by such legacies of the past as an ageing skilled-labour force, commitment to old designs and techniques, superfluous capital or a famous name, this group, most of whom started as garret masters, eventually built up a steady trade in modern upright instruments. Before the onset of war and protection, several of them had succeeded in meeting German competition in the home market, at least in the medium grades of piano, while some had higher aspirations, and a few were even reviving export markets. Exports, which had been virtually dormant for thirty years, doubled in quantity between 1895 and 1905, and then doubled again during the following decade. This still represented only about ten per cent of aggregate production, but in value terms it was probably over twenty per cent, for few shoddy instruments were now exported. While preferential duties in Australia and New Zealand doubtless assisted this success, it was a genuine revival which occasioned comment even outside the trade press.

Table IX   Some Representative English Manufacturers
1. *Firms producing more than 1000 pianos a year during the 1860s*

	Year*	1870	1880	1890	Approximate 1900
Broadwood	1770	(2800)	(2600)	(1000)	(1200)
Collard	1760	2500	1950	1840	1310
Kirkman	1730–1897	1000	900	1300	—

11. *Other firms*

	Year*	1870	1880	1890	Approximate 1900
Allison	1837	800	600	800	800
Barrat & Robinson	1877	—	100	300	300
Berry	1866			150	250
Brasted	1870				
Brinsmead	1837	(500)	(700)	1000	1800
British Piano Mg. Company Ltd.	1887	—	—	(1000)	(2000)
Justin Browne	1864–94	←————(2000?)————→			—
Burling & Burling	1851–94	(500)	(500)	(500)	—
Challenger	1855–96	120	160	800	—
Challen	1804	400	500	680	500
Chappell	1811	400	600	900	1000
Cramer	1824		500	1000	1400
Danemann	1893	—	—	—	1500
Duckson & Pinker	1848	100	100	500	500
Hopkinson	1835	700	800	600	800
Rogers	1843	200	300	400	300
Spencer Murdoch	1886	—	—		1000
Strohmenger	1835				400

Notes

* Year of starting and, where appropriate, ending production.

— No production. (Blank space means no figures available.)

( ) Estimate not based on serial numbers; except for Broadwood where figures are based on ambiguous serial numbers.

The contribution of the three large old-established firms to this revival was negligible. Australian complaints about their indifference to suggestions and complaints have already been noted in Chapter 4, but their entrepreneurial failure was more deeply rooted and therefore more difficult to correct than a mere lack of sales initiative. Conservative attitudes were entrenched at every level, from apprentice to director, and in every branch of activity from fundamental design to retailing. In 1894 the editor of the (American) *Musical Courier* returned from a visit to Europe and reported 'the complete and absolute and even disdainful rejection' of iron frames

annual production						
1910	*1920*	*1925*	*1930*	*1935*	*1940*	*1950*
(1000)	(1000)	(1000)	(1000)	1150	50	400
1205	550	750	250	300	200	200
—	—	—	—	—	—	—
1800	600	600	500	550	400	1300
300	300	300	200	1500	100	1800
300	850	1000	1500	1600	450	200
2000)						
2000	400	400	400	300	100	100
2000)	(1200)	—	—	—	—	—
—	—	—	—	—	—	—
—	—	—	—	—	—	—
—	—	—	—	—	—	—
530	300	500	2000	2500	900	2200
1800	1000	900	550	800	100	200
1500	700	700			100	100
2000	200	500	600	2400	600	1300
700	400	700	400	1100	1000	600
1000	600	600	800	600	(100)	100
900	1000	1200	700	500	(100)	500
2500	1000	1600	500	1200	500	200
290	300	400	100	200	(100)	80

and overstringing in favour of the 'flat scale of forty years ago and all that pertains to it', even the inefficient, unmusical, overdampers for upright pianos.[2] He was referring specifically to Erard's Paris factory and to Broadwood, but similar attitudes prevailed at the two other large London firms, Kirkman and Collard. The former, descended from the eminent eighteenth-century harpsichord maker, was wound up in 1897. The latter was directed by men whose dislike for the new technology was frequently expressed: in 1888 John Collard attacked overstringing as an inferior acoustical system used by good makers 'only when they were compelled to do so by the demand, which is limited'.[3] His partner, C. L. Collard, was also 'essentially a conservative in business matters'.[4]

The cynosure of English piano manufacturers was, of course, Broadwood, whose history during this period illustrates several themes which

are familiar in studies of long-lived family businesses:[5] kinship recruit-
ment and gerontocracy at board and shopfloor levels; a tendency for the
third generation to develop interests outside the business, derived from
an expensive education and new social ambitions; a general willingness to
live on rather than for the firm, with inherited goodwill ensuring a modicum of trade, and inherited capital sustaining a good living without entrepreneurial effort. Its early pioneering history and emergence as the
dominant mid-Victorian firm have already been described. John Broadwood's son died in 1851 at the age of seventy-nine when the firm was at a
peak of prosperity, output and prestige which it never again achieved. Its
annual output of some 2,500 pianos was probably maintained through the
1880s, but by 1890 it had declined precipitously to less than one half of
previous levels. At this extraordinarily late date not a single overstrung
piano had left the Broadwood factory; the first was made in 1897.

Broadwood's principal technician for half a century was A. J. Hipkins,
who joined as an apprentice at the age of fourteen in 1840 and remained
until his death in 1903. He was a musician and scholar with antiquarian
interests, unusual in that age, who contributed to the revival of the harpsichord and clavichord, and was accepted as England's leading authority
on keyboard instruments. His antipathy towards the new technology was
widely publicized in influential articles for Grove's *Dictionary of Music and
Musicians*, the *Journal of the Society of Arts* and the *Encyclopaedia Britannica*.[6]
Hipkins' publications are greatly admired and have influenced the his-
toriography of the piano in England down to the present day, but their
prejudice against technical progress was unacceptable even to knowledgeable contemporaries. American critics, of course, were particularly out-
spoken. Reviewing an 1883 lecture as 'Ancient History', the *Musical
Courier* declared that the 'wonderful improvements of late years' had
made 'not the slightest impression' upon Hipkins.[7] His *Britannica* article
was similarly attacked for antiquarianism and prejudice.[8] The *American
Art Journal* admitted that he designed good pianos but complained that
Broadwood's 'never even look at new inventions'.[9] The London *Music
Trades Review* agreed, reminding its readers that the instrument 'has
entirely changed' during the past twenty years and that failure to recognize this had lost much business to foreigners.[10]

Hipkins was a fine craftsman and a considerable artist. At one lecture
to the Society of Arts he played Bach's Chromatic Fantasy and Fugue on
the clavichord, and some of the Goldberg Variations on the harpsichord,
a rare feat in those days.[11] Doubtless his critics paid scant respect to his
scholarship and authority, but the gravity of their charges cannot be
ignored. Moreover, their significance was greatly increased by the fact
that his conservative designs were unlikely to be challenged by a manage-

ment which was singularly lacking in the training, experience or pre-
dilections which might fit them, as leaders of the largest business of its
kind in the world in 1850, to face a half century of unprecedented technical
and commercial change. Even without access to the firm's archives it is
fairly clear that at Broadwood's during this period there were more
'sleepers' than 'thrusters', more 'gentlemen' than 'players', and that the
'players' were skilled in an obsolete game.[12]

Evidence can be found in the short biographies and obituaries published in the English trade journals, which were rarely less than deferential,
and therefore unlikely to play down appropriate talents. One partner, for
example, died in 1881, leaving £424,000. He 'took no share in the active
portion of the business' but 'was, however, an enthusiastic yachtsman'.[13]
Another, who joined the board in 1890 had been educated at Eton and
Cambridge, was a keen farmer, oarsman and swimmer—'few could equal
him in plunging'. He had travelled extensively and 'shot his tiger', but
apparently visited no piano factories. He was, however, a musician, having performed in the 'varsity minstrel troup'.[14] New blood from outside
the family came in 1899 from a 'nobly born' Etonian who 'finished' his
education in Germany and entered Broadwood's as a 'practical tuner' at
the age of nineteen, becoming a partner three years later.[15]

There were two apparent exceptions to this gentlemanly irrelevance.
Most publicized was Henry Fowler Broadwood (1811–93), educated at
Harrow and Cambridge, the last of the family 'with any practical knowledge and enthusiasm for the art of pianoforte making'.[16] An obituary
described him as 'one of the most conscientious and profoundly scientific
of pianoforte makers'.[17] Certainly he was one of the most conservative,
an open and liberal attitude towards the work of foreign makers, to which
many visitors and observers paid testimony, not affecting the policy of his
own firm. The final and most intriguing partner during this period was
George Rose who joined the firm at the age of seventeen and had allegedly
worked for two years in French and German factories, a rare qualification
in the British trade. In 1901 he became manager of the factory, but left in
1908 to join Herbert Marshall in a new firm bidding for the quality
market.

Broadwood's diminishing competitiveness was offset by the loyalty of a
dwindling group of English and colonial customers, for whom the name
invoked by Kipling ('Broadwood on the Nile') was virtually a synonym
for 'piano'. Fealty was reinforced by the self-interest of some long-
established traders, dependent upon long credit (cf. p. 45) and by a
'tuning connection' which alone was worth over £12,000 a year.[18] The
latter provided both immediate income and future sales since company
tuners were prone to recommend the replacement of old instruments. This

arrangement was so unpopular among less-favoured traders, who were losing income from tuning and who wanted to sell other makes, that it was an important stimulus to the formation of a provincial traders' association.[19]

The style of life (cf. pp. 42–3) and the prevailing ethos among the old English makers were thus overwhelmingly patrician, remote from the worlds of music and commerce from which their fortunes had emerged, and which were later mirrored in William Steinway's diaries and the von Bülow-Bechstein correspondence. It is arguable that such attitudes damaged not only their own prospects of growth, but those of the English piano industry, by failing to provide leadership. Steinway and Bechstein acted as pacemakers of technological advance, spearheads of trade and creators of an image which benefited compatriot manufacturers. None of this could be said of their English counterparts.

In addition to the three old-established large firms, two others rose to a somewhat equivocal prominence before 1900. Justin Browne (1838–1913) is a shadowy but impressive figure whose instruments were greatly admired by contemporaries.[20] After working at Ennever, Broadwood and Erard he started business on his own account in 1864, and allegedly made about 16,000 pianos during the next thirty years. Daniel Spillane, a leading American authority and harsh critic, described Browne's large iron-framed uprights in 1891 as among the best made in England.[21] No specimens appear to have survived, nor any account of the firm's demise. The name and goodwill were sold to Cramer in 1909.

Far better documented was the well-publicized career of John Brinsmead (1814–1908). A farmer's son from Devon who left school at the age of twelve, farmed for a year and was then apprenticed to a cabinet maker, he entered a London piano factory in 1835 as a journeyman case-maker and, after an unsuccessful venture with his brother, began piano making with the assistance of a man and a boy. By the 1870s the firm was expanding vigorously and by 1900, employing more than 200 men, had overtaken Broadwood in the quantity and possibly the value of its output. Prizes were taken at several international exhibitions and an image of high quality was sedulously cultivated; a typical puff of 1878 extols the one-piece frame, division of strings and tone-sustaining pedal, 'as in the Steinway pianos'.[22] But surviving instruments suggest that Brinsmead was never more than a good medium-class maker whose products were not comparable with the best German and American instruments.

Image and reality are peculiarly difficult to separate in the case of Brinsmead because of the elaborate and relentless nature of his puffing, some of which was revealed in a court case brought in 1892 by an advertising agent who had been paid £16,000 during the 1880s to manipulate the press.[23] A rather absurd 'History of the Pianoforte' published by John Brinsmead's son attempted to foster the legend and was rightly chided for its 'superficial knowledge of technical development', 'insular cockney twang' and 'immodest claims for Brinsmead's superiority',[24] although it is still frequently cited as a reliable source. The firm was also prominent in a rather unsavoury jingoistic vendetta against Bechstein, whose instruments it could not hope to oust by other means. Despite, or perhaps to some extent because of, all this, Brinsmead played some part in the renaissance of a demoralized English industry. Starting with nothing, John Brinsmead found his way into the *Royal Blue Book* of 1873 and earned a heroic biography in the reverential *Fortunes made in business: life struggles of successful people*, published in 1901. He died in 1908, leaving a personal estate of £46,000.

Inhabiting a totally different social and economic environment were the garret makers, whose shoddy wares were subjected to a continuing stream of criticism and abuse. 'When a British piano is really shoddy it is shoddy of a sort that cannot be beaten in any part of the world', exclaimed the *MTR* in 1901,[25] and Charles Booth was similarly abusive of 'the third rate maker and his ways . . . working for middlemen, or from hand to mouth, on ill-seasoned material, and shifting out of the class of masters into that of foremen at the bench, or vice versa, as opportunity offers or necessity compels'. Activity was 'always at one extreme or the other; working with feverish energy to sell in haste, or entirely out of work'. The finished instrument might then have to be 'hawked about from dealer to dealer, or money may be borrowed on it where it stands'.[26] These strictures met some criticism in the trade press which seized upon Booth's admission that his account was largely dependent upon 'hearsay', and insisted that some small masters turned out good work.[27] Both views can be accepted for it is practically impossible to give a coherent account of this amorphous sector of the industry. At its centre was the solitary worker with a bench and few simple tools 'putting together' two or three pianos a month. An observer sketched, in words and picture, one such kitchen-workshop, with wife at stove, washing on line, children playing on the floor and pig at door, claiming that it was 'but little overdrawn'.[28]

Some garret makers remained in the seamy areas of the trade leaving no record for the historian save, perhaps, an occasional appearance in court—instruments sold for seven pounds and falsely labelled 'Hopkinson'[29]—or in the outraged commentaries of popular journalism.[30] Old rackets persisted. In 1898 a Mr Pegg was still buying pianos in Birmingham for £13, advertising them as 'property of people living abroad, list price fifty guineas to sell at eighteen guineas', and dumping them in auction rooms as far afield as Dundee.[31] A few small makers aspired to, and sometimes achieved, better things. Those who had acquired technical skills, a knowledge of the trade and perhaps useful business contacts by working at a good factory, were further assisted by a variety of favourable factors: the home market was larger, less discriminating and growing faster than any other in Europe. Labour was cheap, in the absence of alternative occupations, protection by factory legislation or effective trade unions, and accustomed to grim working conditions and highly seasonal employment. Above all there was an abundant supply of pre-manufactured parts available on credit which, if carefully assembled, could result in a useful cheap product. Scarcely a good instrument it would nevertheless, like Hale's maligned products, probably be equal to the musical demands made upon it, and certainly better than the shoddy of earlier generations. In the sketch of a kitchen-workshop described above, it is notable that even the piano there being assembled is iron framed.

Appeals for protection

Against such advantages there was the fact that only England's piano industry was unprotected by tariffs. Some makers inevitably joined the ill-fated 'fair trade' movement of the 1880s.[32] There was a marked lack of unity in the industry, and even the most ardent protagonists failed to produce relevant data, the tendency being to fall back upon the vague rhetoric of protectionist propaganda. At first they were provoked both by German competition and by a short-lived but damaging business depression. 1879 was a bad year when, according to one London observer, there were five bankruptcies, four sequestrations and sixty-four liquidations.[33] Imports of musical instruments were lower than for several years, although it is notable that German imports continued to rise. Prosperity soon returned but several English makers had meanwhile been 'cutting down their expenses, reducing advertisements and limiting their circulars and travellers' while 'the Germans occupied the field'.[34] An embryo trade association was not yet strong or united enough to organize effective propaganda which therefore tended to be sporadic and diffuse. A leaflet addressed to 'the artisans and operatives of the English pianoforte trade' was circulated 'in every shop in the metropolis' urging journeymen to organize and demand protection from France, Germany and America, whose competition had 'cut prices and enforced short-time in half of London's factories'. The widespread nature of this condemnation is curious, for the three countries were competing at very different levels of the market. Working men must act, the leaflet concluded, for it is they 'who send such imposters as Bright and Chamberlain to Parliament . . .

quacking about free trade and the cheap loaf'.[35] While the *Music Trades Review* expressed 'deep sympathy' with these sentiments without actively supporting protection, its contemporary, the *Musical Opinion*, gave short shrift to a correspondence in which similar views were aired. Thus the complaints of a Camden Town journeyman 'with six children, locked out for a fortnight' from 'one of the oldest and largest shops in London' and 'worse off than the last generation' were dismissed by the Editor for 'ignorance of the elementary principles of political economy'.[36]

At intervals throughout the eighties, anti-German propaganda was revived without much effect. The nadir (to be exceeded by the next generation) was reached in a letter from 'Musician' which, on the occasion of an outbreak of cholera in Hamburg, warned parents against 'bringing possibly an instrument of death into their homes for their daughters to strum upon'.[37] More representative of an abundant correspondence was a letter to the *Daily Telegraph* which managed to embody most current prejudices within a short space, but is otherwise representative: 'The introduction of the cheap foreign piano . . . has been keenly felt by English manufacturers for the last twelve years or more owing to a fashionable urge which started in the musical world . . . for German productions. The composition, the performer, the teacher, and the instrument all had to be German to be in the fashion.' England was soon 'deluged with German instruments' and 'English manufacturers . . . surprised to find their goods out of date . . . introduced such improvements as have nearly ousted the Germans from the market. England is getting tired of them and the cheap German piano has nearly had its day'. English makers could not compete in cheapness, solely because German workers slept in the factory 'on a sack of shavings' and were poorly fed.[38] Several letters followed, asserting that English instruments were best, but two struck jarring notes. The first, from 'Mus. Bac.(Oxon.)', spoke up for consumers, claiming that there was no trade in which the British public needed more protection against overcharging 'often coupled with inferior workmanship'. As a musician, he was continually offered a professional discount of forty per cent.[39] The other, from 'an unprejudiced English woman' living in Dresden, assured readers that German workers were well fed and clothed, worked in good conditions and earned adequate wages of eighteen to thirty marks a week.[40]

Protectionist arguments were revived in 1903 under the impetus of Joseph Chamberlain's campaign for tariff reform.[41] The Musical Instruments Trade Protection Association held an extraordinary general meeting which resolved that import duties and preferential tariffs should be introduced, but the movement, though better co-ordinated than at earlier attempts, was rent by discord within the industry and trade. Apart from importers who were obviously attached to the open door, there were many manufacturers whose dependence upon imported supplies made them oppose protection. Nevertheless, the campaign against Free Trade gathered momentum during the last years of peace, helped along by a piano manufacturers' association which was established in 1900. Useful statistics were inserted into the speaker's handbook of the Tariff Reform League; manufacturers and dealers were petitioned for their views and selected extracts published; [42] correspondence was engineered [43] and Members of Parliament lobbied. The level of debate was frequently naïve; thus 'Will Workman' explained that the average price of the twenty-seven (*sic*) English pianos exported to Germany in 1909 was £36 9s. Since the 15,973 German pianos imported by England fetched an average of only £29 2s, then clearly English pianos were more expensive and superior! [44] Considerable impetus came in 1913 from a new journal, *The Pianomaker* which, in its first issue, declared war on German pianos, refusing to carry their advertisements, and inaugurated a new style of venomously jingoistic advocacy in striking contrast to the older trade papers.

In addition to these temporarily unsuccessful attempts to influence government policy, more insidious methods were employed to induce patriotism. A principal target was the Guildhall School of Music whose staff and council were hounded in an attempt to prevent their using German pianos. The campaign, led by Brinsmead, engaged the national press, the Lord Mayor, and, of course, *The Pianomaker*.[45] Even this effort, however, was not crowned with success until war hysteria forced the Guildhall School of Music to part with its Bechsteins in 1914. The dignified rebuke administered by Sir Landon Ronald, the principal of that distinguished institution, is worth quoting for it marks the end of a liberal era: 'Art is cosmopolitan, and a great school of music exists for the purpose of giving a proper education to young musicians. It is not to be confused with a City warehouse . . . nor should it be used as a means of advertisement by any firm under the somewhat laboured excuse of patriotism.' [46]

Reactions to competition

Clamour for protection tended to obscure the different ways in which various sectors of the industry had experienced and responded to the impact of foreign competition. Two groups were undoubted losers: the traditional high class piano makers, and indigenous manufacturers of actions who were utterly unable to meet French and German competition. Even *The Pianomaker*, at the height of its chauvinistic fervour, had to admit that 'pre-war British actions were very poor'.[47] Indeed, when war and protection finally arrived, a shortage of useable actions became the industry's most serious problem. But as the nature of foreign competition came to be understood during the 1880s, many firms discovered that it brought new opportunities. At the lowest level this could take the form of meretricious imitation with false labels, or even a more elaborate simulation of one's betters. A remarkable practitioner in this field was E. Bishop, whose activities can be dimly perceived from his flamboyant advertisements and frequent brushes with the law. Starting business about 1870 he claimed to be making 1,200 pianos a year in 1882 and nearly 2,000 by the late eighties. In 1887 we find him employing 200 hands and faking invoices, putting a '74 guinea ticket' on a £20 'Philadelphia (improved) model' which was then offered for sale in '*Bazaar, Exchange and Mart*', allegedly second hand, for £28.[48] Bishop's approach to a gullible public was sufficiently obvious: other models were christened 'Boston', 'New York', 'California' and 'Philadelphia'. In 1894 he even had the temerity to exhibit at the Chicago Columbian Exposition, and two years later sought incorporation and public support. The company's prospectus was sufficiently outrageous to receive scathing notice in the *Star*, and bankruptcy followed in 1900.[49]

More reputable paths of emulation and expansion could also be taken by small craftsmen rising from factory bench or garret workshop. Genuine attempts were made to copy the new technology. Iron frames were cheap and so easy to adopt that, by the mid-eighties, they were in common use.[50] The Birmingham entrepreneur E. B. Whitfield played a leading role in this development: having visited American factories he began to sell larger, stronger frames in standard sizes at prices below one pound.[51] Overstringing presented much greater problems, requiring improved actions, heavier hammers and an appropriate scale-design based upon a fundamental reappraisal of the instrument's acoustics.[52] None of these were yet available to small masters, though all but the last rapidly became so. The skill and research embodied in the design of new scales could not be generally diffused without a wholesale adoption of standard designs, which was not yet contemplated. Therefore, the standard of quality and price obtainable by such makers was limited.

Contemporary nomenclature was euphemistic and confusing about the size of these firms and the quality of their wares. Firmer evidence comes from accounts of the Music Trade Association's annual private exhibitions, at which its hundred or so members inspected 'pattern pianos' with a view to 'large orders'. Although manufacturers and instruments were described as 'middle-class' prepared to manufacture in 'large quantities', this was confirmed by neither specification, price nor size of order—one hundred a year was thought extraordinary. These events were shrouded in the trade's customary secrecy, particularly about price, but accounts in the American trade press, presumably not read by the English public, were more frank.[53] The typical association instrument sold to dealers for prices ranging from £10 to £24 'cash' (i.e. one month credit). Three month and six month bills were some ten shillings and one pound higher. None of the English instruments, which predominated, were overstrung, but in one year an agent offered a German overstrung model. All would eventually be sold, under the dealer's name or a 'stencil', at prices up to double. The typical maker produced no more than a total of 300 instruments a year in a variety of models. It was, however, precisely the market for cheap instruments which remained comparatively unscathed by German competition. Many small businesses were therefore launched, by means of partnership, extended credit and sub-contracting through a network of highly localized activity, particularly in the area of Camden Town.[54] Both demand and supply conditions were conducive, as the *MTR* remarked, to 'the rapidly increasing business of many who, a few years ago, worked at the bench'.[55]

Promotion therefore was more difficult. It required long term finance and, for real success, a degree of technical and managerial skill which was not easily acquired in England. Nor was the latter much appreciated. It is an indication of parochialism that the *Music Trades Review* should have jeered at Harvard University's introduction of a Master's degree in business administration in 1908: 'Imagination boggles at a prospect which only Harvard could conceive . . . Englishmen will hesitate before advising Oxford and Cambridge to follow.'[56] Capital sometimes came from trade. Thus, in 1898 a Grimsby dealer of fifteen years' standing, T. H. Rushton, opened a 'well equipped factory',[57] and at a more elevated level, when George Rose left Broadwood (p. 147) his partner was Herbert Rose, a prominent Leicester dealer. It seems likely, however, that access to capital as distinct from short-term credit remained a serious problem, becoming more acute as improvements in technology began to offer economies of scale which could not be deflected by 'buying out'. Advertisements began to appear for special machines 'suitable for pianoforte and organ builders' accompanied by books on 'how to manage a steam engine', and 'saw mills, their arrangement and management'. A typical planing-machine was priced at £60.[58] An indication of the demand for capital is the appearance of such advertisements as the following: '£1,000 required by two practical young men for plant and capital to manufacture good, sound reliable pianos—have had large experience in producing same.'[59]

There was a tendency to exaggerate these difficulties in the trade press, and to confuse the problems of the very small maker, recently escaped from the factory bench, with those of the established workshop master seeking expansion and improvement. Thus the *MTR* complained in 1910 that, whereas thirty years before one could start piano manufacturing with a few pounds, now one needed 'large capital', and many small men had 'gone under'.[60] Yet next month it was reporting a speech to the association of manufacturers and dealers in piano supplies which demanded the 'suppression' of men who, with a little practical experience, started workshops without capital, business or general education, and were given long credit.[61] In fact, the flow of garret or 'two pounds a week' masters never stemmed, and indeed was swollen after the war by demobilized soldiers seeking an independent way of life. More significant than this, for it marked what contemporaries described as a 'renaissance', was the accession of a new class of manufacturers.

The new British school

Their coming had been proclaimed at various times during the late nineteenth century. In 1884, for example, the *MTR*, noting the failure of 'the old fashioned English piano . . . now hardly in the market at all', thought it could detect 'an entirely new race of British manufacturers'.[62] Such proclamations were premature, though Brinsmead and Hopkinson (incorporated in 1895) were beginning to produce modern instruments before the turn of the century. During the first decade of the twentieth century, enthusiasm grew apace. 'The New British School' [63] was said to contain at least twelve good makers, whose progress in the 'middle class trade' was 'a direct challenge to those who have for so long dominated the English market'.[64] An American visitor reported that English manufacturers 'hitherto in a profound state of funk about German competition' were cheering up.[65] *Musique et Instruments* detected the 'reveil d'une industrie anglaise', and even the *Economist*, hitherto uninterested in the industry, thought its resurgence worthy of comment, at least 'with regard to the instruments bought by average citizens more or less as pieces of furniture'.[66] In September 1913 a British Music Exhibition where many pianos were displayed was welcomed, with unconscious irony, as a 'first public attempt on the part of British piano manufacturers to pit themselves against all comers, although no foreigners are permitted to enter the lists'.[67] It was claimed to be 'the first collection of pianofortes of all classes made by one country that the world has ever seen', demonstrating that 'for general excellence . . . Britain stands supreme'.[68] Many recitals were given, none by a pianist of international standing, but there was a general air of buoyant optimism.

Such evidence merits caution. Yesterday's journalistic 'dirge of the day', in Landes' apt phrase, transmutes to today's paean, with equal dangers to historical interpretation.[69] Undoubtedly much of this celebra-

tion in print reflected increasingly effective propaganda by an industry
which was becoming better organized and more expert in self-promotion.
Yet there was substance in the claims. We have already referred to the
sudden improvement in export performance. Section II of Table IX
indicates that some firms, whose serial numbers are available, grew fast
during this period. Several manufacturers not listed in the table, because
such data do not exist, were similarly successful. One source of evidence
arises from the continuing debate about protection, for most of the 'new
school' were dependent upon imported parts and were therefore ardent,
and at times articulate, in their opposition to tariff proposals. Thus, the
director of Bansall and Sons claimed to employ between 300 and 400
men throughout the year (i.e. without seasonal unemployment), producing 'about 4,000 instruments'. This was almost certainly an exaggeration,
but half the number would still have made him a substantial maker, and
the rest of his claims had substance. He imported German actions, because
English models were '30% dearer and inferior', and exported good instruments vigorously. New Zealand was a particularly flourishing market
where he could 'beat German pianos by ten shillings a piano'.[70] Another
correspondent named twenty medium class makers whom he claimed to
be producing an annual total of 30,000 instruments. Few of these had
been consulted by the *Daily Express* in its recent agitation for protection
which, if enforced, would ruin them all.[71]

A new manufacturer, who was remarkable both for his origins and
location, was William Sames of Birmingham. Starting in 1855 as a maker
of harmoniums, a trade in which, as we have seen, American competition
became overwhelming, he began to shift to pianos in 1888, and soon
established a local reputation for sound construction. In 1895 a limited
company was formed with a capital of £12,000 subscribed by engineers,
solicitors, organists and the founder. His two sons then apparently spent
four years training in German factories and returned to join their father
as directors. By 1911 the 'Mozart Works', a 'model factory with drying
apparatus', employed 200 men and produced good overstrung uprights,
some of which are still in use.[72]

A few makers attempted to enter the high-quality market, making small
grands or even concert instruments. By far the most important of these
was Chappell and Co. whose rapid expansion is illustrated in Table IX. An
old-established manufacturer and music publisher, it was revivified in
1897 as a limited company with nominal capital of £190,000. In addition
to greater financial resources, and musical connections which were all too
rare in the English industry, Chappell enjoyed the unique advantage of a
Polish factory manager, Mr Glandt, who had been trained at Steinway and
was described as one of the greatest piano makers ever connected with the

Table X   The English Piano Industry: Total Output and Size of Enterprise
1870–1910

	Total Annual Production (in thousands of pianos)			Number of firms making			
	Claimed	*Known firms*	*Serial Numbers*	*More than 2000*	*1000– 2000*	*500– 1000*	*300– 500*
	(1)	(2)	(3)	(4)	(5)	(6)	(7)
1870	20–25	23	10	2	1	3	10
1880	30–35	30	11	1	5	6	20
1890	50–90	30	12	0	10	9	21
1900	70–100	40	13	0	14	4	24
1910	75–100	50	22	5	18	3	24

Notes

Column 1 shows contemporary estimates. The low estimate for 1910 is in Dolge, op. cit., page 434.

Column 2 shows my own estimates, based on general information about known firms, in addition to serial number data. They are therefore probably under-estimates, excluding most shoddy and many 'stencilled' instruments.

Column 3 is based primarily upon production runs taken from reliable serial numbers. A few assessments have been added for those firms on which sufficient information is available to base a reasonable estimate of output. This column therefore represents an absolutely minimum estimate of total production.

The first Census of Production taken in 1907 provides an essential bench mark for these calculations. It gives total output (UK) of pianos as 58,000 valued at £995,000. (Cd. 5545, ci 117, 1911. Census of Production, Part VII, Table I, page 46.)

Columns 4–7 are based on information about 840 firms drawn from music directories, trade journals, piano atlases and stock books.

British trade'.[73] During the 1910 Promenade Concert season, Chappell pianos were used by eleven out of the twenty-one pianists appearing, and their uprights of that period were not significantly inferior to any but the best German instruments.

Table X estimates the industry's overall growth and attempts to quantify this impressionistic account of the 'renaissance'. It will be noted in column three that between 1900 and 1910 there was a remarkable growth in the quantity of pianos for which we have serial numbers, a likely indication of an increasing emphasis upon quality. Columns four and five illustrate the emergence of larger firms. Whereas in 1900 probably no English manufacturer was producing more than 2,000 instruments a year, and only fourteen exceeded 1,000, by 1910 there were respectively five and eighteen businesses operating at these levels.

On the eve of the war, the English piano industry had clearly recovered from its doldrums. Imports had reached a new peak of 24,500 pianos, valued at £757,000. But this still probably accounted for no more than twenty per cent of the domestic market by quantity, thirty per cent by value. Exports had made a spectacular recovery, with values rising faster than quantities, which was partly a reflection of recent price increases but largely a result of improved quality. Some old weaknesses remained: the persistent underworld of garret masters, 'thump boxes', sweating and seasonal unemployment; and the continuing dependence upon foreign actions and parts, and a certain parochialism and philistinism which limited the aspirations and achievements of all but a few firms. A new threat was perceptible, as belated trade union activity, and the attraction of alternative occupations, induced labour costs to rise and the work force to attract fewer new recruits. Some pessimists even warned that the public's new leisure activities would undermine the basic determinants of demand. But, save for a few enthusiasts, the gramophone was still a mere toy, radio a carrier of messages, the cinema a childish pastime and the motor car a perquisite of the rich who were already equipped with their Bechstein grands. Fundamental adjustments had been made to new technology and patterns of trade. The future seemed secure.

Chapter 9

The English Piano Goes to War

A hazard awaits the historian who writes of small matters at a time of great events: a sense of proportion evaporates as his narrative assumes the mantle of self importance affected by his protagonists. In this chapter, therefore, it is advisable to begin with a reminder that the 'great war' was a hideous catastrophe in which millions existed or perished in conditions of unprecedented squalor, while creatures like Bottomley became national heroes. In such a context the achievements and sufferings of piano makers deserve a minor place. Yet the industry's experience of new patterns of demand, supply and governmental interference are part of a wider economic history and its documentation, even its shabby vituperative jingoism, reflects aspects of a fundamental social upheaval.

By 1914 piano manufacture had become so closely attuned to the international economy that war threatened immediate disruption. In England it also offered new opportunities. With German instruments out of the home market and threatened in Australia (until 1916 when they were banned), the best English makers had a chance to consolidate or create a reputation for high quality, while medium class makers, already firmly established, had home and 'colonial' markets at their feet. Moreover home demand grew rapidly as full employment and rising wages enabled a far larger proportion of the working class than hitherto to purchase a long coveted status symbol. The industry failed to rise to these challenges, for reasons which were not all outside its control. Large but temporary inroads were made in South Africa and Australasia, and a handful of firms made genuine attempts to replace the best German makers by earning the allegiance of concert artists and serious musicians. But in general prices rose almost as rapidly as quality deteriorated, reaching a level among 'commercial' instruments which, in the words of Ernest Newman the eminent critic, made 'the name of British pianos stink in the nostrils'.[1] Such products, which tarnished the industry's reputation for another generation, were finally admitted, even by the crassly jingoistic *Pianomaker*, to be 'a disgrace to British industry'.

Myths and propaganda

The primary causes of this débâcle were technical and economic—a delayed, but eventually inescapable, shortage of materials and skilled labour—and will be examined below. But they were intensified by a flood of disingenuous propaganda which attempted to rewrite history, manipulate public opinion and stifle those cosmopolitan and cultural influences upon which the fundamental health of a music industry ultimately depends. Thus, as early as December 1914, a myth-maker 'proved' that German pianos had succeeded merely by 'pushing' and that English superiority was demonstrated by the (implicitly spontaneous) decision of 'leading music schools' to use British pianos.[2] A distinguished economic historian writing about the wartime years advises us to consider 'not only the solid information of the day but also its myths and rumours', for they were 'an essential part of the symbolic popular thinking of the time'.[3] Even the language employed by protagonists, its crass rhetoric and semi-literate embellishment, are evocative and illuminating. In February 1915 'an Englishman' wrote to the *Musical Opinion*: 'What would you of the English maker of instruments? Would you not that he should be our country's pride? If this were so, you would seek ever diligently to find his worth, and would pause thrice ere you passed him by of mere caprice'.[4] The editor of an evanescent trade journal addressed his readers with a 'Prelude'. He had 'penned many introductory pronouncements to budding journals, grave and gay, of many conditions and varieties, for and on behalf of self and the various literary coadjutors enveloped in the all-embracing editorial "we"'. He then got down to business: 'Boycott the Brutes . . . close the door to every German', and so forth. A message from Brinsmead's extolled this 'great enterprise' and pledged to 'have no truck whatever in business with any Hun'.[5] Thus a mean and philistine parochialism, hitherto common only in the industry's lower reaches and inimical to its long term interest, now assumed leadership.

In its vanguard was *The Pianomaker* which, in contrast to the normally decent reticence of its predecessors and rivals, adopted a rabble-rousing stance of eternal vigilance, strengthened by the moral conviction of an old campaigner, welcoming late converts to the true cause: 'Already foreign agents with pianos on hand are contemplating the removal of the German name and the substitution of something misleadingly British. Such action is analogous to clothing one's soldiers in the enemy's uniform for purposes of deceit. There is only one answer for such culprits in war—the bullet.' [6] The editor solicited and abundantly received information from his readers about threats to the Realm. A tireless harangue, alternately vicious and comic in its paranoia, continued month after month, with a special venom distilled for Bechstein: the London showroom's protected windows were photographed and derided for 'funk', while a provincial representative whose windows were broken might seek consolation in condemnation of 'too German an act for an Englishman to perform' but would also be wise to learn 'how the wind is blowing'.[7] Leading musicians were a favourite target: Melba was admonished for singing 'Land of Hope and Glory' in Sydney to the accompaniment of a Bechstein grand. Moiseiwitsch sinned by playing at Bechstein Hall, though his Russian blouse was approved; and a critic who reported that the public had not been 'deterred by any foolish prejudice' against the hall's 'name and connections' was assumed to be of 'Teutonic origin'.[8] Hallé concert programmes, still advertising Bechsteins in February 1915, were deemed to reflect the disloyalty of the 'large German colony in Manchester district'.[9] An old theme was revived when the pianist Madame Janotha was deported: as 'emissary of the Kaiser' she had used 'the German element at Court during Queen Victoria's reign' to popularize German pianos.[10] 'Paying in Blood', one of many similar pieces by Bart Kennedy, poetaster and professional patriot, described the 'horde of German musicians who infested the country' as 'commercial emissaries for German pianos—besides being spies', and dealers who handled German pianos as traitors.

Teachers at the Royal Academy and Guildhall School of Music were again hounded for their nationality or preference for German instruments, and Landon Ronald, an excellent conductor and principal of the School, was subjected to renewed attacks of abuse and harassment. Every number of the paper contained titbits of vital information from the front: Willesden Guardians had bought a second German instrument for a nurses' home.[11] *The Times* was still carrying advertisements for Blüthner.[12] The French government had closed Bechstein's Paris offices. The Czar had struck all German names off the Imperial list, and British dealers could achieve a similar blow for the war effort.[13] Urgent despatches reported a 'mass meeting' of piano workers demanding an end to the Royal warrants and business of Bechstein and Blüthner. Readers were told how one of Blüthner's English workmen, who had attempted to defend his employer's probity and craftsmanship, was denounced as an alien and directed to the trenches in an altercation worthy of the Red Queen in *Alice*. In June 1916 Bechstein closed its London office amid rejoicing at the victory of a campaign which had been waged 'not from a trade jealousy point of view but purely on national grounds'.[14] A favourite rhetorical device was the spurious challenge: 'We will give 10 guineas to the Music Trades Benevolent Society if we cannot produce British made pianos which for tone and touch are superior to the Bechstein.'[15] No item was too trivial or absurd to find a place: a South African correspondent urged the adoption of 'English' rather than 'continental' fingering which 'would give our children a perverted idea of the anatomy of the hand'.[16] ('The continental system, which indicates suitable fingering by numbering the thumb 'one' and the fingers accordingly, is universally adopted. 'English' fingering used a cross to indicate the thumb and called the index finger 'one'.) A British dealer had received Christmas greetings from a German exporter —'the brand of Cain'.[17] A lady whose Fellowship of the Royal Geographical Society was evidently deemed relevant explained 'why German music does not pay' and urged 'the banning of all German composers'.[18]

Some indication of prevailing attitudes and of the paper's vindictiveness and influence is provided by a libel case which the *Financial Times* recommended to connoisseurs of 'patriotic litigation'.[19] Max Lindler, the highly respected representative of Bechstein's who had become a naturalized Englishman, freeman of the City of London, member of the Worshipful Company of Musicians, and a leading influence in Chappell's revival, finally tired of *The Pianomaker*'s unceasing abuse and sued it for libel. The judge who, in a characteristic aside, announced that he himself owned but could not play a Bechstein, awarded Lindler damages of one farthing. *The Pianomaker* celebrated its 'great moral victory' which it compared to Jutland, and even extracted an apology from the *Law Journal* for daring to suggest that its motives had been other than 'pure patriotism and . . . in the best interests of the British Empire'.[20]

No one could rival *The Pianomaker* in sustained virulence, of which only a small representative sample has been quoted, but there can be little doubt that its campaign both reflected and reinforced the attitudes of a substantial proportion of the industry. Indeed, at its inaugural meeting in July 1917, the British Music Trade Convention presented the editor with 'an illuminated address and a cheque in appreciation of his vigorous advocacy'.[21] It was an inauspicious event; whatever its immediate benefits to the industry in war time, and even these were equivocal, the long-term effect of such propaganda were unhealthy. Lulled by the virtual absence of competition or informed criticism, all but a few dedicated English piano manufacturers relaxed standards, forgot the lessons of recent history and basked in the warmth of old, once discredited but now refurbished myths. Thus, when the director of Brinsmead gave his presidential address to the 1916 Convention, he asserted that 'practically all the great improvements in the construction of the modern pianoforte were the inventions of Englishmen'.[22] It became an article of faith that German manufacturers, 'mere copyists', had advanced 'the Kultur of the Hun' through unscrupulous commerce backed by immigrant German professors; even that the 'tubby German tone' of meretricious instruments had been foisted upon a 'Prussianized' English public rendered deaf to the English piano which, through its 'superior delicacy, solidity and workmanship' could now take its rightful place.[23] Even 'expensive' American pianos were said to be failing in Australia because they lacked the tone quality with which British instruments could be assured pre-eminence.[24] It was a magic tone, 'musical in the best sense of the word . . . which, like a good violin, gains an added charm with age'.[25] These quaint beliefs were reiterated, and possibly believed, throughout the war, challenged but undeterred by occasional shafts of truth. In August 1918 a blunt Scottish dealer, amused by the irrelevance of 'originator and improver' myths, feared that many English firms were, 'so to speak, killed with contentment'.[26] A predominant self-satisfaction was doubtless bred by the easy pickings of a sellers' market, but it was greatly reinforced by commercial propaganda, which is never so dangerous to an industry as when it is believed by its own propagators.

Realities

So much for the mythology of the English piano in war time. What of the reality? The industry's changing fortunes during this period must be understood in the context of a national economy which, under persistent and unprecedented strain, was transformed by a series of belated but peremptory changes of policy, from a system of intensive free competition to one of substantial government control.[27] In the first two years, the general level of prices rose sharply as the government failed to curb a swelling civilian demand for consumer goods which were competing with the military for scarce resources. As prices and profits rose rapidly the glaring inequalities which inevitably accompany inflation aroused much discontent. Yet, ironically, this was also a period of material improvement for many working-class families who, after years of impoverishment, were enjoying full employment with rising wages and were spending their money on commodities which were still uncontrolled. Women particularly tended to benefit from these changes, and the increase in their employment and purchasing power added a new stimulus to the demand for pianos. During the second half of the war the government exerted firmer control over the economy, imposing severe controls on the allocation of labour and resources to civilian needs. Inevitably, these fundamental social and economic changes exacted painful adjustments from the piano industry, which was highly labour intensive, dependent upon imported materials and producing a luxury good.

For a few months a sense of new opportunities appeared to outweigh fears of impending difficulties. The prevailing euphoria was well expressed by the *Musical Opinion*, tempered by a notable but sadly evanescent high purpose. 'Secure in the home market, the British manufacturer may be trusted to put forth his best energies to supply the world as well as his own countrymen with instruments worthy of the commendation of the greatest artists.' But he would also remain 'convinced of the futility of war . . . for our whole interests are bound up in peace and cultural progress'.[28] Another contemporary's leading article on 'War and the Music Trade' is further evidence of a surviving liberalism: 'True art stands above the antagonisms of warfare. The music of Wagner, the poetry of Goethe, this belongs to a level of human achievement not to be marred by the latter day ambitions of modern Potsdam. So the very best names in German pianos will undoubtedly survive the shock.'[29] The approach of individual manufacturers to their new opportunities ranged from quiet competence to rabble-rousing opportunism, its vociferousness tending to vary inversely with the manufacturer's true status. Thus Chappell's were content to announce that such leading pianists as Moiseiwitsch, Pachmann, Scharrer and Goodson would henceforth be playing their pianos; and several makers like Rogers and Broadwood simply continued to make good instruments. Burling and Mansfield, claiming to produce 2,000 'Real English Pianos made in England', represent an alternative approach. A typical full-page advertisement claimed that German instruments had been grossly overrated and sold only by name; their own product was 'better than the Germans ever were, made by British men for fifty years in England with British Capital'.[30]

Foremost among the Hun-baiters was Billingshurst, grandson of John Brinsmead and inheritor of that firm, whose propaganda activities were so extensive that they can have left little time for his business, a factor contributing, perhaps, to its ignominious downfall a few years later. Fresh from his Guildhall victory, he poured forth speeches, petitions and letters —one accusing a Belfast dealer of trading with the enemy was effectively blocked in the courts [31]—couched in Bottomley-style rhetoric against those who used the products of 'a nation who have committed the grossest enormity in the whole of the Christian era'.[32] So rosy were his expectations that in November 1916 the Brinsmead Company was reconstructed 'to bring in new capital and new blood to fight Germans'.[33] Representative of this opportunism was an advertisement in *The Times* headed 'Trading with the Enemy (Amendment) Bill'. Established 'in the reign of William IV—long before any of the German invading firms existed', Brinsmead employed tuners who were 'factory trained', unlike enemy manufacturers who 'secured staff more or less at haphazard', and would service 'pianofortes of all kinds'.[34]

Most people in the trade, however, were concerned with more mundane affairs and, since few expected the war to last long, its early months were characterized by the prevailing slogan 'business as usual'. In that first untrammelled season there was no talk of supply difficulties—of pianos for dealers, or of materials for manufacturers. The removal of new German pianos from the market left a shortfall of some 20,000 instruments at current levels of demand. Several English makers could offer acceptable substitutes for those of medium class, and some claimed more. One importer optimistically advertised French instruments by Gaveau, Klein, Burgasser, Kriegelstein and Mussard as 'perfection . . . not excelled in quality and workmanship by any foreign pianos'.[35] Any tolerably good instrument sold well, but there was curiously little increase in American imports, perhaps because they were thought too large and expensive. Abundant rubbish was available at prices which were, for a time, roughly commensurate with quality. C. E. Little, for example, who had assembled some 25,000 instruments since 1878 bearing his own and other names, still advertised a 'Full trichord with iron Frame' for fifteen guineas in April 1915. By the autumn, however, most piano prices had risen by a third, and in June 1916 the general level was at least fifty per cent above that of 1914. Thereafter prices rocketed, but are impossible to chart with any accuracy since the pressures of demand were so greatly in excess of supply that 'black market' transactions became common.

For similar reasons it is difficult to assess the extent of second-hand trading, although undoubtedly it greatly increased. The trade journals eventually recognized this by giving considerable space to advice on repairs, but at first they were more concerned with publicizing the public's alleged rejection of German instruments. Maples, the leading furniture shop in London, 'who once had a never-ending stream of second-hand German pianos', were said by October 1914 to have hidden them 'in cellars deep' or to have covered the fall-board names.[36] Patriotic correspondents fearing contamination were reassured: 'The piano is by a well-known maker and British every inch, except the action, which is by a well-known French maker, one of our allies'.[37] A Yorkshire dealer reported supplying a sensitive customer with a 'transfer' (label) to conceal the 'German spy in front of our piano . . . we cannot bear the sight of the horrible name'.[38] But common sense and the continued appearance of personal advertisements in the newspapers suggest that a thriving second-hand market in German instruments survived discreetly throughout the war. This was monitored by *The Pianomaker* with unceasing vigilance—an advertisement for a Bechstein in the *Daily Telegraph*; a German instrument purchased by a wounded soldier—but apparently without any deterrent effect.[39] After 1916 when good new instruments were unobtainable, it seems unlikely that anyone wishing to sell a second-hand German piano would have had much difficulty. The stock books of our Belfast trader (pp. 106–7) confirm this impression.

Throughout the war the English piano manufacturer's chief problem was the supply of actions. English production, by two nondescript makers of cheap obsolete models, was negligible in quality and quantity, a fact which even *The Pianomaker* was later to admit.[40] A few of the larger piano manufacturers, including Collard, were reputed to make their own actions, but such claims were suspect, stemming in the past from the sedulously cultivated myth of the 'complete maker' and now reinforced by a desire to assert national purity. In any case, there was no question of such firms having actions to spare for their competitors. For a time the better class makers were in a comparatively strong position because they could afford to hold larger stocks which some had prudently built up, and because they already used, or could switch to, expensive French actions which were still available. Costs were rising and future supplies seemed uncertain, but the leading English piano makers, freed from German competition and able to pass higher costs on to prosperous customers, faced buoyant markets with equanimity. The majority of firms, however, and particularly the small men with tiny stocks and limited capital, were wholly dependent upon cheap German materials. Some were rash enough to approach the Board of Trade, unsuccessfully, for permission to continue such imports.[41] A few of the more enterprising makers looked far afield: Broadwood-White's order for 150 Higel actions from Canada to replace his customary supplies from Lexow was probably representative of a general trend.[42] But such temporary arrangements were not an adequate substitute for the abundant supplies of cheap, efficient German actions upon which most European firms had become dependent. Without these it was feared that medium class makers would either be forced out of business, or would supply dealers with shoddy instruments of a kind hitherto confined to the 'auctioneer, pawnbroker and furniture man'.[43]

Since normal demand in the high season was for some 2,000 actions a week, there were obvious opportunities for local enterprise, and while few people in the trade could have shared Billingshurst's optimistic belief that 'English action-making factories would immediately come into being',[44] there was much talk and some activity in this direction. Nine new companies were announced and two actually launched, claiming to have installed sufficient machinery to meet practically all demand.[45] Most notably, Herrburger-Schwander proposed to make their 'union' model in England, and began to train girls to assemble parts imported from their Paris factory.[46] But from the outset there were complaints about shortages of labour. Despite the undoubted market opportunities it was a bad time to launch a new civilian business, for both factory capacity and labour were being rapidly absorbed to equip the armed forces.[47] Probably the trade press exaggerated the extent both of new initiatives and of difficulties in the nascent action-making industry. A correspondent expressed what must have been the dominant questions among potential entrepreneurs as they awaited events: could a protective tariff be secured and buttressed by manufacturers' promising to buy British actions after the war, or would an infant industry be destroyed by the immediate resumption of German competition when peace returned—soon, as men still believed?[48]

A shortage of actions was not the piano manufacturer's sole problem. All materials rapidly became scarce and costly, the price of keys, for example, approximately doubling within a year. For a few months the trade papers expressed a patriotic optimism about supplies, listing English firms which could allegedly produce adequate wire, felt, hammers and veneer, and concluding that an 'all British piano' would soon be feasible.[49] More revealing, however, was a 'Tract for the times' which urged readers to stop complaining about shortages and lamenting the loss of efficient German supplies. It was admitted that quality was falling as prices rose, but angry manufacturers and dealers were urged to be patient and to encourage English firms by 'constructive criticism'.[50] A small but typical and significant example of the disruption caused by breaking established trade channels was the shortage of wrest pins. Approximately 220 were required for every instrument, obtainable before the war from Westphalia, where the use of automatic machinery enabled German firms to undersell all competitors at one shilling a set. Throughout the war it proved difficult to supply adequate quantities of this apparently simple component. In 1916, a trade deputation persuaded the Board of Trade to license manufacture and two Birmingham men began to produce and gradually to improve the quality of the 250,000 pins a week then required. A few months later both were called up for military service, and it was only after considerable protest that one was exempted, saving the trade from extinction.[51]

Protection and Government controls

As piano makers prepared for a second wartime season, apprehension about supplies and optimism about demand were transformed by a dramatic change in government policy. The budget of September 1915 imposed an import duty of thirty-three and a third per cent on certain goods, including musical instruments 'and parts thereof' which, according to McKenna, the Chancellor, were intended not as a protective device but as a temporary measure to restrict expenditure on luxuries. The ensuing debate in Parliament and the press is a useful guide to conflicting interests within the piano industry and assessments of its prospects. Billingshurst welcomed the tax, particularly on components, as promoting 'the nucleus of a new and great industry' though later, under pressure from within the manufacturers' association which he was supposed to represent, he urged exemption for imports from France and the colonies. The traders' and consumers' viewpoint was well argued by Yeo, a Member of Parliament with thirty years' experience as a music dealer, who agreed that manufacturers would indeed 'pay the tax willingly and gladly—with other people's money'. A piano which had sold for eighteen guineas in mid-1914 and earned the trader a ten per cent profit was now, he argued, scandalously priced at thirty guineas. Other MPs described the tax as 'a present to piano manufacturers', allowing them to 'plunder the public'. The bulk of sales were 'cottage pianos purchased by working men', a 'modest and harmless luxury' which brought 'harmony into the home' and kept men out of the public house. McKenna regretted the industry's plight, but expressed the government's determination to restrain the growth of a luxury trade in wartime. In any case, he had been assured that the prices of those pianos which were completely British would not be raised.[52] Since virtually no instrument made in the previous year could honestly have been so described, the promise lacked conviction.

The national press, ever alert to accusations of 'profiteering', reported this debate extensively and provoked vigorous comment from within the trade. The ensuing diversity of opinion offers an interesting glimpse of the industry's state of mind at a turning point in its history. Protection, so long desired by some manufacturers, had come at last and was to be permanent. But its implications were obscured not merely by the few who wilfully ignored difficulties in the hope of gain, but by the many who, even if they were already conscious of wartime scarcities, could not be expected to anticipate their duration and intensity. Reactions to the McKenna duties were therefore confused and sometimes inept.[53] They were opposed most vociferously by shopkeepers dealing in good quality instruments, who offered tart comment on prevailing market conditions. From Edinburgh it was reported that customers were already deterred by high prices and shoddiness; from Nottingham came a prediction that immediately after the war German pianos would resume their dominance. A Birkenhead trader promised to remember the profiteers when normal times returned. Protection was welcomed unequivocally by a few of the larger manufacturers with statements ranging from the jingoistic to the inane: 'The medicine will do us good', claimed Witton and Witton, then making over 1,000 pianos a year. Most of the smaller makers were antagonistic, fearing that the duties would drive them out of business. W. H.

Strohmenger, one of their ablest representatives and a good craftsman, complained that contradictions in government policy should have been more vigorously exposed: the Board of Trade wanted German markets to be captured while the Treasury was making this impossible. The supply of components was totally inadequate for manufacturers' needs and colonial buyers of pianos were already complaining about costs and quality, while short-sighted makers were 'taking advantage of the situation and forcing prices up'. Rogers, operating on a larger scale (500 pianos a year) and also establishing a reputation for good quality, was more optimistic, believing or hoping that the tax on parts would strengthen the industry and make it self supporting.

Meanwhile, the majority of piano makers were less affected by future hopes or fears than by the immediate prospect of easy sales in docile home and export markets, the latter predominantly colonial, always provided they could get materials and were not too insistent upon maintaining quality. 1916 was an excellent season from every viewpoint except that of the consumer. Approximately 40,000 pianos were sold, of which 12,000 valued at £381,000 were exported; £235,000 worth were sent to Australia and New Zealand; £54,000 worth to South Africa. The total value of piano exports set a record which was not to be remotely again approached until after the Second World War. This quintessentially sellers' market encouraged the taking of quick profits and a neglect of quality which was sometimes caused by, and invariably blamed upon, wartime shortages.

The McKenna duties were merely a beginning. After 1916, government regulations really began to bite. Manufacturers could no longer rely upon the open market but were obliged to seek licences from unsympathetic officials who administered increasingly rigorous controls over labour and materials. In 1917, a prohibition against all imports of musical instruments was originally designed to include 'parts' but, after vigorous lobbying, piano manufacturers were allowed a quota of imported components, provided sixty per cent were used in making instruments for export. Apparently this regulation was widely evaded by means of importing through parcel post,[54] but later controls proved less tractable and there were repeated complaints, sometimes justifiable, against bureaucratic rigidity and ignorance. Musical instruments were classified as a 'restricted industry' which severely limited access to labour,[55] and rations of timber and metal were continually reduced until, by May 1918, they were sufficient only for an annual output of 20,000 new pianos and the repair of 4,000 old instruments, approximately equivalent to one fifth the level of pre-war production. Attempts were made to enforce these regulations— one small maker, for example, was fined £50 for 'irregular manufacture' and failing to report his stocks of wire—but the activities of little work-shops were difficult to control.[56] Much bartering of parts and illicit back-street trading continued to take place, giving temporary satisfaction to a public greedy for any sort of piano. By the closing months of the war, government control and scarcity had bitten so deeply that production had virtually ceased, save for a few hundred pianos supplied to the Army and Navy Canteen Board.

In exercising these controls the government needed to communicate with representatives of the industry, and therefore gave a new impetus to the growth of a manufacturers' association. But an industry composed of such disparate elements and conflicting interests was unlikely to reach amicable agreement about representation when so much was at stake. Even in times of peace there had been no semblance of unanimity. The Piano Manufacturers' Association had started life as a Musical Instrument Trades Protection Association in 1900, discarding this cumbrous title in 1908. The fact that only piano manufacturers could get on to its council had led first to complaints [57] and then to the formation of a separate Asso-ciation of Manufacturers and Dealers in Pianoforte Supplies. But this did not prevent the ubiquitous editor of *The Pianomaker* from exerting a force-ful and resented influence upon policy. By 1916 there were sixty-one manufacturers in the PMA, led by Billingshurst and proclaiming a unity which barely papered over deep rifts. It was to this body that all applica-tions by makers for 'metal' were referred by the Ministry of Munitions, and in various other ways the government tended to treat it as repre-sentative of 'the industry'.

Apart from the dealers, whose interests were in many ways directly opposed to those of manufacturers, the principal group of dissidents consisted of small piano makers who felt that their problems and interests were being ignored. In October 1917, their grievances precipitated the 'Islington Revolt', a skirmish hitherto unrecorded in the annals of war. A meeting of cheap manufacturers, some of whom were members of the PMA, assembled to complain about their treatment and to discuss the possibility of forming a separate association. Their immediate complaint was against the size of the metal ration, which was based on makers' previous output and therefore left small and new firms with insufficient material to stay in business. But wartime exigencies were exposing more fundamental weaknesses in such firms. Their inadequate stock and rapid turnover left them dependent upon immediate supplies, and their refusal to adopt standardized models rendered these requirements diverse and inflexible. Because their standards were generally low they were denied access to the remunerative Army and Navy contracts which kept bigger firms in business—an explanation which the Islington group refuted, of course, alleging 'exploitation by a cynical clique . . . dominating the affairs of our trade'.

The group's spokesman was Charles Love who, with six men and four boys, assembled 'thump boxes' selling by now at prices from fifty to seventy-five guineas! In a letter to the *Music Trades Review* he listed the small men's complaints and laid special blame upon the editor of *The Pianomaker* for 'meddling in legislation'.[58] Publication of this letter led inevitably to litigation, with judgement against the worthy editor in a libel case which amply documents the extent of his influence. With acute sensitivity to criticism and blatant disregard for the interests and feelings of those who crossed his path, he had stage-managed a petition to Parliament which, purporting to be representative of the trade, had helped secure the ban on imports of musical instruments. Love's argument that the rationing system was ruining small makers received substantial proof: in his own case it was necessary to make four pianos a week to survive but his ration of material was sufficient for only one a fortnight.[59] Yet the PMA also had a case. If its allocation of rations favoured the 'established', i.e. the bigger firms, many of whom were themselves allowing standards to fall, nevertheless it is probable that the worst trash came from the smallest makers, including several of the Islington rebels who described themselves as 'master pianoforte makers'.[60] The gulf between them and such makers as Chappell, Rogers and Strohmenger was unbridgeable by any association.

Working class affluence and aspiration

The Islington revolt came too late for serious reappraisal of the rationing system which, by 1918, had little to allocate. The death blow was now expected, in the form of a luxury tax similar to those already imposed in Germany and France. This prospect was sufficiently alarming for the furniture and music trades to show some unanimity at protest meetings organized by such bodies as the Hire Purchase Traders' Association. The dreaded tax was never imposed but it occupied a Parliamentary Select Committee and stimulated a debate which, since 1914, had periodically engaged the public and sometimes the government.

Throughout the war, the 'munitions worker's piano' was regarded as symbolic of a new working class prosperity. In February 1915 the *Daily Mail* set the tone: 'There never were such times for the working classes. A new class of buyer is in creation . . . the working class household, with money in the stocking, bethinks of household plenishments. Obtainable at last is that coveted proof of respectability, the piano. Good luck to the British working classes and may Heaven make them thrifty in this, their boom.' [61] The *Manchester Guardian* agreed: 'In this purely working class town the sellers of pianos on the hire system are doing the trade of their lives. The piano, of course, is the token of respectability in every artisan household.' There were interesting economic and social implications. The masses had money beyond their immediate needs for the first time in their lives, but they were unused to institutional saving and this, according to the *Guardian*, explained the government's inability to attract small investors. A typical woman customer earning wages and receiving her husband's allowance was 'using her savings to improve the home against his return. A piano is considered a durable by people who know nothing about stocks and shares'.[62] Many other newspapers followed this lead, attacking extravagant workers and profiteering manufacturers, some unkindly suggesting that shoddy wartime pianos were a poor investment and that it would be both patriotic and sensible to buy war bonds and wait for better pianos after the war.

Striking evidence of the thirst for pianos appears in a social survey of Sheffield which was undertaken in 1917 to assess 'the adequacy of the adult manual workers for the discharge of their responsibilities as heads of households, producers and citizens'.[63] It was an area 'less developed aesthetically' than many, but relatively prosperous in wartime. The survey classified its careful sample of workers (the leading statistician, Bowley, was consulted) into three groups, according to their 'intellectual and educational equipment' for 'home, work, leisure, citizenship and life'. Approximately twenty five per cent were placed into the 'well equipped' group I, another fifty per cent into an 'indifferently or inadequately equipped' group II and the hapless remainder occupied a 'malequipped' group III whose existence was 'a positive evil for the community'. Many people in group I owned and played pianos, including shop girls, housewives and a grinder, dying of dust, who played 'excellently' despite a 'useless school education', and had attended the opera three times in a recent week. Most of those without pianos wanted them, even if the desire was 'chiefly activated by social ambition'. Yet more remarkable was the presence of piano owners in group II, several without books in the house and including a boiler fireman 'strong in arm and thick in head', and a war widow who 'loves ragtime' (the interviewer's sniff is almost audible), 'doesn't know whether Shakespeare was a writer or prize-fighter' and had paid £50 for her 'piano 'in among all the steam and smoke'. A charwoman was buying an instrument on hire purchase for her daughter which dominated the tiny sole living-room. Finally let us record the shop assistant, daughter of a blacksmith, who played 'extremely well', revered Beethoven and was 'indifferent to everything else'.

These eager buyers were ill served by existing supplies. One dealer submitted a detailed report on three pianos which had been supplied at prices which, before the war, would have bought 'magnificent overstrung German instruments'. Among the deficiencies were thin brass hinges with screws clumsily hammered in; joints which could be seen and felt; polish streaked 'as if with treacle'; crudely shaped celluloid keys; and flimsy actions with sticking dampers and 'whiskers as if cut with a rip saw'.[64] The second-hand market was equally hazardous: a Walworth dealer, for example, was successfully sued for recovery of a £5 deposit on a 'wreck' which the court discovered to be a seventy-year-old Wornum pianette.[65]

The trade's response to continual criticism was predictably angry and self righteous, attacking 'extravagance in high quarters whence so much grandfatherly advice is wont to flow'.[66] Resentment became intense as the suspicion grew that 'ignorant newspaper clamour' was being used by the government as a reason, or excuse, for stringent regulation. In its submission to the Board of Trade the Association argued that expenditure upon drink, theatres and other luxuries remained untouched while an industry 'with £36 million capital' was being throttled as a scapegoat.[67] Thereafter, the munitions worker's piano made frequent appearances. National Savings propaganda depicted two men lifting a decrepit instrument and asked 'which is the better investment, a piano at present inflated prices, or War Bonds?' [68] The prevailing gossip can be illustrated by two trivial but representative examples. It was widely reported that Manchester's Chief Constable had observed a mufflered worker purchasing a piano for £80. *The Pianomaker* circularized all Manchester dealers and offered a reward to 'the man in the muffler . . . we trust his fingers were not sparkling with diamonds': there were no takers.[69] A final example of reported extravagance is a story which appeared in the *Evening News* in August 1918: a baby grand bought for £150 was allegedly used as a kitchen table, covered in jam and sold for £25.[70] If government regulation of the industry was primarily determined by genuine scarcities of men, shipping and materials, there can be little doubt that it was reinforced by tattle. Certainly the industry was convinced that it was responsible for hardening the 'attitude of ministers and officials when dealing with the requirements of the trade'.[71]

Survival and standardization

The industry and its supporters put up various forms of defence, changing tack as the war progressed and attempting, despite conflicting interests, to present a united front to mounting public criticism. Talk of high prices and low quality, they pleaded, was greatly exaggerated. Occasional lapses were due to unavoidable shortages of raw materials, or to 'disorderly dealers offering almost any prices for the pianos they desired'.[72] High profits, which were particularly scandalous in 1916, were 'the unforeseen result of war'.[73] *The Pianomaker*, ever ready to push its luck, equated the making and buying of English pianos with high patriotism: it was the nation's duty, in 1915, to support an industry which gave employment to older men and hit Germans by taking their trade.[74] By 1917 a splendid export figure had been achieved, and this enterprise had to be officially encouraged if the capture of German markets was to be consolidated.[75]

Unfortunately for this special pleading, the export record, although quantitatively impressive until 1917, was qualitatively disastrous, as even *The Pianomaker* had to admit. To the old familiar complaints against the government's indifference to the importer's requirements was added a more serious accusation: in dire contrast to the rapidly growing American exports, or even those from Japan where 'a far-seeing race' was subject to rigorous government controls over export standards, English makers, often selling to unscrupulous merchant shippers interested only in quick profits, were freely marketing trash.[76] Complaints were legion and can be fairly represented by the report of a leading Australian importer: 'The cheap British piano is now absolutely worthless as a musical instrument.' Importers refused to accept bills until they had examined the instruments, and many had been 'absolutely refused at any price . . . some of the action work seems almost like a joke'.[77] This letter, which carried extra weight through its publication in *The Pianomaker*, was supported by a series of leading articles raging against the industry's failure to rise to the opportunities afforded by the war: 'Never have such rotten pianos of a certain class been produced in this country.' They had helped to maintain goodwill for Germany.[78] Coming from such a source the verdict requires no further documentation. It also makes nonsense of the industry's final plea for special dispensations, that it represented a priceless cultural and educational heritage and made a unique contribution to social betterment. The sentiment, admissible perhaps in more normal times, was singularly inapt when advanced in 1918, as many angry buyers were eager to point out.[79]

Yet not all was lost. If most manufacturers had done little to enhance their reputation, some had struggled to maintain standards despite the temptations of a sellers' market. In the closing months of the war a few even ceased making pianos rather than damage goodwill. Several of the larger firms survived, and acquired valuable experience by accepting government contracts for various products. The rapid growth of aircraft manufacture from about fifty machines a month in 1914 to 2,700 a month by 1918 was particularly significant. The pianomaker's skills could be adapted to this work, but the demand for rapid production of standardized parts stimulated new ways of management, factory organization, the ordering of traditional processes and use of machinery. The implications of these new methods for the future manufacture of pianos were keenly discussed within the trade, giving a new impetus to the debate on 'Taylorization' (i.e. scientific management) or 'rationalization' which had occupied recent association meetings. At the 1916 convention, there was considerable verbal support for 'the elimination of petty and pottering methods in production' and the provision of 'supplies on a non-wasteful, scientific basis'.[80] By 1918, a typically enthusiastic article envisaged a 'great British piano industry built up from the aircraft movement'.[81]

Cynics might observe that modern procedures had been adopted in America and Germany for more than a generation without much effect on English practice. But two new influences were at work: the virtual elimination of the smallest makers had removed a potent source of conservatism and inefficiency, while the larger firms' practical experience of standardization in war contracts might prove more effective than exhortation in overcoming ancient prejudice and routine. Thus, despite a badly dented public image, English piano makers faced the peace with some equanimity. Protected by the McKenna duties and by fervent declarations 'never again' to trade with the enemy, they contemplated an apparently insatiable and recently unquenched thirst for their product.

Chapter 10

Between the Wars

The post-war decade is an ambiguous and confusing period in the piano's history, a bewildering mixture of genuine and false achievements by men whose major inarticulate assumption—a return to pre-war conditions of demand—was only briefly fulfilled. By European standards, American production had been comparatively unaffected by the war, although the greatest makers were unable to maintain supplies of concert grands. Rather than lower standards they restricted output, and to such an extent that in 1919 leading pianists who wanted instruments by Steinway, Knabe, or Mason and Hamlin were temporarily asked to make other arrangements. Generally, however, the industry continued to thrive.[1] Output rose to a peak of more than 347,000 instruments, valued at 111 million dollars in 1923, and was still high in 1925, after which decline was first rapid and then precipitous. If the 1920s were to be the last great age of piano ownership, nowhere was this more extensive than in the United States: in their classic study of 'Middletown', the Lynds estimated that by 1928 there was a piano in the homes of more than half of America's city dwellers.[2]

In Europe the industry's fortunes were inevitably affected by the political and economic disintegration, and the profound social adjustments of these years. Only the French industry remained relatively stable, or stagnant, maintaining its pre-war production level of some 40,000 instruments a year, of which about ten per cent were exported. Gallic self-esteem remained unsullied. In 1924, Grangier's *A genius of France* explained 'why the Erard piano today occupies in its own country a higher position than any one piano maker in any other country'.[3] Inevitably it was a defeated Germany which experienced the greatest turbulence. There was a major crisis in 1923 when inflation imposed intolerable burdens at home and played havoc with foreign exchange values and international prices. Some indication of the turmoil endured by German industry in these months is provided by the experience of piano trade representatives at the Leipzig Spring Fair in 1923. In January, the mark stood at 200,000 to the pound, but soon appreciated to 100,000. When the fair opened, sales were based on rates between 120,000 and 180,000, but prices fluctuated daily and buyers were naturally cautious.[4] When the inflation ended in November the mark had fallen to one trillionth of its pre-war level.[5] Yet by 1927 production had again passed the 100,000 level, and leading makers had regained much of their former pre-eminence.

The performance of individual firms was better than appears in Table IV (p. 79) which shows only the 1920 and 1930 figures. Both Bechstein and Grotrian Steinweg, for example, produced about 3,000 pianos in 1927, after which output fell rapidly to less than 500 in 1931. But even before the crash, exports never reached their former levels, falling from a post-war peak of 56,000 instruments in 1924 to 31,000 in 1929 and 3,000 in 1932. Moreover her markets were drastically realigned: by 1928 Britain and Australia ranked respectively third and seventh in the list of importers. Exports to Britain consisted almost entirely of the highest quality uprights, and of grands for which Britain was by far the largest market.[6] This indicates both the extent and the limitations of English achievements: success in the medium class of manufacture, failure to retain concert platforms and produce instruments for discerning musicians. But the changes were far more complex than these few words suggest.

Rebuilding a shattered industry: England 1918–28

In its first season of peace and protection from foreign competition, the English piano industry had grounds for optimism. German pianos were expected to reappear but it was thought that they could be defeated, at least in the medium home market, provided that good components became available and the protective McKenna duties could be retained. If the industry were not to resume its pre-war dependence upon imported supplies the two stipulations were obviously interconnected and, after swings in policy and great alarm in the trade, both were ultimately met. The duties, which had been gained in 1915 as a fortuitous by-product of emergency legislation (pp. 167–9), were retained, briefly lost with a change of government in 1924 and then permanently reinstated in 1925. The belated establishment of an action-making industry was one of the least equivocal successes of these years. Among several firms by far the most important was Herrburger Brooks Ltd, which was launched in 1920 with £250,000 capital, an able board of directors and access to Schwander patents and expertise.[7] Supplying a much larger market, of course, than any individual piano manufacturer, it established high standards and paid good dividends, continuing to be profitable even during the 1930s when it took over several rivals.[8] Imports of actions fell rapidly after 1925 and soon became negligible, but other components continued to be imported in sizeable quantities, particularly from Germany.

For pianos the record is more ambivalent. Recovery had to be achieved in the face of hostility from dealers and the public, reflecting a profound disillusion with all but a few English makers. We have already noted Ernest Newman's condemnation of the wartime piano (p. 159). Although materials and men soon became available again, there was apparently little improvement in quality. Articles in the *Star* newspaper reopened the controversy and added fresh indictments. Extensively reprinted in the provincial press, they complained that, despite inferior materials and workmanship, the price of instruments had doubled since 1914, and claimed that demands for continuing protection were 'a form of patriotism which covers profiteering in its worst form'.[9] This released a flood of similar complaints principally from dealers whose latent hostility, muted during the war by patriotic forbearance and a lack of alternative supplies, now burst forth. A Welsh trader represented the general opinion inelegantly but with force: 'The majority are fed up with British manufacturers who prate about patriotism when they have been "doing" the dealers right and left.' He refused 'to sell such stuff to poor people at the present price'.[10]

There were various replies to these attacks: that the price of most goods had doubled; that trade unions should be blamed for high costs; but above all that dealers, who had always exerted a stranglehold over the smaller piano makers, were now complaining simply because their exorbitant profit margins were at last being pared—by manufacturers, not consumers. Most interesting, however, was intervention from a normally uncommunicative source. L. A. T. Broadwood invited a journalist from the *Star* to inspect his firm's books, and explained why the retail price of an upright piano had risen from £45 to £108 since 1913. Broadwood's costs had risen by margins which ranged from 170 per cent for timber, to 100 per cent for frames and actions. The latter still had to be imported from Herrburger in Paris. Despite the fact that only eighty per cent of Broadwood's men had, as yet, returned to the factory its wage bill had already doubled. Out of a total addition to the costs of a piano of £28 9s 3d, labour accounted for eleven pounds and there was little hope of improvement, for the men refused to go back to piece-work rates. The retailer's profit margin was still fifty per cent, forced upon Broadwood in the past by German competition and now retained in anticipation of its resurgence. The manufacturer's profit was calculated at a mere fifteen per cent on the wholesale price.[11]

Such public frankness about costs and prices is rare in the annals of an industry notorious for its secretiveness. Coming from the doyen of English firms, accustomed to a cloistered reticence, it is a measure of sensitivity to criticism. There were well-founded fears that so much adverse publicity would ruin sales, with the return of German competition, despite a thirty-three and a third per cent duty, and might even lead to a reappraisal of tariff policy. Manufacturers were determined to fight for continued protection, differing only in the intensity and style of their lobbying and about the need to tax imported actions and components. But even behind tariff walls they would continue to face difficulties, some old and familiar, others new and barely conceived before they became overwhelming. Among these the profit margins of dealers were least significant. Large discounts to purchasers had long been commonplace, and a return to competition would soon reduce the alleged fifty per cent to retailers. It was in making rather than selling pianos that improvement should be sought, and here the labour question was clearly paramount.

Before the war, industrial relations had achieved a primitive and uneasy equilibrium. Piano making was a comparatively healthy industry, at least in the better shops, as the longevity of its workers suggests. But the majority of firms survived, despite inefficient labour-intensive methods, by paying low wages and offering only seasonal employment under a 'contract system' of piecework.[12] Labour remained cheap because there were few alternative full-time jobs in London, and because the ease with which disgruntled men could start their own business provided a useful safety valve. Apart from a few representatives of the 'new school' (pp. 155–7) most employers were either patriarchs or 'sweaters'. The former were justly proud of the age, skill and loyalty of their workers, but tended to leave the tough shop-floor bargaining to their foremen. 'Sweaters' were usually men whose recent escape from the workbench encouraged a tendency to strike hard bargains. All suffered the pressures of intense competition and a cost structure in which labour was the predominant element. A trivial but illuminating example of working conditions was the practice of exacting 'candle money'. In addition to their own tools workers were expected to provide candles and, when gas lighting was introduced, to contribute sixpence a week in lieu. Even the trade press regarded this imposition as 'indefensible',[13] but as late as 1901 it was still necessary for some workers to seek redress in the courts under the Truck Acts.[14]

In such conditions trade unions could not achieve a continuous reasonable existence, but tended to emerge only at times of acute dispute, as in the strikes of 1878 against the employment of unskilled men, and, more seriously, those of the early 1890s when french polishers led a frontal attack upon the contract system.[15] In piano making as in other industries, the war accustomed men to higher wages and stronger collective bargaining, but a more fundamental threat came from the growth of alternative employment opportunities. Among these, ironically, was the rapidly growing gramophone industry where higher productivity and a buoyant market allowed the payment of higher wages.

It was therefore inevitable that the immediate post-war years should see industrial relations degenerate into open hostility with strikes throughout the industry.[16] The experience was not confined to England: similar outbreaks were reported from America and Germany.[17] But in England they were more widespread and damaging. To retain labour and remain in business, piano firms had to adjust not merely wages but their whole approach to industrial relations. It was failure to do this which precipitated the most spectacular event in the trade during these years—the collapse of Brinsmead in January 1920—although fundamental weaknesses in management had probably undermined for many years the foundations of this self-ordained leader of the industry. The subsequent bankruptcy proceedings revealed a chaotic state of affairs: productivity had fallen to a quarter of the level of comparable firms and many of the pianos auctioned by the Receiver were of very poor quality.[18] The effect upon public opinion was so serious that the British Associated Pianomakers, which included such reputable firms as Broadwood, Chappell, and Marshall and Rose, had to issue a reassuring statement that the public was not being 'generally bled'.[19] Brinsmead's name and goodwill, if that is the correct term, were acquired by another firm which, two years later, was advertising: 'When customers see "John Brinsmead and Sons, London" on the fall, they know they are purchasing a genuine and real Brinsmead piano and not a fraudulent imitation.'[20]

The labour problem was a question not merely of productivity, costs and post-war intransigence, but of the quality of the workforce. When the distinguished economist, Alfred Marshall, assessed the advantages of Germany's excellent system of public education in promoting 'the growth of a scientific proletariat', he chose piano workers as one of his most telling examples: 'The thoroughness and universality of the musical training of her people have given her piano manufacturers a large choice of designers and workers apt to judge tones with a true and fine instinct.'[21] No comparable system of musical or technical education was available in England, but a few enlightened piano manufacturers attempted to repair some of the deficiencies with a scheme of evening classes for apprentices in 1913. Boys from Cramer and Chappell attended between 7.30 and 9 in the evening, and even *The Pianomaker*, urging employers to allow time off for study, argued that in this case it was wise to imitate Germany.[22] A more elaborate system was started four years later at the new and conveniently located Northern Polytechnic, which included a research department under the direction of Dr R. S. Clay aiming to raise standards and 'recover trade that has been lost by bad workmanship'.[23] The timing of these creditable initiatives was cruelly inopportune. In wartime, neither available resources nor the prevailing climate of opinion in a sellers' market were conducive to a spirit of open enquiry and progress. Thereafter only a few years remained before the industry's declining fortunes became sufficiently obvious to deter recruits. Nevertheless, during that period the training scheme made great progress and was applauded abroad.[24]

Meanwhile competition from Germany had recommenced. Exports began a few months after the Armistice and, by May 1919, instruments using makeshift materials but acknowledged to be of 'good quality and workmanship' were already reported in Holland and Belgium.[25] In the same month the British government allowed a resumption of piano imports, up to twenty-five per cent of 1913 quantities.[26] A few thousand instruments and a flood of advertising material arrived, precipitating agonized reappraisal within the English trade. Recent pledges 'never again' to deal with the enemy were forgotten, and those retailers who deigned to answer attacks upon their lack of patriotism explained that refusal to handle German instruments would merely place lucrative agencies into the hands of 'the stores and private speculators'. Moral outrage and campaigns of rumour against such alleged deficiencies as the use of 'artificially dried timber' failed to deter the public from embracing treason.[27]

The speed of German recovery is demonstrated by the trade statistics. Before the war Britain had imported approximately 20,000 German pianos a year. In 1920 the figure was 4,500, and by 1922 it had risen to 15,000. High average values indicate a return to pre-war trading patterns, with even greater emphasis upon first class instruments. Further evidence of this is the reappearance of Bechstein, who reopened their London agency in 1923 to the disgust of *The Pianomaker*, which attempted to reopen old wounds, reiterating its invective against Max Lindler and disloyal musicians, but this time without much response.[28] Our Belfast dealer's activities were probably representative of the better class trade in these years. During the first two seasons of peace the only good instruments he could secure were Chappells, which he bought at prices between £70 and £90 and sold for £90 to £120. In July 1920, he imported his first post-war Bechstein, a model 8 upright. Since the firm's London agency was still closed, he had to import directly from Berlin, paying £84 plus £37 for duty and freight and selling easily for £170. By autumn 1924, temporarily free of import duty, he was getting the same instruments directly from London and could sell at a greatly increased profit for £130. The smaller, more popular model 9 cost him £80 and retailed for about £115, more than double the pre-war price but still eagerly purchased. No English pianos were in this class but there was a steady demand for Chappell's excellent model V instrument, at approximately £80, giving him a gross profit of about £18. It was a busy season because the repeal of the McKenna duties had been announced in May and carried out in August. This was the first and, as subsequent events proved, the last post-war opportunity to buy foreign pianos free of tax. He therefore placed large orders for German instruments, particularly the more expensive models, for which there was a considerable pent-up demand.

After protection was reimposed he sold a smaller proportion of German instruments, but no English maker succeeded in taking over the market for the highest quality instruments. Every disinterested observer agreed that this was generally the case throughout the United Kingdom, a failure which elicited much comment. Even the *Daily Express*, scarcely likely to underrate national achievement, was reduced to a rather lame commendation: 'The British manufacturer has been reaching nearer and nearer the standards set by those Teutonic giants, Steinway, Bechstein and Blüthner . . . if our ancient rivals in Germany must look elsewhere for markets, they can console themselves with the thought that the standard set by them played no inconsiderable part in the splendid development of the British piano.'[29] Others were less generous, remarking that German and Austrian pianos continued to dominate concert platforms. The reference to Austria is an early indication of the resurgence of Bösendorfer, a firm which henceforth was to figure prominently in professional music making. An analysis of concert announcements in October 1928 revealed that less than ten per cent used English pianos. Against inevitable protests that this was merely a function of makers' subsidies to pianists,[30] the *MTR* stated flatly that 'no one who has moved in British artistic circles with his eyes open will deny that the classic German piano is still the most coveted and the most used'.[31]

This failure of leadership was important for the whole industry. The concert grand's role in establishing an image and settling standards had long been appreciated. It was the highest embodiment of a maker's skill, a 'crucial test of claims to produce an art-product' and demonstrated that the best makers were patrons of music, 'not mere furniture constructors'.[32] Such leadership was sorely needed in an industry which contained elements whose distrust of 'mongrel professors' (pp. 97 and 105) and indifference to musical values sometimes degenerated into outright antipathy. A long-standing tradition of philistinism was manifest in part of the trade's press and in the banality of its chosen entertainments: 'smoking concerts' at association meetings, for example, or the 'grande soirée' which celebrated John Brinsmead's golden wedding with tawdry drawing-room music.[33] Nurtured by parochial ignorance and reinforced by isolation from the highest musical standards, it threatened during the war years to dominate the industry: a speaker at the 1917 music trades convention, who urged his audience not to regard pianists as 'cranks and pro-Germans', and attempted to demonstrate the performer's requirements by playing Chopin's B-flat Minor Scherzo, was greeted with derisory laughter.[34]

It is impossible to judge how representative this barbarous attitude was of the trade in general. Presumably some manufacturers and shopkeepers were cultivated men, but there is little evidence of firm cultural leadership. In 1921, the president of the piano manufacturers' association was still at war, asserting that 'nearly every improvement in piano construction has been devised by British craftsmen . . . and some of the best known foreign instruments are merely imitations of native pianos'. A fondness for jingoistic myth was enhanced by technological naïvety: 'a good piano will improve with use, like a good violin', said the same speaker.[35] In 1919, a Federation of British Music Industries was established with the laudable purpose of representing all branches of the trades in the advancement and spread of music. At its inaugural banquet Neville Chamberlain proposed the toast of 'the British Musical Art and Industry', attacking the national predilection for 'German players, German composers and German pianos', but also advocating musical appreciation for the masses, and reminding his audience that Birmingham was the first city to subsidize an orchestra from the rates.[36] Subsequent proceedings tended to dwell upon the first of these themes. A principal speaker at the 1922 meeting was convinced that one 'could not popularize music on German pianos; it could only be done by means of British pianos, British military bands and British orchestras' and 'jazz music should never appear in a programme'.[37] Among piano men, in contrast to their colleagues from the gramophone industry, debates tended to be stale and parochial. The 'problem of the professional musician' still referred to trade discounts.[38] When protection was temporarily abandoned in 1924, traders were urged to 'emulate the British Tommy when he lost his rifle and went for his enemy with his fists'.[39] Even after protection had been restored, the Convention's secretary continued to lament that 'for some aesthetic reason'— as if it were an ailment—musicians preferred German pianos.[40]

There can be little doubt that a section of the industry had fallen into the trap of believing its own propaganda. This was the opinion of J. L. Stephen, who was better informed than most of his contemporaries and had no particular axe to grind. A good craftsman and ardent student of the piano, his breadth of knowledge is demonstrated by his vast collection of documentary material bequeathed to the British Museum. Despite suffocating self-esteem, wrote Stephen, most of England's 'so-called factories' required a complete overhaul. No foreign dealer would accept such antiquated designs as vertically strung uprights, but demanded 'something at least as good as the American, Canadian, German and Japanese [*sic*] pianos'. Reform necessitated the education of manufacturers, dealers and public to 'appreciate a real musical instrument—not bits of furniture with tensioned wire'.[41] That was written in 1921. Seven years later, the *Music Trades Review*'s editor reported a conversation with 'a leading English pianoforte manufacturer' who was indignant at talk of German superiority: 'Whilst of course in our hearts we must admit these facts, there is no need to put them into cold print'. Such men, added the editor, 'live in a fool's paradise, with the soft light from the magic lamp of the McKenna Duties gently beaming on them'.[42]

Certainly much rubbish continued to be made. In 1921 there were 'more garret workshops than ever before', employing unskilled men to produce 'something with which well-ordered factories cannot compete'.[43] A year later, *The Pianomaker* confessed that 'more shoddy goods have been sold since the Armistice than ever before'.[44] But failure to produce the highest quality pianos did not in itself constitute a fool's paradise. Those firms, including Challen, Chappell, Hopkinson (under new management after its collapse in 1924), Rogers and Strohmenger, which concentrated upon good medium class instruments, were making a modest but rational response to existing resources and opportunities. Their success was based upon modern industrial practices which are epitomized in two catchwords of the period, 'rationalization' and 'standardization': a more rational use of labour and machinery; a smaller range of models, abandoning idiosyncracies which had rarely done much to enhance the product but had greatly increased costs. Standard sizes, frames, scales, actions and interchangeable parts were a belated adoption of the American system, necessary if wages and prices were to be kept at a competitive level. Unfortunately, the large and expanding market which was the essential prerequisite for such developments was about to disintegrate.

The fallen idol

The piano industry was crippled by alternative sources of entertainment, erosion of the instrument's social status, and by the crash and depression of the 1930s. It must be emphasized that the blows came in that order. Fundamental changes in consumption patterns do not happen overnight, nor is their timing identical in different countries and at various levels of society. This revolution took about twenty years before it was apparent everywhere, to all but the most obtuse. It was first clearly perceived in America when, in 1909, a year after Ford's introduction of the

Model T, motor cars were recognized as the most formidable of rivals because 'a greater visible show can be made than with the piano'.[45] The comment was more perceptive than contemporaries could have realized. There were more utilitarian reasons, of course, for the car's popularity, but its place in modern family budgets is no mere question of utility. Not for another generation did the car become a middle-class obsession in England, less still a target-good for the common man. Yet in 1925, traders were already complaining that young married couples were buying cars, at prices no higher than before the war, while they said that they could not afford pianos.[46] Again we have a precursor of present-day expenditure attitudes.

A more obvious rival, for entertainment if not status, was the gramophone. In 1887 the *Musical Times*, facetiously noting the antics of Edison, enquired if future musicians would 'scatter examples of their skill all over the globe to order? Will Rubinstein or little Hofmann make a tour of the world by phonogram, sitting quietly at home and preparing new specimens?'[47] Twenty years later the 'toy talker' was being hailed as a musical instrument.[48] It was not yet quite respectable: when the Holborn Guardians were offered one they were urged to reject 'a vulgar instrument' but relented when the records of De Reszke, Melba and Calvé were invoked.[49] A luxury model was designed, soft in tone and topped with porcelain figures, to 'appeal mostly to an educated class . . . and those who do not desire that their next door neighbours should be acquainted with the fact that there is a talking machine in the adjoining house'.[50] As techniques improved and repertoire widened, the machine was taken more seriously. 'Novelties' and popular songs were joined by operatic arias—Caruso and the gramophone became 'twin institutions', each increasing the other's popularity.[51] The piano recorded less well than the voice, but as early as 1908 records by Backhaus were acclaimed because they enabled listeners to appreciate, 'some for the first time in their lives, the extraordinary effect of the piano in the hands of a master'.[52] The experience could be demoralizing. While records were a stimulus to musical appreciation, they were also a deterrent to amateur fumbling, reinforced in time by the virtual disappearance of rewarding music which the untalented or poorly trained could hope to master. There was even an attack, more symbolic than practical to be sure, upon one of the amateur's most coveted roles: ten records were issued of accompaniments to ballads which were said to 'supersede the piano'.[53]

Gramophones had long been cheaper than pianos, in so far as a direct comparison could be made. After the war, the gap widened alarmingly and comparisons of the satisfaction to be derived from alternative expenditures became more meaningful. In 1921, the cheapest piano worth buying cost £60, while good gramophones cost upwards of £15 and record prices were falling.[54] Music traders who, in the past, had left the new product to bicycle dealers and the like, began to switch loyalties. Many discovered that it could be sold on hire purchase—initially they had feared it might be too portable—and that turnover was so much greater that they were indifferent to falling piano sales.[55] The once despised toy was taking over the market for home music. It was a world-wide transition, most rapid in the United States: in 1914 output of phonographs and records was valued at $27 million against $56 million for pianos; by 1919 the figures were respectively $158 million and $95 million. At Federation meetings in England, representatives of the two industries could hardly have presented a greater contrast. English gramophones and records were acknowledged to be among the world's leaders. Prices were falling as quality improved, reflecting enormous strides in technology (notably the transition from acoustic to electric reproduction), skilled management, mass production and increasing productivity. By 1928, shares in gramophone companies were 'the liveliest of stock exchange propositions'—the Columbia Graphophone Company declared a dividend of forty-eight per cent.[56] Moreover, their links with international music were intimate and inspiriting. At the 1927 Convention they provided a concert by Chaliapin, Isolde Menges, De Greef, Peter Dawson and Gerald Moore.[57] Nothing remotely comparable was in reach of the piano manufacturers. Within the musical instrument trades was a paradigm of British industry in the 1920s, sharply divided between old contracting and new expanding sectors.[58]

There was a natural reluctance to acknowledge this parting of the ways: 'Despite the wonderful figures attained by the gramophone and record industry,' said the *MTR* in 1927, 'it is probable that most of us still regard the pianoforte industry as the basic factor of music trade prosperity'.[59] The prevailing air of wounded bewilderment and futile hope was well expressed by a Scottish trader at the 1928 Convention: 'At one time no one set up a home without purchasing a piano, sooner or later. Now a smoking lounge with a gramophone and a garage are all that is necessary. But this cannot endure, and soon there will be a return to the true home, with children at the piano.' [60]

There were many attempts, trivial and ambitious, to fight back, all eagerly reported in the trade press. One dealer sent his chauffeur to convey prospective customers: car rides were a novelty for the working class.[61] Another offered three months' free lessons with pianos at 2s 6d a week and no deposit.[62] In 1927, a British Pianoforte Publicity Committee raised £2,000 to 'create the idea that the piano is still a necessity in every home'. No manufacturer's name was mentioned in its propaganda, which was designed 'to benefit the maker of the commercial piano in an equal degree to the maker of the branded instrument'.[63] Window dressing competitions and a training school for piano salesmen were advocated, and 'salvation' was also sought through a system of 'group piano teaching', which was the main activity of the Federation's 'educational department'.[64] The most successful event was a national piano playing competition, launched by the *Daily Express*, which offered seventy-two British pianos as prizes. William Murdoch recorded some nondescript test pieces by contemporary English composers to guide the 20,000 contestants.[65] The winner was Cyril Smith, who emerged from a working-class background similar to the 'group I' described on page 172 to join a new generation of artists, including Myra Hess and, above all, Solomon, who rescued English piano playing from its long tradition of mediocrity. Second prize was taken by Alec Templeton, the blind pianist who was to make a reputation in jazz.

By encouraging talent and focusing public interest, the competition undoubtedly assisted music and the piano industry, but it could not stem the tide. Further intrusions upon consumers' expenditure came from the cinema (by 1939, weekly attendances were nineteen million) and the radio. In 1923 there were only half a million holders of wireless licences, confined primarily to the middle class. Within three years this figure was quadrupled, and by 1939 there were seventy-three licences for every hundred households in the United Kingdom.[66] The pattern of development was similar to that of the gramophone, but far more rapid and wide-ranging: 'It has caught on like an epidemic', declared the *MTR* in 1929.[67] Lord Reith's BBC transformed the country's musical culture with little assistance from the musical establishment or appreciation by later historians. But as one of them remarks, it 'replaced the piano in the front parlour'.[68]

Crash and recovery, 1929–1939

The process of displacement, gathering momentum by 1929, was greatly accelerated by the economic crisis and succeeding depression, which afflicted other piano-making countries even more seriously than England. If total industrial production in 1929 is represented by an index of a hundred, the subsequent fall by 1932 was to eighty-four in England, seventy-two in France and fifty-three in Germany and the United States.[69] With falling incomes and extensive unemployment, the purchase of expensive durable goods which, in any case, were likely to become cheaper, ranked low among consumers' preferences. In Germany between 1927 and 1933 the number of piano manufacturers fell from a hundred and twenty-seven to thirty-seven and their work force from 17,000 to less than 3,000. Output, in thousands of instruments, plunged from a hundred to six and exports from forty to three.[70] The American collapse was equally humiliating, annual production falling, over the same period, from 250,000 to 25,000. English piano statistics for these crucial years are more comprehensive than in the past, but probably misleading. They were based upon returns made to the Board of Trade by manufacturers of iron frames, as follows:

1927	92,000	1929	86,000	1931	55,000	1933	40,000
1928	97,000	1930	86,000	1932	36,000	1934	50,000

Critics of these figures argued that 1928 was a depressed year, with many bankruptcies in the trade, so that production was unlikely to have increased, and that stocks of frames held by their manufacturers and by piano makers made nonsense of the annual quotations.[71] All the evidence suggests that piano output was already declining by 1928: the labour force, for example, fell from about 10,000 in 1925, when output was said to be 100,000, to 4,000 in 1931, with at least twenty per cent of the latter working only twelve hours a week.[72] It is therefore probable that annual output fell to little more than 30,000 pianos in 1931 and 1932.

In 1914 at the height of the piano's popularity, a journalist attempted to forecast its future market. Previous generations, he argued, had expected demand to be satiated long before 1900, yet it had enormously increased and would continue to do so. 'A population of forty million', he concluded, 'has an absorptive capacity of 120,000 pianos a year'.[73] Surveying the wreckage of 1932, W. H. Strohmenger, president of a decimated manufacturers' association, postulated a 'rock bottom demand' for 25,000 pianos a year which would be required as 'professional tools' for musicians, schools, teachers, hotels and steamships. The desire to possess an instrument 'as a hallmark of respectability or even of social standing' was dead, but with economic recovery there would also be a 'fashion demand'.[74] He did not enlarge on this concept, nor could he foresee that social standing might be divorced from respectability and attached to fashion. Yet a new image was already in the making, tentatively at first in the form of the baby grand and then, with far greater potency, in the miniature upright.

Baby grands were less than five feet in length, at least one foot shorter than the boudoir grand or *Stutzflügel*. With few exceptions they were inferior in sound to a good upright, and the smallest ones were little more than toys. Their short bass strings required adjustments in tension and gauge which made it virtually impossible to secure good quality of tone. If the strings were too thick and heavily overwound, the result was a 'tubby' bass characteristic of the genre. Thinner strings required low tensions which gave a feeble evanescent sound. A restricted soundboard, limiting in itself, also meant that the bridges had to be brought too close to its rigid edges, again debilitating the tone. Even the finest designers and craftsmen could do little to overcome these inherent limitations; in lesser hands the product was a meretricious object which sacrificed everything to save a few inches. In America its popularity was already waning by the late 1920s (p. 140) when it became fashionable in Europe. Discriminating musicians were unanimous in their antagonism. A typical comment dismissed it as a creature of 'vanity . . . fit only for strumming "In a Monastery Garden"'.[75] But this did not deter many German and English manufacturers who, in their desperate search for custom, strained to reduce the size of their offspring. A representative English cohort of the early 1930s included Broadwood's 'Elfin' (4 ft 6 in., 123 gns.), Allison's 'Peter Pan' (4 ft 3 in., £90), the 'Metzler Midget' (4 ft, 65 gns.) and a dwarf which sold for sixty-five guineas and was less than four feet long.

Baby grands tapped a new market which survived the crash, but at these prices they could not revivify the piano industry; nor did subsequent price cutting attract many new customers. By 1933 Monington and Weston were offering the 'Babette grand for the million' at forty-eight guineas, and intense competition was being attacked as 'a menace to the whole industry'.[76] But as the British economy slowly pulled out of depression, the market for musical instruments alone among household goods stubbornly refused to expand, despite a housing boom which in earlier years would have inevitably stimulated the demand for pianos. A fundamental change in consumption habits is revealed in the following remarkable figures. It will be noted that expenditure increased in all categories except musical instruments in which pianos were the predominant element, and that sales of gramophones and radios expanded more than twice as fast as any other group. All estimates are rounded to the nearest million pounds.[77]

Estimated consumer expenditure on furniture and furnishings in the United Kingdom (£ million)

	1924	1930	1935
Wood furniture	39	55	62
Soft furnishings	11	14	15
Carpets	22	25	25
Radios and gramophones	7	18	27
Musical instruments*	9	6	5

* Pianos and other musical instruments, including sheet music.

Faced with these market conditions, surviving piano manufacturers had three alternatives. A few continued to make good conventional instruments; others were content to produce gimcrack pianos, some straight strung, all with overdamper actions, in which everything was sacrificed to cheapness. Anonymous or stencilled with fanciful German sounding names, they were mostly retailed through furniture shops which knew and cared nothing for the properties of a musical instrument. A third alternative was to attack the 'fashion' market with a new product which, by evangelizing modernity, would not merely attract new buyers but might even stimulate the eviction of old family pianos as unwanted heirlooms from a rejected past.

There were rational arguments for reducing the upright's size, weight and power to conform with small rooms, low ceilings and thin walls. But arguments of utility and convenience alone cannot explain the miniature piano's extraordinary success, for its technical and musical deficiencies far outweighed these attributes. In order to reduce its height below three feet, actions had to be drastically modified, resulting in a 'spongy' unresponsive touch. Its sound was tinny ('sweet and small' according to a recent euphemistic account [78]), its construction so peculiar that repairs, or even tuning, were a formidable task. But undoubtedly it looked different, and these looks could easily be modified by enclosing its mass-produced innards within various types of box. Style was of the essence, even at the cost of function. For generations, piano makers had been accused of neglecting fashionable taste—making objects which required draping to hide their ugliness (p. 130)—and now they were to lead it.

The pioneer in this extraordinary enterprise was Percy Brasted whose Associated Piano Company had the resources to mount a large scale attack on the market but lacked a suitable product. It was Brasted's considerable achievement to recognize the possibilities of an unprepossessing Swedish design, adapt it for mass production and cleverly name it the 'minipiano'. In 1934, the first year of English production, 7,000 of these six octave bichord instruments were sold, defying all conventional understanding of design and market possibilities. An improved, seven-octave trichord model was introduced with a more conventional action, though the touch remained poor, and Brasted then secured an even more remarkable triumph by selling the American manufacturing rights to Hardman Peck.[79] Thus for the first time in a century, the direction of technological diffusion was reversed: Americans adopted a British product.

Meanwhile in England a miniature boom took place. Other firms designed small pianos, advertising extensively and provocatively: one did not require 'contortionist tuners'; another was 'the only genuine minipiano' as used by the Princesses Elizabeth and Margaret Rose. There was no attempt to suggest that serious musicians were interested: the

entire emphasis of advertising was upon novelty and association with the
glamorous world of show business. Miniature pianos were as 'thrilling and
inevitable as a streamlined car' commended by such 'Great artistes' (*sic*)
as Harry Roy and Charlie Kunz.[80] Pianos, said Brasted, are 'like perambulators . . . they will not go unless they are pushed'.[81] Fifty minipianos
appeared together at the 1936 Radiolympia Show, played by fifty pretty
girls. More than 100,000 people saw this 'sensational act' which later
toured the Paramount cinema circuit. Cernikoff the 'world's largest
pianist' played the 'world's smallest piano'.[82] A new frame was advertised
as 'the greatest achievement of all time in the art of pianoforte construction'.[83] Traders were urged to avoid second-hand business which merely
perpetuated old images, and keep up with fashion.[84] Puffs were discreetly
placed where they would have maximum effect. The *News of the World*
discovered a 'most extraordinary change in two years': in the past a
piano only sold if it looked like a piano. Now people wanted 'pianos that
do not look like the old pianos'. While foreign makers still concentrated
on 'big heavy instruments', the English industry had captured its home
market save for a few people who 'prefer the continental tone'.[85]

   In truth, the fashion had spread to foreign parts. In Germany Mannborg
and Feurich announced new small instruments, and in France Erard
offered the 'Vog', Pleyel the 'Elite' and Gaveau 'Le Menuet'. In America
the transformation was significant enough for the 1937 census to introduce a new classification distinguishing 'conventional' uprights from
'console models, flat top, drop action'. 32,000 of the latter type were sold,
valued at nearly five million dollars, approximately twice the sales of
conventional uprights. The favoured design was rather different from
European patterns and remained so (later miniatures were called 'spinets').
But the essential features were the same—smallness, a complete break
with the past appearance and a 'drop', as distinct from 'direct blow',
action. In America, as in Europe, these changes were never accepted by
discerning purchasers despite subsequent improvements: as recently as
1967 an independent consumers' report advised against the purchase of
small pianos, especially those with drop actions,[86] but this did not affect
their success with the public and by the late 1930s they dominated markets
everywhere. Which is not to say that those markets had regained much of
their former buoyancy. In America, where propaganda had been similarly
extravagant, total sales increased in number between 1937 and 1939 from
103,000 to 111,000, but declined in value from $20 million to $18 million.
In England there was talk again of the piano's declining popularity, with
blame attached to the various influences already discussed, plus some new
culprits: piano accordions, a decline in domestic hospitality and the lack
of music playable by amateurs.[87] In the trade papers' anxiety to note and

encourage every hopeful sign there is a hint of desperation. Nothing was too trivial to escape notice: a businessman who included a picture of a girl at the piano in his firm's calendar received congratulations from *The Pianomaker*'s editor for 'giving the piano a boost'.[88]

Good instruments were still being made. Indeed, some pianists regard the 1930s as the last golden age, when many skilled craftsmen still remained in an industry which was no longer able to attract or train enough men of similar quality to guarantee the continuance of such standards. In England there were two newcomers to the ranks of serious piano makers: Welmar began in 1934 when Blüthner's former London agents started to manufacture on their own account. A director of the new firm had been apprenticed at Blüthner, and long association with the highest standards encouraged a respect for craftsmanship and music which rapidly earned Welmar a reputation for quality. No such advantages accrued to the other newcomer, who was to become one of the most remarkable figures in the history of English piano making. Alfred Knight (1898–1974) was educated at a central school, apprenticed at Hicks and, after working with Squire and Longson, started a business under his own name in 1935. The qualities of the man and his instruments soon became evident from his patents and advertisements. The former are for sensible improvements in action and soundboard,[89] the latter are unpretentious and unfanciful, claiming merely good sustained tone and sound workmanship. By 1938 he was making over 800 pianos a year. Apart from an unsuccessful baby grand which was soon withdrawn, these were mainly small but not minuscule uprights whose modern appearance required little compromise with good technology. A large (4 ft 3 in.) upright selling at ninety guineas is further proof of Knight's ambitions.[90]

We have already referred to the BBC's difficulties with influential musicians who, as its historian records, tended to 'pursue sectional interests' and to be 'more cautious and protectionist in their outlook than the BBC's own Music Department'.[91] It was therefore inevitable that the Corporation's selection of foreign pianos should come under attack, for coveted business and prestige were at stake. In fact, the procedure for selecting pianos for broadcasting, at a series of tests conducted in 1936, could hardly have been more thorough and fair. The experience of juries at international exhibitions had demonstrated how difficult it was to appraise and grade instruments objectively, apart from questions of mere mechanical efficiency. Judgment of quality, particularly of 'tone', is inevitably affected by preconceptions, prejudices and myth. At the BBC tests, here was a genuine attempt to neutralize these influences: any maker was free to submit instruments which were played and judged under conditions of strict anonymity. The panel included academic musicians and the pianist Frank Merrick, and the Piano Manufacturers' Association was invited to send a 'referee and observer'. Three categories of grand piano were judged: instruments at least nine feet in length, those between seven feet six inches and nine feet, and small grands over six feet. Bösendorfer was selected in the first and third categories, and Steinway and Challen in the second. Contracts were awarded to these makers, dependent upon future good service under heavy wear. There were protests through the BBC's Musical Advisory Committee led, ironically, by Sir Landon Ronald, who had once experienced similar pressures (p. 152). *The Pianomaker*, of course, found the decisions 'worse than deplorable. Art for Art's sake . . . is just sheer sophistry'.[92]

Chapter 11

Conclusion

The Second World War was less disruptive to piano making than the first because there was less to disrupt. Some factories were destroyed in air raids, including Blüthner's, and some firms were forced out of business by shortage of men and materials. But many small or weak makers had been eliminated during the depression, and further concentration through market forces or government decree merely continued an existing trend. In Britain, the most important difference was that the industry no longer depended upon foreign components, which again eased adjustment to wartime conditions. Production was diminished, of course, and standards tended to decline, which disturbed musicians but had little effect on a general public for whom pianos no longer occupied a central place in expenditure and aspiration. Occasional incidents, such as the purchase of a second-hand instrument in which the action's tapes had been replaced by elastic bands,[1] were illustrative of a sellers' market, but people were not sufficiently eager to buy for a 'munition workers' scandal to develop comparable to that of 1915–19.[2]

Post-war austerity dictated a continuation of the piano shortage. Exports were encouraged at the cost of the home market where, until 1950, pianos were subject to a hundred per cent luxury tax. Britain then entered a period of rising incomes and full employment: during the subsequent decade the standard of living rose faster than at any other time in the twentieth century. The removal of the luxury tax, and the release of pent-up demand for instruments after more than a decade of acute shortage, therefore ensured a buoyant market. It was at this stage that Knight moved firmly into leadership of the industry, opening a new factory in Loughton, Essex, and expanding production to nearly 2,000 pianos a year by the mid-fifties. Wartime advances in machine technology and materials were embodied in his instruments. New plastics were utilized to strengthen moving parts and to provide an acceptable substitute for ivory in covering keys—a development which earlier use of celluloid had failed to accomplish. New adhesives replaced glue, speeding up assembly, allowing greater use of laminates and increasing the instrument's resistance to central heating. Above all, the designs were excellently conceived and executed, so that Knight's became the first English pianos in a century to win international acclaim. The 1967 American consumers' report placed the larger Knight uprights in its first 'recommended' category, describing them as 'brilliant . . . equal in tone quality to a small grand'.[3] Commercial success accompanied prestige: by 1968 total sales approached £300,000, nearly half of which were exported. The only limitation on Alfred Knight's burgeoning enterprise was his refusal to woo the concert platform. His pianos were unique in acquiring a world-wide reputation without this and his decision was doubtless soundly based, but one cannot avoid a touch of regret that he died without trying for the highest accolade. A similar prosperity was enjoyed throughout the English piano industry. In 1972, production reached a post-war peak of 19,000 instruments; slightly lower than West Germany's output—and approximately seven per cent of Japan's.

We now arrive at the most significant development in modern piano history. The speed of Japan's emergence is at first sight astonishing: in 1953 total output was less than 10,000 instruments; within a decade it increased tenfold and in 1969 Japan became the largest piano manufacturing country in the world with an output of 257,000 instruments, some 35,000 more than the United States. This predominance was based, however, upon much longer experience than is generally appreciated. The two leading firms, Yamaha and Kawai, were founded respectively in 1887 and 1925, while Japanese interest in western music, as in other aspects of 'modernization', dates back to the Meiji restoration of 1868. It was introduced through the Church, the military band—a navy band performed at the opening of the first railway in 1872—and, most significantly, through the state schools. The government's curriculum for training teachers, established in 1880, included lessons in piano, organ and violin as well as in traditional instruments. Indeed, students who specialized in piano tended particularly to go into the state schools and 'exerted a powerful influence on the musical habits of young Japanese'.[4]

The evolution of Japanese piano making is to be understood against this background. Its history has not yet been written from indigenous sources, but an outline can be perceived from sporadic comments in the trade press. We have already recorded the appearance of a square piano at the 1878 Exhibition (p. 67) and some early American comments on Japanese manufacture and inquisitiveness (p. 142). Western reactions tended to alternate between ridicule and apprehension. In 1885, an English correspondent in Yokohama disparaged Japanese self confidence and assured his readers that 'these people know absolutely nothing of music'.[5] Five years later Americans were informed that although Japanese trade would 'never compare with that of America or any European nation' there would eventually be 'quite a demand for foreign instruments' and Japan would produce 'some of the finest musicians in the world'.[6] In 1895 Algernon Rose, whose views on Australia have previously been noted (p. 87), alleged that Japanese girls were 'indifferently taught the piano in mission schools and forget it when they leave, such an instrument being beyond the means of their parents to buy. The beloved samisen is more to their taste'.[7] A letter to the *American Art Journal* warned that cheap Japanese bicycles 'of superior material and workmanship', which were already being imported, would soon be followed by harmoniums and pianos. But a leading article entitled 'Imitative Artisans' was confident that imitation 'has never risen and . . . never can rise to the high level of the original'.[8] *Presto*, investigating an American harmonium manufacturer's loss of Japanese sales to a local firm, agreed that fears were exaggerated: 'There is little likelihood that the Japanese will ever become competitors in the piano industry.'[9] The import of actions into Japan was noticed in 1899 without alarm,[10] and in 1900 Shinkichi Matsumoto was acclaimed as the pioneer of Japanese piano manufacture. Starting as the country's first tuner, he had made a few harmoniums and pianos but, realizing his lack of experience, he visited several American factories and trained with Bradbury, whose manager produced a glowing testimonial to his 'discipline, eagerness and endurance'.[11]

The first Japanese pianos to appear abroad were summarily dismissed: 'either assembled from imported parts or simply rehashed imported crocks with an extra coat of varnish'.[12] But by 1906 *Presto* had shifted ground sufficiently to admit the possible emergence, some time in the future, of 'formidable rivals',[13] and the *Zeitschrift für Instrumentenbau* reported that competitive instruments were already appearing in India, Australia and the Philippines.[14] The English *Musical News* was more confident: 'It is inconceivable, of course, that the English, German and French firms will be affected at home. No sane European would be likely, except for the novelty of the thing, to purchase an experimental instrument from far off Japan.' In any case, the instruments would probably fall apart and were fit only for such customers as 'Coreans' who required them for show.[15] The *Musical Opinion* was alarmed but vague, repeating rumours 'from a German source' that Japan was 'preparing a large and comprehensive piano industry'.[16] These views were expressed in 1907 which was a boom year for alarmist talk of the 'yellow peril', since Japan's defeat of Russia was alleged to have encouraged 'exotic and yellow races' to welcome a new leader. Thus, argued *Presto*, their pianos could command prices disproportionate to their deficiencies'.[17] The dilemma of a newcomer to international trade was manifest: high prices were 'disproportionate', low prices constituted 'dumping'. The American Consul in Shanghai, where pianos were also being assembled in a factory established in 1896 and employing sixty Chinese workers, was more generous: several 'well equipped factories' in Japan, managed by men trained in America, were producing 'handsome pianos' at about half the price of American instruments.[18]

Information was becoming more specific. The German Consul General in Yokohama reported in 1910 that Yamaha employed 800 hands to make harmoniums and several hundred pianos, including a few small grands 'following the Steinway model'.'[19] An American article described two factories in 1911: Nishikawa and Son (the latter was apprenticed with Estey in New York) who made 200 pianos a year, 1,300 harmoniums and several hundred violins; Yamaha were said to be producing 600 pianos, 8,000 harmoniums and 13,000 violins annually. Both firms made complete instruments, importing only strings, leather and felt.[20] In 1916, Professor Shoji Iwanoto of the Tokyo Imperial Musical Academy added further details: Japanese pianos had replaced foreign instruments in the schools soon after the turn of the century and were now exported for the same purpose to China, India, Siam and Australia, at an average retail price of twenty-five dollars. High quality German pianos were still imported in large quantities.[21]

Admonition and abuse continued to appear sporadically in the trade press throughout the 1920s and thirties, conveying a general impression that Japanese pianos were improving, assisted by Germany's difficulties, with the government taking a direct interest in the quality of exports, and that an expanding home market was providing the essential base for production.[22] Increasing respect is apparent in the few reports which reflect direct experience. Thus, in 1939, an Australian trader described a visit to Yamaha's factory, 'so comprehensive as to include every process for the casting of frames onwards' and the manufacture of 'accordions, harmoniums and western-style furniture'. [23]

This mosaic of assorted facts and opinions suggests that some of the leading features of Japanese piano making had emerged long before the efflorescence of the 1960s. Production was based largely on the home market—even the huge exports of modern times account for less than twelve per cent of total output—and was intimately connected with education. This practice continues today in, for example, the 6,000 Yamaha 'music schoolrooms' throughout Japan.[24] 'Imitation', a sincere and re-warding flattery, began with the ancient tradition of the craftsman's *wanderjahre*, but Japanese manufacturers rapidly emancipated themselves from subservience to foreign components and expertise. For concert work, independence came more slowly: a photograph of the Japan

Philharmonic Orchestra dating from about 1926 prominently displays a Bechstein piano, although a 1911 report specifically refers to Japanese 'grands, semi and baby grands'. [25] In more recent years, of course, both Yamaha and Kawai concert grands have been played by the world's leading pianists.

A final unique feature of Japanese piano manufacture is the size of firms and the extent of product diversity. Yamaha's recent annual production of some 200,000 pianos is by far the largest in the history of the industry, while its variety of products gives resilience and flexibility to an industry notoriously subject to cyclical fluctuations in demand. Although no detailed figures are available, productivity is obviously high and this, rather than low wages or inferior materials, explains the low level of prices. Belief that mass production, or association with boats and motor cycles, must sully the pristine quality of musical instruments, is mere superstition. Japanese methods are a logical extension of the 'American system' which, it will be recalled, once came under similar attack. Few disinterested observers question the quality of Japanese pianos, particularly the larger uprights and grands (above six feet), in terms of mechanism and robustness. About 'tone' there will always be disagreement among discerning musicians once a certain standard has been reached. The American consumer report of 1967 reached similar conclusions, praising design, workmanship and 'outstanding quality in relation to price'. [26]

☙❧☙❧☙❧☙

What is the piano's status at present? The figures in Appendix II suggest a surprising answer. By 1970, world production, including an estimate for smaller manufacturing countries not listed in the table, was over 750,000 instruments, at least 100,000 more than in the years of the piano's supremacy before the First World War. This apparently remarkable fact is less impressive, however, if we remember the enormous growth in population, incomes and consumption which the developed world has experienced since 1914. For the output of pianos to increase by twenty per cent in sixty years is a small achievement in comparison with the performance of virtually any other product which has continued to attract consumers. Moreover, the most rapid growth occured during the 1960s, due in some measure to pent up demand after decades of shortages. The continuation of this trend would require a considerable extension of the market and an industry capable of supplying good pianos at competitive prices. At this point, generalization tends to break down because economic, social and musical conditions vary enormously between the piano manufacturing countries. Russian expansion has been almost as remarkable as Japan's— a tenfold increase between 1953 and 1970. In both countries the demand for pianos reflects improved living standards, an insatiable thirst for music which is stimulated by consistent education, and perhaps by 'Victorian' patterns of social aspiration.

In Europe and America, the household god was dethroned at least forty years ago and subsequent attempts at resurrection have met with only limited success, despite wishful assurances that 'the piano is coming back'.[27] Old social habits, like pianos, are slow to die. In 1937, the winner of an English Sunday paper's competition for the best account of obsolescent customs listed top hats, church going and playing the piano.[28] Yet twenty years later, a sociologist discovered that half the working class parlours he investigated contained pianos. New householders were admittedly replacing them with tiled fireplaces, which sometimes cost the equivalent of one year's rent, but he believed that this was because modern instruments were not then available. The main requirements of a new home, he concluded, were that 'it should conform to the approved social norms'.[29] A few years later both fireplaces and pianos were evicted by television, transforming society's leisure habits, and today the symbolism of status has been diffused over a wide range of consumer goods with which the piano has to compete.

Its ability to do so has been greatly weakened by mounting costs of purchase and servicing. A good upright costs nearly £1,000 in England, and first class instruments are much more expensive. This represents a serious fall in the consumer's 'piano purchasing power' (compare the discussion on pp. 41 and 107) and is in striking contrast to what has happened to the real cost of other manufactured goods despite inflation. (Gramophone records, to take a relevant example, have improved in quality and fallen in price.) Tuning and repairs are also expensive and often inadequate. Even at public concerts there are occasional signs of falling standards, which probably arise less from intrinsic deficiencies in the instruments concerned than from a lack of skilled finishers and tuners to maintain them in excellent playing condition: the finest pianos will only play and sound as well as their last 'service' permits. The fact that prices have doubled in recent years is not solely a result of scarce labour. Productivity is low—at least outside Japan piano making remains a labour-intensive industry—and profits have probably not been much affected by competition. The abolition of resale price maintenance, which has greatly benefited purchasers of other consumer durables, appears to have left the piano trade unscathed. If the worst excesses of mid-Victorian marketing have been curbed—although there are occasional examples of ancient rackets—the consumer in no way enjoys those advantages of competition which accrued to his Edwardian predecessors.

But in the last analysis the piano's status depends upon what is happening to music, and here it is difficult to reach a balanced judgment. There are abundant signs of vitality, particularly in England, where musical standards have risen immeasurably since the 1920s, and the piano has benefited from this. It has never been better played or, to be more precise, has never been so well played by so many professionals. Schnabel, Horowitz and Tatum have been succeeded by Brendel, Ashkenazy and Peterson, who reach a far greater audience through records, radio, and occasionally television. The *conservatoires* produce an endless stream of graduates whose virtuosity and range of repertoire (as displayed at international competitions, which are another recent innovation) would shame an earlier generation. More pianists can play Balakierev's 'Islamey' than in the composer's lifetime, and there are more good performances of the Mozart concertos and Schubert sonatas than ever in the past. Fewer amateurs learn the piano but they are better taught, thanks to more qualified teachers and the exertions of such institutions as the Associated Board. Moreover, their repertoire is more likely to reflect a broader musical culture, thanks to the influence of records and the waning but still beneficent influence of broadcasting. Many schools are equipped with adequate instruments, and some attempt to inculcate an appreciation of music which rises above commercial pop.

Yet doubts remain. One is expressed by the distinguished publisher Ernest Roth, who believes that domestic music making was defeated not by mechanical reproduction but by changes in 'music itself'. Amateurs who had coped with the increasing difficulty of nineteenth century music were finally vanquished by the 1920s.[30] Even professionals were nonplussed. The piano is 'no longer a *sine qua non* of musical existence' asserts an enthusiast for contemporary compositions, who invokes their 'confusion, excitement and endless variety'.[31] Most pianists and music lovers have primarily experienced the first of these emotions. The piano is merely one casualty in 'the agony of modern music',[32] displaying open wounds at the hands of Cage and his followers and gaining few advocates among serious modern composers. It is a commonplace that pianists subsist on an inexhaustible but dying repertoire.

Nor is this the sole reason for disquiet. In 1955, Arthur Loesser was sanguine because he considered that 'high adventures' were less important to the piano's future than the fact that it was still at the centre of popular music.[33] This is no longer the case. The rise of teen-age culture and electronic noise has not merely debased popular music from the heights of Gershwin, Porter and Kern, but has shifted the piano to at best a peripheral role. Talent and technique have retreated to the control room, charisma resides in the untutored, for whom pelvic gyrations and a few strummed chords suffice. The immediate effects are an erosion of that rock-bottom demand for pianos which Strohmenger described in 1932 (p. 188): 'discos' and pop groups replace dance bands and jazz musicians; hotels and halls need only electric plugs and spare fuses. The indirect effects are more obscure. But if culture heroes sell pianos then the descent from Anton Rubinstein to Led Zeppelin is not without significance for the trade. The piano is not doomed, and its history contains enough premature obituaries to deter Cassandras. For musicians and musical people, it will survive through its marvellous repertoire and because it remains the master key to a vast literature. But a wider revival will require changes in culture and leisure habits of which, at present, there are few signs.

Appendix I

A List of Piano Makers since 1851

The following conventions have been adopted:

| 1861–1895 | = dates of establishment and closure. |

fl. 1861–*fl.* 1895 = firm existed in 1861 but may have begun at an earlier date; closed some time after 1895.

1861–1926 *et fl.* = original firm ceased business in 1926, then rose phoenix-like from the flames. Since old names were considered valuable this practice was common but is obviously misleading as to longevity. Any classification will have an arbitrary element, but this represents an attempt to depict a firm's genuine life-span. For information before 1851 see R. Harding, op. cit., Appendix G.

Piano makers since 1851

United Kingdom (LONDON unless otherwise indicated)

Abbott, J. H. *fl.* 1900
Acourckia Piano Co. 1924–1929
Adam, J. *fl.* 1862
Adams, H. D. *fl.* 1862
Adamson, G. F. *c.* 1916–1929
Adlam, J.
Aeolian Co. 1917–1939 (*see* Orchestrelle)
Agate & Pritchard. *fl.* 1880
Ajello, G. 1862–*c.* 1890
Alberg.
Albion. 1871–*c.* 1910
Alberti. 1896
Aldrich, R. *fl.* 1862
Alexander & Ward (BIRMINGHAM). *fl.* 1900
Allen, A. *c.* 1916
Allen, F. *c.* 1880–1894
Allen & Caunter.
Allen & Taylor. *c.* 1880–*c.* 1890
Allison & Allison. 1837–1848
Allison, R. 1850–1910
Allison Ps. 1911–1929
Ambridge, H. 1890–1918
Anderson, W. *fl.* 1862
Angelus.

Anola Piano Co. –1928
Anglo-German Piano Co. *c.* 1900 (later W. A. Green)
Apollo Player & Piano Co. 1922–1925
Armitages & Tanfield (BRADFORD). *fl.* 1850
Armstrong & Sheppard. *fl.* 1930
Arnall, H. B. *fl.* 1900
Arnold, J. 1879. *fl.* 1902
Arnsby, F. *fl.* 1916
Ascherberg, G. –1883
Ascherberg, Hopwood & Crew. *fl.* 1916
Ashton, J. *fl.* 1908
Associated Piano Co. 1927–
Avill, W. S. *fl.* 1862
Avill & Smart *c.* 1820–*c.* 1900

Bachan, J. *fl.* 1862
Bacon, J. 1847–1869
Bagnall, J. 1862
Bailey, C. R. 1874–1891
Ballinghall, J. 1847–1869
Bannister. *fl.* 1933
Bansall. 1883–*fl.* 1938
Barber, J. 1892–*fl.* 1908

Barker, J. *fl.* 1903
Barnadel. *fl.* 1840–*fl.* 1860
Barnem, R. *fl.* 1916
Barnes & Mullins. *fl.* 1916
Barnett, S. 1832–*fl.* 1910
Barrat, J. 1840–1887
Barratt & Robinson. 1877–
Bartholomew & Earl. *fl.* 1900
Bateman, A. *fl.* 1862
Bates, T. *fl.* 1862
Bath, M. *fl.* 1862
Batsford, G. & H. *fl.* 1925
Battershall, W. *fl.* 1903
Beadle & Langbein. *fl.* 1903–*fl.* 1921
Beckhardt. *fl.* 1910
Begg, C. (ABERDEEN). 1849–1861
Bell. 1899–1921
Belmont. *fl.* 1916–*fl.* 1926
Benthin, T. *fl.* 1862
Bentley (WOODCHESTER). 1906 *et fl.*
Berry, N. 1866–
Binckes, L. 1835–1866
Bishop, A. *fl.* 1903
Bishop, E. *c.* 1870–1900
Bishop, J. 1877–*fl.* 1903
Bishop, R. C. *fl.* 1933
Blackall, C. J. *fl.* 1862
Blackman, J. *fl.* 1862
Blake, W. *fl.* 1862
Blankenstein. *fl.* 1909
Blazdell, A. *fl.* 1862
Bochenek, Z. 1914–1923
Böhmer, H. B. *fl.* 1880
Bourlet, W. S. *fl.* 1880
Boyd. *fl.* 1916–1927
Brasted, H. & R. 1870 *et fl.*
Brewer, S. *fl.* 1880
Bridgeport. 1878–*fl.* 1916
Brinsmead, E. G. S. *fl.* 1903–*fl.* 1916
Brinsmead, H. 1839–1880
Brinsmead, J. 1837–1920
Brinsmead, S. 1920
British Piano Co. *fl.* 1903–*fl.* 1911
British Piano Manufacturing Co. 1887–
    1924
British Woodcraft. *fl.* 1934
Broadwood, J. 1795 *et fl.*
Broadwood White. 1879–1915
Brock, A. J. 1894–1919
Brock, B. 1890–*fl.* 1910
Brock & Vincent. 1897–1911
Brockbank, J. 1841–1874
Brockbank, W. C. *fl.* 1882
Brockley, G. 1847–1862
Brooks, R. (SHEFFIELD). *fl.* 1878

Brown, J. *fl.* 1862
Brown, P. 1846–1868
Browne, Justin. 1866–1909
Browning. *fl.* 1862
Bruce, F. *fl.* 1924–1927
Bryson, T. 1849–1885
Buchan, T. 1820–1866
Buckland, G. A. *fl.* 1920
Bull, W. H. *fl.* 1862
Bunting, J. 1840–1883
Burkitt & Lawrence. 1924–1928
Burling. 1857–1894
Burling & Mansfield. 1881–1933
Button, E. *fl.* 1862
Byers. *fl.* 1920
Byers, W. C. 1896–1924

Cadby, C. 1839–1885
Calenberg & Vampel. *fl.* 1882
Campbell, P. *fl.* 1862
Caperoe & Hastelow. 1851–1894
Capra, Rissone, & Detoma. *fl.* 1881
Care, W. H. *fl.* 1881
Castle, G. (LOUGHBOROUGH). *c.* 1890
Cathie, J. 1851–1852
Challen. 1838–1926 *et fl.*
Challenger, G. 1855–1882
Chalton. *fl.* 1922–*fl.* 1926
Chandos. 1923–1927
Chaple, C. *fl.* 1862
Chapman & Chapman. 1899–*fl.* 1903
Chappell. 1811 *et fl.*
Chard, E. *fl.* 1862
Chepstow. 1919–1930
Chesterman, C. *fl.* 1862
Child, D. *fl.* 1862
Child, E. *fl.* 1903
Chisholm, W. J. 1923–1924
Clark & Boothby. 1839–1856
Clark, A. 1892. 1901–1924
Clarke, R. 1851–1858
Cocks, H. *fl.* 1862
Cocks, R. 1823–*fl.* 1883
Cohen, P. 1893–*fl.* 1909
Cole, R. *fl.* 1903
Cole, T. *fl.* 1862
Collman, L. W. *fl.* 1876
Collard. 1832–1918
Collings, F. 1919–1921
Collins. *fl.* 1903
Cons & Cons. 1815–*fl.* 1903
Cook, R. *fl.* 1862
Coombe, C. 1839–1854
Cooper, J. 1850–1866
Cooper, T. 1844–1893

Cooper-Southam. *fl.* 1918–*fl.* 1932
Cotsford, E. *fl.* 1862
Cottam, H. (RAVENSTHORPE). 1918
Coventry & Hollier. 1840–1852
Cowley, J. (HULL). *fl.* 1885
Crabb, F. *fl.* 1903
Cramer, J. B. 1824–1960
Cramer, Beale & Wood. *fl.* 1862
Creber, R. 1840–1863
Creber, W. 1842–1882
Croft, B. *fl.* 1862
Crosswell, J. *fl.* 1862
Crowley, J. (WATFORD). 1912–*fl.* 1922

Dainty & Harrison. 1843–1871
Dale, D. 1850–1874
D'Almaine. *fl.* 1862–*c.* 1874
Danemann. 1893 *et fl.*
Darnton, W. 1845–1858
Darter, G. 1846–1858
Davies, W. H. (LIVERPOOL). *fl.* 1881
Dawkins, T. *fl.* 1916
Day, A. 1913–
Deacock, T. 1841–1860
Deardon & Wood. –1903
Denham, C. *fl.* 1903
Dicks. *fl.* 1871
Dixon, H. *fl.* 1903
Dobson. *fl.* 1898
Dodson, W. 1867–*fl.* 1903
Douse, T. *fl.* 1862
Drake, H. (BOURNEMOUTH). 1919–1927
Drake, J. *fl.* 1862
Drake & Skerrat. (BOURNEMOUTH). 1916–1927
Dreaper, W. & G. (LIVERPOOL). *fl.* 1878 *fl.* 1884
Dreher, C. 1849–1858
Ducat, Wilmot. 1920
Duckson & Pinker (le Bath). 1848–1960
Duff & Hodgson. 1843–1860
Dunckley, W. 1865–*fl.* 1903
Dunmo, Ellis & Hill, 1890–*fl.* 1903

Eason, A. 1864–1894
Eastman, J. *fl.* 1923–*fl.* 1934
Eavestaff, W. *fl.* 1862
Eavestaff, W. G. 1862–1925
Ebblewhite, J. *fl.* 1862
Edwards, A. *fl.* 1903
Edwards, R. 1844–1889
Edwards & Button. *fl.* 1903
Ekstedt, M. 1835–1883
Ellis, J. 1888–*fl.* 1903

Elman. *fl.* 1903
Empire. 1892–*fl.* 1903
England. 1926–1928
English (Noble & Hall). 1922–1927
Ennever, W. 1848–*fl.* 1903
Erard, S. & P. 1786–1890
Esdaile, J. *fl.* 1887
Eungblut. 1865–1933
Evans, H. (BLOCKLEY). 1857–*fl.* 1903
Evestaff, W. 1838–1874

Fabian, J. *fl.* 1862
Fairchild, J. 1846–1852
Fancourt. *fl.* 1862
Feord, G. *c.* 1890–*fl.* 1903
Ferdinand, G. *fl.* 1862
Fitzsimmons, R. 1879–*fl.* 1903
Fitzsimmons & Sharpe. *fl.* 1884
Fleming & Barker. *fl.* 1909
Forrester, J. 1912–1932
Forster, J. *fl.* 1862
Fosh. *fl.* 1921
Foster, G. *fl.* 1903–1924
Foulston, A. (BIRMINGHAM). 1905–1924
Foxton, W. ('Premier' and 'Hertman'). 1922–1928
Fricker & Chudleigh. *fl.* 1862
Frood, J. *fl.* 1862

Gange, G. 1833–1887
Gautier, J. 1866–*fl.* 1903
Geary, J. *fl.* 1862
Geaussent, E. *fl.* 1862
George, L. *fl.* 1862
Gibbs, J. 1835–1871
Gilbert, T. 1880–*fl.* 1927
Gladman (STROUD) ('Steindl'). *fl.* 1912
Godfrey, H. *fl.* 1882
Gonin, L. *fl.* 1862
Goodburn & Rooke. –1881
Gorden, D. *fl.* 1862
Gough (HULL). 1856–1896
Goulden & Wind (ASHFORD). 1891–*fl.* 1893
Graddon, M. 1847–1855
Graham, W. *c.* 1880–*fl.* 1908
Grantone. *fl.* 1903
Green, W. 1908–*fl.* 1927 ('Wagmar')
Green & Savage. 1876–*fl.* 1903
Grice, C. *fl.* 1862
Grogan, Fairbanks. *fl.* 1903
Grover. 1830–1923
Groves & Deare. 1879–*fl.* 1922
Gunther, H. 1819–1878

Haig, J. 1842–1854
Halley, J. 1845–1854
Hammond, W. 1842–1880
Hampton, C. *fl.* 1862–*fl.* 1879
Handford, W. 1847–1854
Hannington, A. *fl.* 1903
Hardcastle, J. *fl.* 1903
Hardie, W. 1843–1857
Hardy, H. *fl.* 1888
Harland, A. 1879–*fl.* 1903
Harold. 1909–1922
Harold & Denson. 1883–*fl.* 1903
Harper, T. 1880–1925
Harper, W. 1834–1887
Harris, J. *fl.* 1862
Harrison, F. 1887–*fl.* 1903
Harrison, J. 1850–1864
Harrison, T. 1890–*fl.* 1903
Hart, J. 1838–1858
Hartley, S. (HALIFAX). 1857–*fl.* 1903
Harwar, J. 1839–1854
Hastelow, H. *fl.* 1862
Hattersley, W. 1845–1857
Hawkesley, J. *fl.* 1862
Hawkins, R. 1879–1925
Hayes. 1927–1930
Healey & Richards. 1886–*fl.* 1908
Heath, A. –1928
Hemingway & Thomas. 1862–1903
  ('Reeve's Pianos')
Henderson, J. *fl.* 1862
'Hertman' (Foxton)
Hickey, T. *fl.* 1901–1922
Hickman, C. 1849–1865
Hicks, H. 1860–1913
Hill, R. 1847–1856
Hillier, E. 1855–*fl.* 1903
Hilton (LEEDS). *fl.* 1887–1916
Hoare, P. *fl.* 1881
Hodge, J. 1851–1852
Holcombe, P. *fl.* 1862
Holdernesse, C. 1851–1906
Holman, E. 1851–1874
Holman, J. *fl.* 1862
Holmes, J. 1850–*fl.* 1862
Hooker, W. *fl.* 1862
Homan, A. *fl.* 1923–1925
Hopkinson, J. 1835–1919
Horsfall. 1919–
Howard, C. 1840–
Howard, S. (MANCHESTER). *c.* 1888
Howett, T. *fl.* 1862
Hulbert, J. 1863–1894
Hulbert & Jones. 1884–*fl.* 1938
Hull, W. *fl.* 1862

Humphrey, J. *fl.* 1916
Humphreys, A. & E. 1883–1924
Hund, F. 1851–1880
Hunton, R. 1875–1890
Hunton & Crocker. *fl.* 1881
Hutchison, G. *fl.* 1862
Hutchinson, T. (CARDIFF) *fl.* 1893

Iliffe & Rintoul, 1859–*fl.* 1878
Imhof & Mukle. *fl.* 1862
Imperial Organ & Piano Co. ('Best
  Pianos'). *fl.* 1903–*fl.* 1928
Ingleton. *fl.* 1903
Ivory, H. *c.* 1860–1881

Jack, S. *fl.* 1883
Jackman, E. *fl.* 1862
Jackson, J. 1838–1854
Jackson, T. 1843–1878
Jackson & Paine. *fl.* 1862
Jacob, C. *fl.* 1922
Jacobs, H. 1844–1852
Jacobs, T. *fl.* 1862
James, H. 1878–*fl.* 1903
Jarrett & Goudge. 1871–*fl.* 1894
Jarvis, J. *fl.* 1862
Jenkins, W. 1835–1862
Jenman & Atkins. *fl.* 1862
Jenn. 1874–*fl.* 1903
Jewell, J. *fl.* 1862
Johnson, B. *fl.* 1862
Johnson, E. *fl.* 1903
Johnson, G. *fl.* 1862
Johnson, J. *fl.* 1862
Jones, J. 1846–1884

Kelly, C. *fl.* 1862–1863
Kelly & Lion. 1851–1855
Kemble. 1916 *et fl.*
Kemmler, Bénard & Co. *fl.* 1914
Kennay, J. 1840–1857
Kennt, H. *fl.* 1903
Keogh, F. 1870–*fl.* 1886
Kessels. *fl.* 1916–*fl.* 1924
Kilvert, J. *fl.* 1880
King & Adams. *fl.* 1862
King, 1899–*fl.* 1934
Kirkman. J. 1822–1896
Knapton. 1896–*fl.* 1903
Knapton & Vaney. 1894–*fl.* 1897
Knight. 1936–*et fl.*
Knoll, C. 1852–*fl.* 1862
Kohler. *fl.* 1864
Kohlson (Cole). 1928

Lacabra, J. 1845–*fl.* 1862
Lambert, F. 1881–1929
Lambert, W. *fl.* 1862
Lamert. *fl.* 1954–*fl.* 1957
Larkins, M. 1845–*fl.* 1903
Latham, J. 1850–1855
Laurence, A. (LEICESTER). *c.* 1864–1913
Lawler, L. ('Howard'). *fl.* 1923–*fl.* 1933
Lawrence, J. *fl.* 1862
Layton, E. 1850–*fl.* 1862
Leaman, F. 1851–1860
Legg, J. 1848–1887
Leswein. *fl.* 1939
Levesque, J. 1839–1875
Levesque, Edmondes. *fl.* 1856–*fl.* 1862
'Lion' (Shenstone). *fl.* 1903
Little, C. *fl.* 1862
Little, C. E. 1878–*fl.* 1909
Livie, R. *fl.* 1862
Livingstone & Cook. 1897
Llewellyn, E. *fl.* 1862
Locke (MANCHESTER). 1849–*fl.* 1880
Locke & Barker. *fl.* 1862
London Music Publishing Co. *fl.* 1887
London Piano Co. 1879–*fl.* 1913
London Piano & Organ Co. *fl.* 1903–*fl.* 1909
Longman & Bates. 1825–1862
Love, C. 1897–1926
Lovell, R. *fl.* 1862
Lucas & Pyne. 1860–*fl.* 1882
Luck, W. *fl.* 1885
Lucraft, G. 1911–1927
Luff, G. 1839–1862
Lyon, F. *fl.* 1862
Lyon, G. 1875–*fl.* 1903
Lyon & Duncan. 1812–1855

Machells (GLASGOW). *fl.* 1939
Macintosh, G. (DUBLIN). –1881
Mackie, R. 1848–1854
Madell, A. 1873–*fl.* 1881
Magnus, M. 1916–1928
Manktelow, J. 1841–1886
Manuel. *fl.* 1887
Marchant, W. *fl.* 1862
Marks, M. *fl.* 1862
Marr (ABERDEEN). 1847–*fl.* 1887
Marshall & Rose. 1907–1931
Matthews, J. 1839–1855
Matthews, S. *fl.* 1862
Matthews, W. 1845–1852
Maurice & Benedetto, *fl.* 1885

May, H. 1850–1862
McCulloch (BELFAST). *fl.* 1851
McVay, C. 1879–*fl.* 1916
Merrington, A. (SOUTHEND). 1920–1924
Merrington. *fl.* 1905–1937
Metzler, G. 1839–1880
Miall, J. 1851–1870
Middleton, J. *fl.* 1862
Middleton, R. *fl.* 1862
Milgrom, A. 1903–1933
Miller, J. *fl.* 1862
Mills, H. *fl.* 1862
Milward, J. 1924
Moggridge, F. 1882–*fl.* 1891
Monington, J. *fl.* 1862
Monington & Weston. 1858–*et fl.*
Monk & Schuppisser. 1887–*fl.* 1903
Montague. 1880–*fl.* 1936
Montrie, *fl.* 1878
Moore, J. 1839–1854
Moon (PLYMOUTH). *fl.* 1915
Morley, R. 1890. *et fl.*
Morley, W. *fl.* 1862
Morris, H. *fl.* 1903
Mott, J. 1820–1863
Moutrie, G. *fl.* 1862
Moutrie, W. 1851–1918
Muggeridge & Ulph. 1893–1897
Munnew, W. *fl.* 1862
Munt, W. 1873–1933
Murdoch, J. 1862–*fl.* 1903
Murphy, G. *fl.* 1855–*fl.* 1862
Murray, J. 1848–1856

Neumeyer. *fl.* 1883
Newman & Parkinson. *fl.* 1903
Newsome (RAVENSTHORPE). *fl.* 1913
Nichols-Richmond (EDINBURGH). *fl.* 1885
Nightingale, J. 1860–*fl.* 1903
Noble, J. 1825–*fl.* 1862
Noble & Hall. *fl.* 1916
Norman, J. *fl.* 1862
North London Piano Co. *fl.* 1903
Northfield, G. *fl.* 1862
Nutting & Addison. *c.* 1845–1866
Nutting & Normington. 1866–*fl.* 1877
Nutting & Wood, 1843–1854

Oakey, H. 1839–*fl.* 1862
Oetzmann. *fl.* 1862
Oetzmann & Plumb. 1846–1928
Offer, J. *fl.* 1924
Offord, W. 1922–1930

Orchestrelle Co. (After 1917 Aeolian)
Orillion. *fl.* 1923–*fl.* 1926
Owen & Stodart. 1835–1867

Paget, T. 1849–1869
Pain, W. *fl.* 1862
'Palace' (SOUTHPORT). *fl.* 1884
Papps (PORTSMOUTH). *fl.* 1885–*fl.* 1924
Parker & Smith (PLYMOUTH). 1866–
fl. 1882
Payne, H. *fl.* 1851–*fl.* 1862
Payne, T. & G. 1892–*fl.* 1913
Peace, R. *c.* 1890
Peachey, G. *fl.* 1850–*fl.* 1862
Pearson, J. *fl.* 1862
Peele, T. *fl.* 1862
Penso, V. *fl.* 1903
Penton, C. *fl.* 1862
Peppercorn, W. *fl.* 1862
Perkin. 1888–
Perkins & Fielding. *c.* 1840–*fl.* 1862
'Phillips' (Allen). 1918–1926
Pickett, J. *fl.* 1862
Pike & Gradridge. *fl.* 1882
Pinnock, E. *fl.* 1862
Piper & Manton. *fl.* 1862
Pocock, J. 1848–1854
Pohlmann (HALIFAX). 1832–*fl.* 1881
Portman. *fl.* 1915
'Premier' (Foxton). 1922–1928
Priestley, J. 1857–1887
Prowse, T. 1845–1854
Pugh, J. *fl.* 1903
Pull & Field. *fl.* 1898–*fl.* 1903
Pyle, H. *fl.* 1924
Pyrke, C. 1895–*fl.* 1903

Rand, J. 1848–1855
Rayner & Allen. *fl.* 1903
'Realms'. *fl.* 1920
Redfern, J. *fl.* 1862
Reed, J. 1868–*fl.* 1903
Reave, W. 1881–*fl.* 1903
Regale, J. *fl.* 1924–*fl.* 1927
Regent Pneumatic. *fl.* 1919
Regester, H. 1909–1929
Regester & Fellowes. 1897–1905
Reid, J. 1848–1854
Renn, Honnan. *c.* 1920–*fl.* 1926
Rhodes, J. 1835–1870
Rhodes, M. *fl.* 1862
Richards, C. *fl.* 1862
Richmond, G. *fl.* 1862
Rintoul, J. 1880–1887
Robertson. *fl.* 1905

Robins, J. *fl.* 1862
Robinson, R. *fl.* 1862
Rodewell, R. *fl.* 1862
Rogers, D. *fl.* 1862
Rogers, G. 1858. *et fl.*
Rogers, S. *fl.* 1862
Rolfe, W. 1800–*fl.* 1883
Rowed, J. 1846–*fl.* 1862
'Royal'. *fl.* 1903
Rudall, Rose Cart. *fl.* 1862
Rudd, E. 1837–*fl.* 1903
Rushton, T. (GRIMSBY). 1898
Russell, G. 1842–1899
Rust, 1850–*fl.* 1862
Rust, R. *fl.* 1862

Saggs, J. *fl.* 1862
Salter, C. *fl.* 1862
Sames, W. (BIRMINGHAM). 1888–1926
Samuel, B. 1882–*fl.* 1912
Sanders, H. *fl.* 1880
Sanderson, J. *fl.* 1862
Sandon & Steedman. 1880–1895
Sayers, P. 1918–1929
Schreiber. 1877–*fl.* 1903
Schucht & Schonewald. 1856–*fl.* 1903
Schumann Piano Manufacturing Co.
fl. 1903
Schuppisser, A. 1852–1890
S.D.H. Pianoforte Manufacturing Co.
fl. 1923
Scipeo. 1881–1899
Scipeo, J. *fl.* 1862–1881
Scotcher, C. 1844–1871
Scotcher, T. *fl.* 1862
Seager. 1897–*fl.* 1903
Seager, H. (LIVERPOOL). 1866–1960
Seager, T. *fl.* 1862
Sebastik, G. 1920–1929
Seeley, R. *fl.* 1862
Segar, W. *fl.* 1862
Serquet, E. 1850–1860
Shand Piano Co. (WOODCHESTER)
Sharp, J. *fl.* 1862
Sharpe. *fl.* 1881
Shaw, R. 1852–*fl.* 1870
Shelford, E. *fl.* 1882
Shelford, T. –1903
Shenstone. 1899–*fl.* 1924
Shepherd, A. 1835–1871
Shepherd, J. *fl.* 1862
Shepperd & Wigget. 1919–1928
Shipman. 1887–*fl.* 1903
Silsby, T. 1899–1908
Simon, H. *fl.* 1908

Simpson, S. *fl.* 1862
Slater, R. *fl.* 1862
Smart, C. *fl.* 1883
Smith, G. F. *fl.* 1862
Smith, G. J. (BIRMINGHAM). 1885–*fl.* 1903
Smith, J. Muir. 1859–1890
Smith, P. *c.* 1870–*fl.* 1884
Smith, R. *fl.* 1862
Smith, W. *fl.* 1862
Smith & Jeffery. *fl.* 1903
Snell, H. *fl.* 1903–1924
Solomon, H. *fl.* 1862
Southam, C. *fl.* 1913–1918
Southwell, W. 1844–1857
Spademan, J. 1838–1869
Sparks, W. 1845–1891
Spencer, J. 1883–*fl.* 1903
Spencer Murdoch. *fl.* 1886–1953
Spiegl, M. 1920–1925
Spikins, J. *fl.* 1862
Spiller, Boult. *fl.* 1903
Sprague, W. 1847–1883
Squire, B. *fl.* 1881
Squire, H. *fl.* 1862
Squire, J. *fl.* 1862
Squire, W. 1835–1856
Squire & Longson. 1884–*fl.* 1903
Standard Pianoforte Manufacturing Co. (BIRMINGHAM). –1915
Statham, T. 1841–1866
Steers, E. *fl.* 1862
Steinmetz, F. *fl.* 1903
Stephen, J. *c.* 1872–1886
Stewart, J. *fl.* 1852–*fl.* 1862
Stickland, J. *fl.* 1903
Stiles, C. *fl.* 1862
Stodart, M. 1775–1862
Stokes & Holt (LEICESTER). *fl.* 1912–*fl.* 1916
Stratford, H. *fl.* 1862
Strohfeldt, E. *c.* 1892–
Strohmenger, J. 1835–1937
Strong, J. 1850–*fl.* 1880
Strong & Jackson. *c.* 1880–1927
'Stroud' (Gladman) (GLOUCESTER). 1906–1960
Sugden, L. 1835–1854
'Supertone' (LONG EATON). 1920–*fl.* 1933
Symons, S. *fl.* 1862

Taylor, A. 1890–*fl.* 1926
Taylor, C. *fl.* 1908
Taylor, J. *fl.* 1862

Tennessee Piano Co. (Ivory). *fl.* 1903
Theobolds, W. 1835–1854
Thomas, W. 1869–1894
Thomas & Rogers. *fl.* 1856
Thompson, C. *fl.* 1886
Thompson, H. *fl.* 1862
Thorp, J. *fl.* 1862
Tindall, G. 1850–1857
Tidder, W. *fl.* 1903
Tippins, W. *fl.* 1862
Titford, G. *fl.* 1862
Tolkein, H. 1845–1889
Tomkinson. *fl.* 1862
Tow. *c.* 1855–*fl.* 1862
Towns, T. *c.* 1839–1862
Transposing Pianoforte Co. *fl.* 1903
Trinder, W. *fl.* 1862
Tripp, W. *fl.* 1862
Turner, J. 1840–1860
Turner & Phillips (PLYMOUTH). *c.* 1902

Underhay & Lovendahl. *fl.* 1887
Upton & Gill (BRADFORD). *c.* 1907–*fl.* 1919

Vanckorden. *fl.* 1862
Vaney, L. *fl.* 1920
Van Gruisen (LIVERPOOL). 1845–1912
Veitch, A. 1845–1852
Venables, C. *fl.* 1862–*fl.* 1881
Vincent, T. 1894–*fl.* 1916

Waddington (YORK). 1896–*fl.* 1929
'Wagmar' (Green, W.). 1908–*fl.* 1927
Walker, R. *fl.* 1862
Wallis, J. 1848–1928
Walter, W. 1850–*fl.* 1903
Walters, W. *fl.* 1862
Ward, A. 1921–1925
Ward, H. 1848–1903
Warwick, J. *fl.* 1862–*fl.* 1882
Watkins, W. *fl.* 1862
'Weber' (Orchestrelle Co.). *fl.* 1916
Weekly & Box. *fl.* 1862
Welmar (Whelpdale-Maxwell). 1934 *et fl.*
Wernem, W. 1879–*fl.* 1903
Wesson, D. *fl.* 1862
West Green Piano Works. *fl.* 1903
Weston. *fl.* 1903
White, A. 1896–*fl.* 1916
White, T. 1895–*fl.* 1903
Whitebread & Payne. 1894–*fl.* 1903
Whitely, R. *fl.* 1903

Whittingham, W. 1885–1903
Wigget, J. *fl.* 1862
Wiggett, W. *fl.* 1862
Wilcocks, H. 1844–1869
Wilkie, W. 1851–1874
Willcocks, C. *fl.* 1903–*fl.* 1906
Williams, R. 1879–*fl.* 1903
Willson, W. 1862
Wilson, T. *fl.* 1862
Winbourne. *fl.* 1930
'Windover'. (Brit. P. Mfg. Co.)
Windus, J. *fl.* 1862
Witton. 1838–*fl.* 1918

Wonder Pianoforte Co. 1893–1908
Wood, J. *fl.* 1903
Wood, R. *fl.* 1903
Woolway, A. 1897–1900
Wornum, R. 1798–*fl.* 1878
Wright, W. 1879–*fl.* 1887
Wright, W. *fl.* 1892–*fl.* 1904
Wroot, J. *fl.* 1862
Wuest, T. 1842–1866

Yates, W. 1852–*fl.* 1903

Zender, S. *fl.* 1898 *et fl.*

France

Aucher. *fl.* 1820–*fl.* 1881
Aurand & Bohl. *fl.* 1830
Avisseau, E. *fl.* 1850

Baudet, H. 1876
Bernard, Champ. 1849–
Blondel, A. 1839–
Boisselot. 1844–*fl.* 1882
Bord, M. 1840–1919
Bucher. 1848–
Burgasser, L. 1846–*fl.* 1952

Caunt, Moritz-iser. 1863–*fl.* 1881
Champ, B. 1849–
Cocquet, L. 1865–

Debain. 1853–*fl.* 1881

Elcke. 1846–*fl.* 1960
Erard. 1785–1960

Focké. 1860–1910
Frantz, J. 1852

Gaveau, J. 1847–1960
Gouttière, E. 1846–
Guillot, A. *fl.* 1900–1938

Hamm. *fl.* 1915–*fl.* 1945
Hansen. 1873–*fl.* 1940
Herz, H. 1825–*fl.* 1930
Herz, P. *fl.* 1881

Klein, G. *fl.* 1875–*fl.* 1960
Klein, H. 1879–
Kriegelstein, C. 1831–*fl.* 1930

Labrousse. 1876–*fl.* 1960
Lafontaine, J. 1878–*fl.* 1889
Leguerinais. 1856–*fl.* 1940
Lorpheul. 1871–

Mag. *fl.* 1935–*fl.* 1940
Mangeot, E. 1859–*c.* 1888
Mussard, E. 1822–1910
Mustel. 1855–

Oury, A. 1860–*fl.* 1932

Pleyel. 1807–*fl.* 1960
Pruvost, H. 1850–

Roller & Blanchett. 1827–
Ruch, J. 1869–*fl.* 1930

Schotte. 1850–
Soufleto, C. *fl.* 1881
Staub, J. 1848–

Therson. *fl.* 1885–*fl.* 1940
Thibout, A. 1840–*fl.* 1891
Thomas & Avarsun. *fl.* 1840–*fl.* 1855

Van Overburg. *c.* 1850
Vuillemin-Didion. *fl.* 1846

Germany

Ackermann, F. 1882–
Adam, F. 1864–
Adam, G. 1828–1940
Andre, C. 1828–
Andre, J. 1837–
Angerhofer, H. 1869–1940

Arnold, H. 1830–
Arnold, K. 1830–
Ascherberg, E. *fl.* 1883

Baldner. 1872–
Baldur. 1872–

Barthol, R. 1871–*fl.* 1903
Bechstein, C. 1853 *et fl.*
Beckmann, W. 1806–
Behnken, N. 1873–
Berdux, V. 1871–*fl.* 1960
Berles, C. –1886
Berndt, T. 1837–
Beyer-Rahnefeld. 1852–*fl.* 1903
Biehl, J. 1868–
Biese, W. 1851–*fl.* 1960
Bing, F. *fl.* 1883
Blasendorff, C. 1898–
Blüthner, J. 1853 *et fl.*
Bock & Hinrichsen. 1869–
Boekh, H. 1866–
Böger, W. 1860–
Bogs & Voigt. 1905–
Bonecke, H. 1906–
Borkenhagen, M. 1892–
Brinkmann & Goebel, 1879–*fl.* 1960
Buschmann, G. 1805–

Concordia. 1869–*fl.* 1883
Crasselt & Rahse, 1881–

Dassell, A. 1859–*fl.* 1882
Deesz. J. 1820–
Dethleffs. 1874–*fl.* 1897
Döhnert. 1876–*fl.* 1945
Donadoni & Pohl. 1880–*fl.* 1903
Donath, M. 1882–
Dorner, F. 1830–1948
Dornheim, F. *fl.* 1903
Dreyer, M. 1896–*fl.* 1908
Dührkopf, C. *fl.* 1909
Duysen, J. 1859–*fl.* 1955

Ecke, K. 1843 *fl.* 1952
Eckermann, C. *fl.* 1881
Eigborn & Hoffmann. 1907–
Elias, E. 1875–
Engelmann & Günthermann. 1888–
   fl. 1903
Erbe, J. 1881–*fl.* 1904
'Eroica'. *fl.* 1903
Euphonie. 1906–
Euterpe. 1860–*fl.* 1960

Fahr, A. 1887–*fl.* 1953
Felschow, A. 1875
Fehn, A. 1900
Feurich, J. 1851–*fl.* 1960
Fiedler, G. 1871–*fl.* 1903
Finger, A. 1887–*fl.* 1960

Förster, A. 1859 *et fl.*
Förster, H. 1840–*fl.* 1903
Fortner, G. 1871–
Francke, A. 1865–*fl.* 1903
Freytag, A. 1889
Fuchs & Mohr. *fl.* 1938–*fl.* 1957

Gawenda, F. 1888–
Gebauer, G. 1819–
Gebauhr, C. 1834–*fl.* 1903
Geil, F. 1904–
Geissler, F. 1878–*fl.* 1903
Gerbstädt, O. 1888–*fl.* 1960
Gerhardt, T. *fl.* 1881
Gerold, F. 1875–
Gerstenberger, J. 1864–*fl.* 1881
Gertz, W. 1873–
Geyer, A. 1877–*fl.* 1903
Giese-Reinecke. 1888–
Glaser, F. *fl.* 1903
Glass, C. 1879–*fl.* 1900
Gleick, C. 1843–
Glück, C. 1843–
Goebel, W. *fl.* 1881
Görs & Kallmann. 1877–*fl.* 1960
Goetze, C. 1866–*fl.* 1903
Grabau, M. 1880–
Grand, A. 1869–*fl.* 1960
Grotrian-Steinweg. 1856 *et fl.*
Gruss. *fl.* 1873
Gschwind, I. 1858–
Guckel, O. *fl.* 1890–*fl.* 1945
Gude, M. 1886–
Gunther, C. 1819–*fl.* 1896
Gunther, O. 1880–

Haake, E. *fl.* 1881
Haake, K. 1836–
Haegele, H. 1846–*fl.* 1956
Hagspiel. 1851–*fl.* 1903
Hahmann, G. 1884–
Hain, S. 1892–*fl.* 1960
Hanck, J. 1865–
Hancke, C. 1890–
Hanne, P. 1861–
Hansen, J. 1838–
Hardt, C. 1855–*fl.* 1903
Hasche, W. 1914–*fl.* 1946
Hegeler & Ehlers. 1895–*fl.* 1903
Heidrich, H. 1881–
Heilbrunn, K. 1875–
Heiser, H. *fl.* 1883
Held, H. 1867–
Helmholz, F. 1851–
Hermann, A. 1835–*fl.* 1960

Heyl, G. 1828–*fl.* 1903
Hilger, E. *fl.* 1885–*fl.* 1900
Hilse, C. 1876–
Hilse, W. 1876–
Hinke, A. 1901–
Hintze, C. 1898–1911
Hofberg, M. 1892–1955
Hoffman, F. *fl.* 1881
Hoffmann & Kühne. 1899–1945
Hoffmann, W. 1888–*fl.* 1960
Hohne & Sell. 1885–*fl.* 1903
Hölling & Spangenburg. 1843–*fl.* 1903
Hoof, L. 1882–
Horn, A. 1905
Horugel, M. 1893–1952
Hundt, F. 1850–*fl.* 1887
Hupfer, R. 1874–*fl.* 1903
Hüttner, A. 1896–

Ibach, R. 1794–*fl.* 1960
Imhof & Muckle, 1848–
Irmler, J. 1818–1958

Jacob, A. 1862–*fl.* 1903
Jaschinsky, A. 1879–*fl.* 1903
Jehle. *fl.* 1950–*fl.* 1960

Kaim. 1819–1930
Kaim & Günther 1845–*fl.* 1883
Kanhäuser, E. 1844–*fl.* 1881
Kaps, E. 1858–1931
Karn, D. 1865–*fl.* 1903
Kemmler, C. –1914
Ketnath, F. 1836–
Kewitsch, J. 1878–*fl.* 1903
Klemm, R. *fl.* 1881–1883
Klimes, Schwitalla. 1905–
Klingmann, G. 1869–
Klusmann & Wenzel. *fl.* 1887
Knabe & Thal. *fl.* 1903
Knake. 1808–*fl.* 1903
Knauss, H. 1821–*fl.* 1886
Knöchel, A. 1876–
Koch, E. 1896–
Kohl, H. 1855–
Krause, H. 1860–
Krauss, C. 1868–
Krauss, E. 1870–*fl.* 1945
Kreugel, H. 1906–
Kreutzbach, J. 1874–*fl.* 1903
Kriebl, H. 1863–1934
Krietzsch, H. 1847–
Krumm, J. 1900–
Kuhla, F. 1872–*fl.* 1882

Kuhse, J. 1874–*fl.* 1903
Kulb, J. 1873–

Lammerhirt, E. 1880–
Laurinat. 1879–
Langfritz, C. 1889–*fl.* 1903
Lehmann, A. 1890–*fl.* 1903
Lehnhardt & Emmer. *fl.* 1903
Lenz, A. 1876–
Liedcke, W. 1872–
Liehr, F. 1871–*fl.* 1925
Lindholm, O. 1894–1954
Lindner, J. 1825–*fl.* 1882
Lipp, R. 1831–*fl.* 1960
List, E. 1888–
Lochow & Zimmermann. 1900–*fl.* 1903
Lubitz, H. 1875–

Maas, W. 1891–
Machalet, T. 1862–
Mädler, G. 1857–
Maetzke, E. 1862–
Mand, K. 1835–1928
Mann, T. 1836–*fl.* 1903
Mannborg. 1889–*fl.* 1961
Mannsfeldt & Notni. 1867–
Manthey, F. 1868–*fl.* 1960
Manthey, W. *fl.* 1882
Marquadt, O. 1905–
Mattaes, T. 1888–
Matthaes, C. 1883–
Matz, H. 1869–
Mayer, J. 1826–*fl.* 1903
Menzel, W. 1890–*fl.* 1903
Mentzler, W. 1890–
Merkel, W. 1845–*fl.* 1903
Meyer, R. 1871–*fl.* 1950
Mobes. 1869–
Möller, E. 1819–
Morenz, B. 1891–
Mörs, C. 1869–*fl.* 1937
Müller, C. 1877–
Müller, M. 1905–
Müller-Schiedmeyer. 1874–*fl.* 1942

Nagel, G. 1828–
Nesener & Segret. 1803–
Neufeind, R. 1888–
Neufeld, C. 1872–*fl.* 1881
Neugebauer, A. 1878–
Neuhaus, W. 1840–
Neumann, C. 1897–
Neumann, F. 1854–*fl.* 1912
Neumayer, F. 1861–*fl.* 1903

Neumeyer, E. 1905–
Neumeyer, M. 1906–
Neupert, J. 1868–*et fl.*
Nieber, A. 1885–*fl.* 1900
Niendorf. 1896–*fl.* 1960
Noeske. 1888–

Oehler. 1857–
Otto, C. 1866–*fl.* 1886

Pachmann. *fl.* 1904
Pepper, W. 1863–*fl.* 1957
Pfeiffer, C. 1862–*fl.* 1960
Phillip, G. 1872–*fl.* 1945
Phillips, J. 1877–
Prein, F. 1857–

Quandt, C. 1854–*fl.* 1948

Rachels, M. 1832–*fl.* 1957
Rene, C. *fl.* 1882
Renner, C. 1882–
Rheinische Pianofort Fabriken
    (Knauss. 1832; Kappler. 1911,
    Mand. 1835–)
Riese-Hallmann. 1919–*fl.* 1960
Rissmann, C. 1846–*fl.* 1903
Ritmüller, W. 1795–*fl.* 1961
Ritter, C. 1828–1934
Rohlfing. 1790–*fl.* 1942
Röhm, O. 1869–
Roloff. *fl.* 1855–*fl.* 1870
Römhildt, C. 1845 *fl.* 1925
Rönisch, C. 1845 *fl.* 1957
Rösener, F. 1839–
Rosenkrantz, E. 1797–*fl.* 1882
Rösler, G. 1868–*fl.* 1957
Roth & Junius. 1889–*fl.* 1960
Rubner, E. 1875–

Sauer, T. 1863–
Sauter, C. 1819–*fl.* 1960
Schake, H. *fl.* 1881
Schaaf, F. 1872–*fl.* 1903
Schaaf, H. 1932–1944
Scharf & Hauk. 1870–
Scheel. 1846–*fl.* 1882
Scheipe & Newman. 1897–
Schemelli, R. 1900–
Schiedmayer & Söhne. 1809–*fl.* 1952
Schiedmayer, J. 1853–*fl.* 1960
Schiemann & Madsen. 1870–
Schiller, J. 1884–*fl.* 1956
Schilling, F. 1871–*fl.* 1882
Schimmel, W. 1885–*fl.* 1961
Schleip, B. 1816–

Schmidt, C. *fl.* 1881
Schmidt, L. 1865–
Schmidt, P. 1876–*fl.* 1903
Schmidt, R. 1887–
Schneider, A. 1907–
Schnell, H. 1872–
Scholze. 1876–*fl.* 1957
Schönlein, E. 1895–
Schötz, H. 1907–
Schroeder, C. 1856–
Schroether, R. 1914–*fl.* 1930
Schubbe. 1894–
Schultz, H. *fl.* 1903
Schumann, C. 1857–
Schuppe & Newmann. 1897–
Schustering, C. 1869–
Schütze, H. 1877–
Schwechten, G. 1853–*fl.* 1960
Seiler, E. 1849–*fl.* 1960
Selinke & Sponnagel. 1866–*fl.* 1886
Siegel, R. 1849–*fl.* 1903
Simon, C. 1880–
Skibbe, M. 1905–
Soph, F. 1902–
Spaethe, W. 1859–*fl.* 1903
Spira, C. 1892–
Sponnagel, E. 1866–*fl.* 1903
Sprunk, F. 1839–
Stapel, G. 1848–*fl.* 1903
Steck. 1857–
Steinberg. 1908–
Steingraeber. 1852–*fl.* 1960
Steinmayer. *fl.* 1883
Steinway. 1880– *et fl.*
Steuer, W. 1894–
Stichel, F. 1877–*fl.* 1903
Stoessel, Gertler. 1880–
Strauss & Wiener. *fl.* 1882

Taubert, K. 1920–*fl.* 1952
Tempe, R. 1868–
Tetsch & May. 1867–
Thein, O. 1863–*fl.* 1960
Thürmer, F. 1835–*fl.* 1929
Tietze, R. 1890–
Trau. *fl.* 1881
Traugott. 1836–

Uebel & Lechtleitner. 1871–*fl.* 1960
Ulbrich, H. 1876–
Ulbrich, R. 1888–
Urbas, J. 1894–

Vierling, R. 1879–
Vogel, I. 1828–1883

213

Wagner, H. 1844–
Wahren, C. 1902–
Walsmann, M. *fl.* 1903
Weber, F. 1860–*fl.* 1905
Weber & Fuchs. 1905–
Weidig, G. 1890–
Weissbrod, R. 1884–*fl.* 1903
Welte, M. 1883–1930
Werner, E. *fl.* 1881
Werner, F. 1845–
Werner, P. 1810–*fl.* 1908
Westermeyer, E. 1863–*fl.* 1938
Westphall, R. 1894–

Wetzel, P. 1879–1952
Wiedenslaufer, T. 1860–1887
Winkelmann. 1908–
Wittenberg & Herman. 1900–
Wittig, E. 1863–
Wohler, A. 1885–
Wolffram, H. 1872–*fl.* 1960
Wolkenhauer, G. 1853–*fl.* 1903

Zahn, F. 1885–
Zeiter & Winkelmann. 1837–*fl.* 1903
Zierold, G. 1882–
Zimmermann. 1884–1926

Austria-Hungary

Albert, E. 1868–*fl.* 1918
Audreys, A. *fl.* 1919–*fl.* 1935

Baumbach, J. 1842–*fl.* 1959
Baroitius, K. 1898–
Belehradek, J. 1870–*fl.* 1915
Berger I. *fl.* 1900–*fl.* 1910
Bösendorfer, C. 1828–*et fl.*
Bremitz, E. 1874–*fl.* 1915

Cafol, A. *fl.* 1875–*fl.* 1885
Chmel. 1835–
Czapkas, J. 1842–*fl.* 1926

Dalibor. 1905–*fl.* 1958
Dehmal, K. 1888–
Dörr, K. 1817

Eder, A. 1848–
Ehrbar, F. 1857–*fl.* 1957

Fritz, J. 1801–
Fuchs, F. 1903–*fl.* 1925

Gossl, J. 1854–
Graf, C. *c.* 1810–1851

Hajack, F. *fl.* 1900–*fl.* 1915
Hamburger, K. 1874–*fl.* 1938
Havlicsek. *c.* 1895–
Heckenhast, G. 1865–
Heinisch, J. *fl.* 1920–*fl.* 1951
Heitzmann, O. 1839–*fl.* 1949
Hofbauer, G. 1850–
Hofmann, K. 1876–*fl.* 1881
Hofmann & Czerny. 1902–*fl.* 1960
Holze & Heitzmann. 1868–*fl.* 1933
Holzl. *fl.* 1881

Karbach, F. 1856–
Karoly, D. 1900–
Karoly, T. A. 1898–
Karoly, V. V. 1896–
Koch & Korselt. 1891–*fl.* 1920
Krauss, A. 1898–
Kreuter, L. *fl.* 1945–*fl.* 1956

Littman, J. 1869–*fl.* 1909
Lorenz, W. *fl.* 1895–*fl.* 1915
'Luner'. 1868–*fl.* 1953
'Lyra'. 1885–*fl.* 1952

Mayer, W. *fl.* 1930–*fl.* 1941
Mayr, F. 1885–
Magrini & Figlio. 1870–*fl.* 1920

Nemetschke, J. 1898–*fl.* 1950
Neuberger, A. 1890–*fl.* 1915
Novak, V. *fl.* 1900–*fl.* 1910

Oeser, F. *fl.* 1881

Pallik & Schniker. *fl.* 1920–*fl.* 1940
Pallik & Strasny. 1894–*fl.* 1920
Papperberger, A. 1912–*fl.* 1949
Parttats, A. 1868–
Paukert, *fl.* 1895–*fl.* 1900
Pawleck, J. 1894–*fl.* 1915
Petrof. A. 1864–*fl.* 1960
Peukert. *fl.* 1880–*fl.* 1905
Pokorny, A. *fl.* 1890–*fl.* 1920
Proksch, A. 1864–*fl.* 1915
Proskowetz, P. *fl.* 1890–*fl.* 1910
Protze, J. 1905–*fl.* 1911
Produktiv-Genossenschaft 1873–*fl.* 1952

Reinhold, R. 1890–*fl.* 1914
Rösler, G. 1878–1945

Schambe, W. 1870–
Schmetterer, J.
Schmid, H.
Schmid & Kunz. 1880–
Schneider & Neffe. 1839–
Schweighofer. 1792–*fl.* 1924
Seuffert. *c.* 1850–1855
Skop, J. *fl.* 1915–*fl.* 1928
Spira, C. 1892–
Stary, J. 1892–
Stein, A. 1812–
Stelzhammer, A. 1848–*fl.* 1960

Stenzel & Schlemmer. 1898–
Stingl. 1887–*fl.* 1950
Streicher, J. 1794–*fl.* 1871

Waldhausel, R.
Warbinek, R. 1906
Wasniczek, I. *fl.* 1910–*fl.* 1920
Weinbach. *fl.* 1900–*fl.* 1960
Wendl & Lung. *fl.* 1910–*fl.* 1925
Windhofer, R. *fl.* 1890–*fl.* 1910
Wirth, F. 1880–*fl.* 1928
Wolck, F. 1878–

Italy

Aggio. *fl.* 1916
Agmonino. 1850–
Anelli. 1836–*fl.* 1961
Audreoli. *fl.* 1881
D'Avenia, L. *fl.* 1882

Berra, I. 1850–*fl.* 1916
Berzioli. 1836–*fl.* 1916
Brizzi & Nicolai. *fl.* 1882–*fl.* 1903

Cessato. *fl.* 1881
Chiappo, F. *fl.* 1916
Colombo, A. *fl.* 1916

Deponti, C. *fl.* 1916
Dequoco, N. 1893–
Dondi, P. *fl.* 1916

Fabrici It. Pf. 1917–1924
Fea, G. 1880–*fl.* 1916
Fischer, C. *c.* 1850–*c.* 1910
Frederico. *fl.* 1882

Gillone. *fl.* 1881

Lachin, N. 1830–*fl.* 1916
Lefonti, L. *fl.* 1882
Levi & Diena. *fl.* 1916

Meglio. *fl.* 1882
Migliani & Borello. *fl.* 1916
Mola, G. 1862–*fl.* 1881

Otturo & Pollandi. *fl.* 1916

Perotti, G. 1870–*fl.* 1916

Quatero, V. *fl.* 1916

Racca. *fl.* 1916
Raffaele, F. *fl.* 1916
Ricordi & Finzi. *fl.* 1882
Roeseler, C. *c.* 1850–*fl.* 1916

Savi, R. *c.* 1905–

Volpi, N. *fl.* 1916

Spain

Charrier. 1875
Chassaigne. 1864–*fl.* 1960
Estela, P. 1830–
Guarra, H. 1860–
Hermanos, G. 1860–
Izabel, P. 1860–

Montano. *c.* 1864–
Ortiz & Cusso. *fl.* 1903
Sociedad Franco-Hispano-Americana.
  1898
Ten, R. 1902–
Vidal, J. 1879–

Belgium

Berden, F. 1815–*fl.* 1878
Berger, F. –1885
Bernard. 1898–
Berrens, A. *fl.* 1881
Boone. 1839–

Campo. *fl.* 1881
Derdeyn. 1846–
Frin, N. 1833–
Gevaert, V. 1846–*fl.* 1928
Gunther, J. 1845–*fl.* 1960

Hainaut. 1840–
Hanlet, A. 1866–*fl.* 1960
Hantrive. 1887–1959
Lacroix, M. *fl.* 1853
Minot, H. 1850–*fl.* 1870

Oor, J. 1850–
Oor, L. 1907–*fl.* 1928
Renson. 1857–
Van Hyfte. 1839–*fl.* 1960
Vits, E. 1838–

Holland

Allgäuer & Zoon. 1830–*fl.* 1883
Brinkmann, F. 1870–
Cuijpers, J. 1832–

Leijser & Zoon. 1854–
Mes, A. 1874–
Rijken & de Lange. 1852–

Switzerland

Bieger, J. 1842–*fl.* 1920
Burger & Jacobi. 1872–*fl.* 1955
Hüni. 1860–
Kunz, H. 1949–*fl.* 1960
Rordorf, N. 1847–*fl.* 1889
Schmidt, A. 1830–

Sabel. 1920–*fl.* 1957
Schmidt-Flohr. 1830–*fl.* 1960
Suter, H. 1875–
Trost. *fl.* 1881
Wohlfarth. 1905–*fl.* 1955

Scandinavia (Denmark, Finland, Norway, Sweden)

Billbergs (S). 1868–
Christensen, A. (D). *fl.* 1918–*fl.* 1960
Ehlert, J. (D). 1867
Fazers, A. (F). *fl.* 1950–*fl.* 1960
Felumb, E. (D). 1872–
Geisler, A. (D). 1876–
Hals, Brodrene (N). 1847–*fl.* 1922
Hansson, D. (S). 1854–
Hindsberg, H. (D). 1853–*fl.* 1952
Hornung & Moller (D). 1827–*fl.* 1960
Jensen, S. (D). 1893–
Jorgensen, B. (D). 1913–
Knudsen, J. (N). 1896–
Landschultz, C. (D). 1865–
Larsen, J. (D). 1855–

Löfmark, J. (S). 1903–
Löfmark & Hoglund (S). 1899–
Malmsjö, I. (S). 1843–*fl.* 1893
Nystroms, J. (S). 1865–
Ostlind & Almquist (S). 1888–*fl.* 1960
Peterson, H. (D). 1854–
Petersson, J. (S). 1889–
Ralins, A. (S). 1885–
'Standard' (S). 1904–
Svanquist, C. (S). 1899–
Walther, M. (N). 1954–*fl.* 1956
Wedell & Aberg (D). 1881–
Wennberg (S). *fl.* 1897
Westerlund (F). 1875–*fl.* 1960
Zwicki, L. (D). 1933–*fl.* 1957

Russia

'Apollo'. 1899–
Becker, J. 1841–1904
Betting, T. 1887–*fl.* 1903
Diederichs. 1810–*fl.* 1900
Dütz, A. 1873–
Fibiger, A. 1878–
Hellas, O. 1901–
Ivanovsky, E. *fl.* 1916
Johannsohn, T. 1855–
Kapustin, I. *fl.* 1916
Kehrer, H. 1872–
Kerntopf. *fl.* 1875
Kopp, A. 1887–
Koretsky, F. 1887–
Lappenberg, G. 1888–*fl.* 1916

Mayr, H. 1870–
Offenbacher. 1897–*fl.* 1916
Rathke, R. 1868–
Rausch, M. 1856–
Reinhard, W. 1874–
Rönisch, C. 1898–*fl.* 1913
Schmidt, P. 1880–
Schoen, A. 1843–
Schröder, C. *fl.* 1895
Schroeder, J. F. 1818–1885
Simuleit, J. *fl.* 1916
Smidt & Wegener. 1880–*fl.* 1916
Uslall & Mickina. *fl.* 1885
Ushall, A. 1878

Japan

Hamaguku ('Diapason'). 1948–*fl.* 1970
Kawai. *fl.* 1925–*et fl.*
Nishikawa. *c.* 1885–*fl.* 1916
Ono ('Horugel'). 1919–*fl.* 1970
Otsuka. 1920–*fl.* 1964

Tenryu. 1941–*fl.* 1970
Toyo. 1956–*fl.* 1970
Yamaha (Nippon Gakki). 1887–*et fl.*
Zen On. 1950–*fl.* 1964

U.S.A.

Aeolian. 1887–*fl.* 1933
Aeolian American Corpn. 1932–*et fl.*
  (incorporating American Piano Co.
  and Chilton, Stuyvesant, Technola)
Ahlstrom. 1875–*fl.* 1890
American Piano Co. 1909–1932 (incor-
  porating Brewster, Chase, Chicker-
  ing, Cook, Duo-Arte, Ellsworth,
  Emerson, Fischer, Foster-Arm-
  strong, Franklin, Gabler, Haines,
  Holmes, Knabe, Laffargue, Linde-
  man, Mason & Hamlin, Marshall
  & Wendell, Normandie, Pianola,
  Primatone, Steck, Stratford, Stroud,
  Vox Ward, Weber, Wheelock)
Amphion. 1901–
Anderson. 1900–
Archer. 1906–
Auto Grand. 1905–
Autopiano. 1903–1926

Baldwin. 1862–*et fl.*
Bailey. 1901–
Bauer, J. 1857
Baumeister. 1894–
Baus. 1880–*fl.* 1890
Bayer. 1906–
Becker. 1902
Behning. 1861–*fl.* 1956
Behr. 1881–*fl.* 1953
Behre. 1881–
Bellevue. 1906–
Bennett. 1900
Bent. 1889–*fl.* 1900
Bentley. *fl.* 1895–*fl.* 1904
Biddle. 1861–
Billings. *c.* 1876–1886
Bjur. 1887–1928
Blasius. 1855–
Boardman & Gray. 1837–*fl.* 1890
Bogart, E. 1899–
Bollerman. 1880–
Bourne. 1846–
Bradbury. 1861–*fl.* 1890
Brambach. *fl.* 1900–*fl.* 1957
Braumueler. *c.* 1887–*fl.* 1890

Brewster. *fl.* 1900–1933
Brockmeier. 1908–
Brockport. 1893–
Brooks. 1850–1918
Brown & Simpson. *c.* 1880–1910
Bush & Gerts. 1882–
Bush & Lane. *c.* 1900–
Butler. 1910–
Byrne. 1862–

Cable. 1880–*fl.* 1964
Cable, Hobart. 1900–
Cable-Nelson. 1903–*fl.* 1965
Callenberg & Vaupel. 1858–*fl.* 1890
Chase, A. B. 1875–*fl.* 1938
Chase Hackley. 1889–
Chickering Bros. 1892–
Chickering & Sons. 1823–*fl.* 1965
Christman Church. 1859
Chute & Butler. 1901–
Clarke, M. 1900
Colby. 1887–
Collins & Kindler. 1910–
Columbus. 1904–
Concord. 1907–
Conrad. 1910–
Connor. 1877–
Conover. 1870–*fl.* 1890
Cornish. 1876–
Cote. 1890–
Cunningham. 1891–*fl.* 1964

Davenport Treacy. 1873–*fl.* 1957
Daynes-Beebe. *fl.* 1908–1915
Decker. 1856–
Decker Bros. 1862–*fl.* 1890
Deitemeier. 1892–
De Rivas & Harris. 1905–
Detmer. 1907
Doll. 1871–
Dubois, Bacon & Chambers. 1836–
Dusinberre. 1884–*fl.* 1890

Ebersole. 1910–
Ellington. 1890–1930
Emerson. 1849–1940

Emerson. 1849–
Engelhardt. 1889–
Erhadt. *fl.* 1904–1917
Everett. 1883–*fl.* 1964
Estey. 1885–*fl.* 1965 (made 'Alexan-
der', 'Anderson', 'Bellman', 'Chase
& Baker', 'Drachmann', 'Lan-
caster', 'Malcom Love', 'Meldorf',
'Metropolitan', 'N.W. Nelson',
'Purcell', 'Schumann', 'Settergren',
'Soward', 'Vough', 'Wegman')

Farrand. 1884–
Fay. 1880–
Fischer. 1840–
Florey. 1909–
Foley & Williams. 1870–
Foster-Armstrong. *fl.* 1896–1932
Franklin. *fl.* 1900–1933
Fuehr & Stemmer. 1903–
Furlong. 1910

Gabler. 1854–1931
Germain. 1895
Gibbons & Stone. 1821–
Goetzmann. 1905
Gilbert. 1907
Gordon-Laughead. *fl.* 1948–*fl.* 1960
Gran–Richsteig. *c.* 1900–
Greve. 1896–
Grinnell. 1879
Guild. 1861–*fl.* 1890
Gulbransen. *c.* 1906–*fl.* 1965

Haddorff ('Brooks-Evans'). 1901–1920
Haines. 1898–1942
Hale. 1860–*fl.* 1880
Hallet & Davis. 1843–*fl.* 1890
Hamilton. 1889–*fl.* 1964
Hardman, Peck. 1842–*fl.* 1964
Harrington. 1886–*fl.* 1964
Harvard. 1885–
Hasbrouck. 1886–
Hazelton. 1849–*fl.* 1957
Holmes. *fl.* 1906–1924
Homer. 1907–
Hornung. 1880
Howard. fl. 1894–*fl.* 1964
Hughes. 1866–
Hume. 1902–
Huntington. 1894–

Ivers & Pond. 1880–*fl.* 1965

Jacob. 1878–
James & Holmstrom. 1874–*fl.* 1890

Janssen. 1898
Jewett. 1899
Johnson. 1907–

Kaiser. 1891–
Kaufmann. *fl.* 1909–*fl.* 1924
Kayton. *fl.* 1905–1910
Keller Bros. 1892–1927
Keller-Dunham. 1909–
Keller, G. F. *fl.* 1914–1929
Keller, H. *fl.* 1900–1915
Kellmer. 1883–1926
Kelso & Co. 1891–
Kimball. 1885 *et fl.*
Kindler & Collins. 1910–
King. 1903–
Kirchnoff. 1901–
Kleber. 1841–
Knabe & Gaehle. 1839–1854
Knabe. 1854–*fl.* 1965
Knight-Brinkerhoff. 1907
Kohler & Campbell. 1894–*fl.* 1964
(took over several firms, including
Davenport-Treacy, 1916)
Kraft. 1903–
Krakauer. 1878–*fl.* 1965
Kranisch & Bach. 1864–*fl.* 1964
Krell. 1889–
Krell-French. 1898
Kroeger. 1879–*fl.* 1957
Kurtzmann. 1848–

Laffargue. 1896–1932
Lauter. 1862–
Lawson. 1906–
Leckerling. 1886–
Lehr. 1890–
Leins. 1889–
Lester ('Betsy Ross'). 1888–*fl.* 1960
Lighte & Newton. 1848–
Lindeman. 1887–
Lockhardt. 1892–
Ludwig. 1889–
Lyon & Healy. 1864–

Macfarlane. 1902–
Mansfield. 1906–
Marquette. 1905–
Marshall & Mittauer. 1867–1871
Marshall & Wendell. 1836–*fl.* 1953
Mason & Hamlin. 1883–*fl.* 1965
Mathusek. *c.* 1865–*fl.* 1890
Maynard. 1905–
Mauzy. 1884–
Mehlin. 1888–*fl.* 1964

Melin-Winkle. 1909–
Meyer. 1829–*fl.* 1890
Miller, H. 1863–*fl.* 1890
Miller, S. W. 1896–
Milton. 1892–
Monarch. *c.* 1894–1941

Narvsen. 1845–1880
National Piano Co. 1911–
Needham. 1846–
Nelson ('Karlbach'). 1908–*fl.* 1923
Netzow. 1885–
Newby & Evans. 1884–*fl.* 1890
Newmann. 1880–

Packard. 1871–
Painter & Ewing. 1893
Palmer. 1906–
Peek. *c.* 1878–*fl.* 1890
Peerless (Player). 1889–
Peters. 1902–
Pizarro. 1908–
Poole. 1893–*fl.* 1959
Prescott. 1869–
Pond. 1847–*fl.* 1890
Price & Teeple. 1902

Radle. 1898–
Randenbush. 1883–
Raymond. 1856–
Reed. 1842–
Ricca. 1891–
Rogers & Borst. *fl.* 1877–
Ropelt. 1901–
Rudolf. 1903–
Salyer-Baumeister. 1907–
Schaaf, A. 1873
Schaeffer. 1873–
Schaff. 1866–
Schiller. 1893–
Schimmel. 1892–
Schleicher. 1878–
Schomacker. 1838–
Schubert, *c.* 1885–*fl.* 1890
Schulz. 1869–
Seeburg. 1907–*fl.* 1970
Segerstrom. 1900–
Shoninger. 1850–
Singer. 1894–
Smith. 1884–*fl.* 1890
Smith, Barnes & Strohber. 1884–
Sohmer. 1872–*fl.* 1965
Solingen. 1910–
Sporer, Carlson & Berry. 1861–
Stadie. 1899–

Stark. 1891–
Starr. 1872–
Steck. 1857–*fl.* 1965
Steger. 1879
Steinway. 1853–*et fl.*
Sterling. 1885–*fl.* 1964
Stieff. 1842–
Story & Clark. 1869 *et fl.*
Straube. 1878–
Strich & Zeidler. 1889
Stroud. *c.* 1902–1939
Stultz. 1909–
Stultz & Bauer. 1880–*fl.* 1957
Stultz & Co. 1905–
Sturz. 1871–
Stuyvesant. 1884–*fl.* 1890
Swan. 1907–

Telelectric (Player). 1906–
Tonk. 1881–
Trowbridge. 1888–
Tryber. 1881–

Universal. 1908–

Valley Gem. *c.* 1870–1925
Van Dyke. 1880–
Virgil Practice Clavier. 1889
Vose. 1851–1930

Waldorf. *fl.* 1900–1926
Walters. 1899–
Waltham. 1885–
Warde. 1909–
Waters, Horace. 1845–
Weaver (Davis). 1870–1930
Weber. 1852–*fl.* 1965
Wegmann. 1882–
Werner. 1902–
Weser. 1879–
Western Cottage. 1865–
Wheelock. 1877–1941
Wick. 1886–
Wilcox. 1877–
Wilson. 1909–
Wing. 1868–
Winkler. 1875–
Winter ('Brooks'). *c.* 1900–*fl.* 1964
Wissner. 1878–
Woodward & Brown. 1843–*fl.* 1890
Wissner. 1886–
Wuertz. 1893–
Wurlitzer. 1856–*et fl.*

Zech. *fl.* 1860–*fl.* 1870
Zellman-Socol. *fl.* 1906–1919

Other Countries

Beale (Australia). *c.* 1911–*fl.* 1924
Bell (Canada). 1864–*fl.* 1891
Bevan (India). 1883–*fl.* 1937
Close (Australia). *fl.* 1882
Consolidated Crossin (Canada). *fl.* 1908
Doherty (Canada). 1875–
Dominion (Canada). 1870–*fl.* 1891
Heintzmann (Canada). 1850–*fl.* 1922
Hoerr (Canada). *fl.* 1891
Karn (Canada). 1868–*fl.* 1961
Lazaro (Shanghai). 1896–*fl.* 1947
Lipczinski (Danzig). 1890–
Makrodt (India). *c.* 1890–
Mason & Risch (Canada). 1871–*fl.* 1922
Mendelssohn (Canada). 1885
Morris (Canada). 1892–
Morrison (Hong Kong). *fl.* 1921–*fl.* 1957
Nardelli (Brazil). *c.* 1894–*fl.* 1929
Newcombe (Canada). *fl.* 1891
Nordheimer (Canada). *fl.* 1891–*fl.* 1922
Shanghai. 1924–
Sherlock-Manning (Canada). *fl.* 1935–*fl.* 1964
Thomas (Canada). 1832–
Uxbridge (Canada). *fl.* 1891
Wertheim (Australia). 1909–
Williams (Canada). *fl.* 1891

Appendix II

Estimates of Production (in thousands of pianos) 1850–1970

Approx. Year	England	France	Germany	U.S.A.	Japan	Russia
1850	23	10		10		
1870	25	21	⟨15	24		
1890	50	20	70	72		
1910	75	25	⟩120	370		10
1930	50	⟨20	20	120	⟩2	
1935	55	⟨20	4	61	⟩4	
1960	19	2	16 (West) 10 (East)	160	48	88
1970	17	1	24 (West) 21 (East)	220	273	200

Note: Estimates for 1960 and 1970 are taken from *United Nations*, 'Growth of World Industry'. For earlier years cf. notes to Table IX p. 144.

Appendix III

Exotica

Unconventional pianos have appeared at various times in the instrument's history. Some were merely eccentric or too trivial in function to merit more than a passing reference: Blüthner made a light grand piano with a leather case for the airship *Hindenburg*. To celebrate George v's silver jubilee, Challen created the largest piano in the world, 11 ft 8 in. long and weighing one ton. In 1888 the German maker, Mann, produced an instrument with interchangeable keyboards, one with smaller keys for children. And another practical but unsuccessful idea was Ajello's upright introduced in 1908 with a keyboard which could be removed to enable the instrument to be carried easily up awkward stairs.

More fundamental attempts to change the piano have taken two forms: radical transformation of the keyboard, and a change in the means by which its string tone is amplified. Among the former the most remarkable example was patented by a Hungarian, Paul von Janko, in 1882. The Janko keyboard was banked like a typewriter's, its keys shaped like steps, which enabled the player to place his thumbs on lower rows while his fingers, in a natural hand position, had far greater scope than is possible on a conventional piano. This allowed an unprecedented facility; 'skips', as in Liszt's 'Campanella', and huge chords were child's play. The general effect, as described by a German critic, was of 'four able bodied virtuosi hammering away at four different grands'.[1] The first instrument with the new keyboard was made by R. W. Kurka and demonstrated in Vienna by Janko in 1886. The programme included Chopin's 'Funeral March' Sonata, several Liszt arrangements of Schubert songs, and Janko's own concert transcription of Delibes' *Naila* Waltz—obviously chosen for bravura display.[2] There was much criticism: the disposition of keys enforced the use of oblique levers which were said to result in a dull tone, but many deficiencies were probably due to Janko's granting Austrian monopoly rights of manufacture to an inexperienced maker. Failing to get support in Vienna, Janko was welcomed in Germany where several manufacturers, including such illustrious firms as Blüthner and Kaps, began to sell instruments with the new keyboard. Modifications improved touch and tone, instruction manuals were published, and Janko lectured and toured throughout Europe with an Ibach concert grand.[3] Hopkinson was the first English maker to adopt the keyboard in an instrument which was exhibited at the Royal College of Music in 1888 and inspected by Grove.[4] Advocates of the new system compared it to the revolution effected by chromatic brass instruments, and urged 'all lovers of progress' to espouse its cause.[5] Classes at the Leipzig Conservatoire were reported to be so popular that there was a shortage of keyboards.[6]

Yet enthusiasm soon waned. In 1894 a Berlin professor attributed the neglect of 'the greatest invention of the age' to conservatism among musicians who refused to learn the new fingering.[7] By 1900 *Musical News*, noting the end of Janko's patent rights, feared that, despite the 'misfit' of conventional keyboards to the human hand, 'keyboard reform' had failed.[8] Janko retreated to Constantinople where he died in 1919. Was conservatism the sole reason for the failure of his device? Certainly it was rejected by concert pianists whose view was expressed by one of Liszt's greatest pupils, Emil von Sauer: those who could play 'straight' had no need of 'terrace'.[9] But apart from the vested interest of established virtuosi there was a musical case to be made against the innovation, as contemporaries were quick to appreciate, even at the height of its popularity. Its facilitation of technical problems was self defeating. 'Skips' were written to produce a daring effect; making them easy to play removed tension and ruined the effect. In so far as the new system had any effect upon composers it would merely encourage them to 'crowd still more into their pieces' at a time when clarity of line was already threatened by congested sonority. Finally, the commonest deficiencies among pianists were musical rather than technical: a truly desirable invention would be 'a patent mind attachment for brainless virtuosi'.[10]

Another Hungarian, Emanuel Moor, was responsible for the next important attempt to change the keyboard. His design, introduced in 1921, was a double keyboard with a coupling device and the two manuals placed close enough together for one hand to play notes on each. Its devotees included Tovey, who considered that it might become 'the exhaustive modern concert room translator of Bach's harpsichord', and Carroll Gibbons whose Savoy Orpheans Band employed it to introduce 'a new kind of rhythm which is only made possible by the use of the double piano'.[11] Like Janko's invention and probably for similar reasons, Moor's piano was soon forgotten. An example still exists at the Royal Academy of Music and can occasionally be heard at public concerts.[12]

Of potentially greater significance than experimental keyboards is the electric piano. As early as 1890 an enterprising journalist argued that the main invention required of piano manufacturers was a means of prolonging tone, 'probably by means of electricity'.[13] As radio developed it was inevitable that attempts be made to replace the piano's soundboard by a system of amplification through loudspeakers. By far the most important example was the neo-Bechstein. The fundamental tone was produced with a conventional action and hammers, but only one or two strings were used for each note, and the tiny sound was amplified and reproduced electronically. Since low tensions sufficed, no iron frame was required and the entire structure could be lighter and smaller. The right hand pedal was conventional, but the left pedal acted as a volume control. This led some musicians to attack the concept as the antithesis of piano tone which, of course, has an intrinsic diminuendo [14] (see p. 11). A Bechstein director denied that so distinguished a house would be 'associated with anything that vulgarized or distorted great masterpieces of music'.[15] Yet recitals by John

Hunt and a gramophone record of Debussy's 'Clair de Lune' failed to convince enough musicians to take up the new instrument. Its failure must also be attributed to unfortunate timing—it was launched during the depression.[16] Similar attempts in later years met with little success. Several electric pianos appeared in America, and in England Chappell introduced the 'Pianotron' claiming 'the tone of a concert grand . . . from an instrument that occupies only the space of a pianette'.[17] 1939 was, again, an unhappy time for new ventures. But even the great improvements in post-war electronics, including cheap transistorized circuits and efficient small speakers, have failed to establish the electric piano.

An interesting recent innovation is Baldwin's 'Electropiano laboratory' designed for class instruction and particularly useful for beginners. Resembling the more familiar language laboratory, it allows up to twenty-four students to play 'silently', hearing their efforts through headphones. Meanwhile the teacher sits at a control centre from which he can communicate with and demonstrate to individual students or to the whole class.

Select Bibliography

Trade journals, newspapers and piano atlases

AAJ   *The American Art Journal* (New York)
BCA   *The British Colonial and Allied Countries Music Trade Directory*
DPM   *Directory of the Provincial Music Traders' Association* (1888)
Fed.   *Federation of British Music Industries Annual Reports*
FG   *The Furniture Gazette*
FR   *The Furniture Record*
H   *Hale's Piano Atlas* (Boston 1966)
HT   Herzog, H. K. *Taschenbuch der Pianonummern* (Berlin 1961)
I   *Internationales Hand und Adressbuch für Instrumentenbrache* (Leipzig 1883)
MTR   *The London and Provincial Music Trades' Review*
Me.   *Menestral* (Paris)
M   Michel, N. E. *Michel's Piano Atlas* (California 1957)
MM   *Monde Musical* (Paris)
Mu.   *Music*
NYMTR   *The Music Trade Review* (New York)
MC   *The Musical Courier* (New York)
MJ   *The Musical Journal*
M Mag.   *The Musical Magazine*
MN   *Musical News*
MO   *The Musical Opinion* and *Music Trades Review*
MS   *The Musical Standard*
MT   *The Musical Times*
MW   *The Musical World*
MI   *Musique et Instruments* (Paris)
PDG   *The Piano Dealers' Guide*
PM   *The Pianomaker*
PO   *The Piano, Organ, and Music Trades' Journal*
P   *Pierce Piano Atlas* (Long Beach 1965)
POD   Post Office Directories
Pr.   *The Presto* (Chicago)
R   *Revue et Gazette Musicale*
W   *Weltadressbuch der Musikinstrumenten Industrie* (Leipzig 1903)
Z   *Zeitschrift für Instrumentenbau* (Leipzig)

Select Bibliography

Books, articles, reports and pamphlets

ALEXANDER, D. *Retailing in England during the industrial revolution.* (1970).
ANDRÉ, K. A. *Der Klavierbau.* (Frankfurt 1855)
ASLIN *Nineteenth-century English Furniture* (1962)
AYARS, C. M. *Contributions to the art of music in America by the music industries of Boston 1640 to 1936.* (New York 1937)
BACH, C. P. E. *Essay on the true art of playing keyboard instruments.* (Translated and edited by W. J. Mitchell 1974)
BACKUS, J. *The Acoustical Foundations of Music.* (1970)
BADURA-SKODA, E. and P. *Interpreting Mozart on the keyboard.* (1962)
BAINTON, H. G. *The piano, its construction and care.* (Providence R.I. 1915)
BAMBERGER, L. *Memoirs of sixty years in the timber and pianoforte trades.* (undated: c. 1930)
BENNETT, J. *A short history of cheap music.* (1887)
BENT, G. P. *Tales of travel, life and love.* (Los Angeles 1924)
BENTON, R. 'The early piano in the United States' in *Hinrichson: Music, libraries and instruments.* (1961)
BEST, G. *Mid-Victorian Britain.* (1971)
BIE, O. *A history of the pianoforte and pianoforte players.* (1899)
BLACKHAM, E. D. 'The physics of the piano'. *Scientific American* (December 1965)
BLESH, R. (Ed.) *Classic piano rags.* (New York 1973)
BLESH, R. and JANIS, H. *They all played ragtime.* (New York 4th edition 1971)
BLOM, E. *The romance of the piano.* (1928)
BLONDEL, M. A. 'Le piano et sa facture'; chapter in *Encyclopédie de la Musique et Dictionnaire du conservatoire.* (Paris 1925)
BLÜTHNER, J. and GRETSCHEL, H. *Der Pianofortebau.* (Berlin 1909)
BOALCH, D. H. *Makers of the harpsichord and clavichord 1440–1840.* (2nd edition 1974)
BODE, C. *The anatomy of American popular culture 1840–1861.* (California 1959)
BOOTH, C. *Life and labour of the people in London: second series: Industry.* Vol. 2. (1903)
BOOTH, W. *In darkest England and the way out.* (1890)
BOSWELL, J. *The rise and decline of small firms.* (1972)
BRADY, V. A. *Music for the millions: the Kimball piano and organ story, 1857–1957.* (Chicago 1957)
BRANCOUR, R. *Histoire des instruments de musique.* (Paris 1921)
BRIGGS, G. A. *Pianos, pianists, and sonics.* (Bradford 1951)
BRINSMEAD, E. *The history of the piano.* (1889)
BRODER, N. 'Mozart and the clavier.' *The Musical Quarterly* (1941)
BÜLOW, H. von. *Neue Briefe.* (Munich 1926)
BURN, J. D. *Commercial enterprise and social progress.* (1858)
BURNEY, C. *An 18th century musical tour.* (Ed. P. Scholes, 1959)
BUSONI, F. *The essence of music.* (Translated and edited R. Ley, New York 1957)
CAIRNS, D. *The memoirs of Hector Berlioz.* (1969)

CASELLA, A. *Il pianoforte*. (Milan 1937)

1888–9 CENTENNIAL EXHIBITION, MELBOURNE. *Official Record*. (1890)

CHAPMAN, D. *The home and social status*. (1955)

CHASE, G. *America's music*. (New York 1955)

CIEPLIK, T. *Entwicklung der deutschen Klavierindustrie bis zu ihrer heutigen Bedeutung als Exportindustrie*. (Ph.D. dissertation, Giesen 1923)

CLAPHAM, J. *An economic history of modern Britain. Vol. III*. (1938)

CLAY, R. S. 'The British pianoforte industry'. *Journal of the Royal Society of Arts* (January 1918)

CLOSSON, E. *La facture des instruments de musique en Belgique*. (Brussels 1935) *History of the piano*. (1947, 1974)

CLUTTON, C. 'The pianoforte'; chapter in A. Baines (Ed.) *Musical instruments through the ages*. (1961)

COGGINS, J. *The governess's musical assistant*. (1822) *A companion*. (1824)

COLEMAN, D. C. 'Gentlemen and players'. *Economic History Review* (February 1973)

COLT, C. F. 'Early pianos, their history and character.' *Early Music* (January 1973)

COMETTANT, O. *Histoire de cent mille pianos*. (Paris 1890)

CORPORATION OF LONDON *Music committee minute books*. (Guildhall)

COUPERIN, F. *L'Art de toucher le clavecin*. (Paris 1717)

CROWEST, F. J. *Phases of musical England*. (1881)

COURT, W. H. B. *British economic history 1870–1914: Commentary and documents*. (1965) *Scarcity and choice in history*. (1970)

CURTI, M. 'America at the world fairs.' *American Historical Review* (1950)

DENT, E. J. 'The pianoforte and its influence on modern music'. *The Musical Quarterly* (1916)

DODD, G. *Days at the factories*. (1843)

DOLGE, A. *Pianos and their makers*. (Covina 1911)

DUTTON, R. *The Victorian home: some aspects of 19th century taste and manners*. (1954)

DYSON, T. G. *The pianoforte*. (1888)

THE EQUIPMENT OF THE WORKERS: *An enquiry by the St Philips education and research council*. (1919)

ERARD *Erard's new patent action grand pianoforte*. (1836) *Exposition universelle de 1855. Notice sur le travail de M. Erard*. (Paris, 1855)

FAUST, O. C. *The piano tuner's pocket companion*. (Boston 1902)

FAY, A. *Music study in Germany, 1880*. (New York 1965)

FÉTIS, F. J. *Exposition universelle de 1867 à Paris: Rapports du jury internationale. vol. 2, classe 10. Rapport de M. Fétis*. (Paris 1868)

FISCHOF, J. *Besuch einer Geschichte des Clavierbaues*. (Vienna 1853)

FORTUNES MADE IN BUSINESS: *Life struggles of successful people*. (1884)

FREYGANG, H. *Die Produktions und Absatzbedingungen der Deutschen Klavierindustrie*. (Ph.D. dissertation, Berlin 1949).

GALPIN, F. W. *A textbook of European musical instruments*. (1937)

GOEBEL, J. *Grundzuge des modernen Klavierbaues.* (Leipzig 1952)

GOODBAN, T. *Complete instructions for the pianoforte.* (1814)

GOUGH, H. 'The classical grand pianoforte.' *Proceedings of the Royal Musical Association* (1951)

GRAFING, K. G. 'Alpheus Babcock's cast iron piano frames.' *Galpin Society Journal* (April 1974)

GRANGIER, C. *A genius of France—Sébastien Erard.* (1924)

GREAT EXHIBITION 1851 *Catalogues and jury reports.*

GREELY, H. *The great industries of the United States.* (Chicago 1872)

GREW, S. *The art of the player piano—a textbook for student and teacher.* (1922)

GROVE'S DICTIONARY OF MUSIC AND MUSICIANS. (1879, 1904, 1927, 1954)

THE GUARD: *Instruction for the purchase of pianofortes.* (1854)

de GUCHTENAERE, M. *Le piano, son origine, sa facture.* (Paris 1926)

HALL, P. *The industries of London since 1861.* (1962)

HANSING, S. *Das Pianoforte in seinem akustischen Anlagen.* (New York 1888, 1906)

HARDING, J. *Saint-Saëns and his circle.* (1965)

HARDING, R. E. M. *The pianoforte: its history traced to the Great Exhibition of 1851.* (1933)

HARRISON, F. and RIMMER, J. *European musical instruments.* (1964)

HAWEIS, H. P. *Music and Morals.* (1871)

HEDLEY, A. *Selected correspondence of Frederyk Chopin.* (1962)

HELMHOLTZ, H. L. F. *On the sensations of tone.* (1862, 1870, 1877)

HEMMINGS, F. W. J. *Culture and society in France 1848–1898.* (1917)

HIGEL, O. *Illustrated and descriptive catalogue of actions, keys . . . supplies.* (Toronto 1906)

HILL, W. G. 'Noise in piano tone.' *The Musical Quarterly* (April 1940)

HIPKINS, A. J. Articles on the pianoforte in Grove's dictionary (1879), *Journal of the Royal Society of Arts* (1883) and *Encyclopaedia Britannica* (1889)

HIRT, F. J. *Meisterwerke des Klavier.* (Berlin 1955)

HOBBS, H. *The piano in India: How to keep it in order.* (Calcutta 1899, 1914)

HOLLIS, H. R. *The piano. A pictorial account of its ancestry and development* (1975)

HOOVER, C. *Music Machines, American style.* (Washington 1971)

HUBBARD, F. *Three centuries of harpsichord making.* (Harvard 1965)

HUGHES, T. P. *The development of western technology since 1500.* (New York 1964)

HULLAH, J. P. *Music in the house.* (1878)

HUME, A. W. J. G. O. *Player Piano* (1970)
   Clockwork music. (1973)

HUNEKER, J. *Chopin, the man and his music.* (New York 1900)

HUNTLEY, L. *The Language of the Music business.* (Nashville 1965)

IBACH *Das Haus Rudolf Ibach Sohn.* (Barmen 1894)

1862 INTERNATIONAL EXHIBITION *Reports of the juries and illustrated catalogue. Class XVI, musical instruments.* (1862)

JACKSON, A. A. *Semi-detached London.* (1973)

JAMES, P. *Early keyboard instruments.* (1930, 1970)

JANKO, P. VON. *Eine neue Claviatur.* (Vienna 1886)

JOACHIM, J. *Letters to and from Joseph Joachim.* (Translated and edited N. Bickley, 1914)

JOHNSON, D. *Music and society in lowland Scotland in the 18th century.* (1972)

JONES, G. S. *Outcast London.* (1971)

JOPLIN, S. *Collected piano works* (Ed. J. B. Lawrence, New York 1971)

JURAMIE, G. *Histoire du Piano.* (Paris 1948)

KAISER, J. *Great pianists of our time.* (1971)

KENNEDY, M. (Ed.) *The autobiography of Charles Hallé, with correspondence and diaries.* (1972)

KIRBY, F. E. *A short history of keyboard music.* (New York 1966)

KNIGHT *Cyclopaedia of the industry of all nations.* (1851)

KREHBIEL, H. E. *The pianoforte and its music.* (1911)

LANDES, D. *The unbound Prometheus.* (1969)

LANDOWSKA, W. *Landowska on music.* (Ed. Restout 1965)

LOCARD, P. and STRICKER, R. *Le piano.* (Paris 1966)

LOESSER, A. *Men, women and pianos.* (1955)

LONDON REPORT 1862 *International exhibition: Reports of the juries. Class XVI.*

MCCLOSKY, D. N. (Ed.) *Essays on a mature economy: Britain after 1840.* (1971)

MCKENDRICK, N. 'Josiah Wedgwood: an eighteenth century entrepreneur in salesmanship and marketing techniques.' *Economic History Review* (April 1960)

MACKERNESS, E. D. *A social history of English music.* (1964)

MAHILLON, V. *Amsterdam international exhibition 1883. Reports of juries.*

MARCUSE, S. *Musical instruments: a comprehensive dictionary.* (1966)

MARMONTEL, A. *L'Histoire du piano.* (Paris 1885)

MARTIN, J. *Reminiscences of Morris Steinart.* (New York 1900)

MARWICK, A. *The Deluge.* (1965)

MASON, H. C. *The modern artistic pianoforte.* (New York 1900)
    How has the pianoforte as an instrument developed since 1876? (Cleveland 1928)

MATTHEWS, D. *In pursuit of music.* (1966)
    (Ed.) *Keyboard music.* (1972)

MELVILLE, D. 'Beethoven's pianos.' Chapter in D. Arnold and N. Fortune (Eds.) *The Beethoven Companion.*

MICHAELS, M. I. Chapter on musical instruments in *The new survey of London life and labour. Vol. VIII. 3.* (1934)

MOULD, C. 'The Broadwood Books'. *The English Harpsichord Magazine* (October 1973 and April 1974)

MOZART, W. A. *The letters of Mozart and his family.* (Translated and edited by E. Anderson 1938)

MUSICAL DIRECTORY, REGISTER . . . CALENDAR. (1857–70)

THE MUSICAL GAZETTE (1899–1902)

MUSICAL INSTRUMENT TRADE'S PROTECTION ASSOCIATION *Report of an extraordinary general meeting . . . tariff reform* (1903)

MUSIC TRADE CREDIT RATING BOOK AND DIRECTORY (Boston 1910)

THE MUSIC TRADES DIARY

NALDER, L. M. *The Modern Piano.* (1927)

Select Bibliography

NETTEL, R. *Music in the five towns 1840–1914.* (1944)

NEUPERT, H. *Vom Musikstab zum modernen Klavier.* (Bamberg 1926)

NEWCOMB, E. *Leschetizky as I knew him.* (New York 1967)

NEWMAN, W. S. 'Beethoven's piano versus his piano ideals.' *Journal of the American Musicological Society.* 1970

NEW SURVEY OF LONDON LIFE AND LABOUR Vol. VIII, part III, ch. VII (1934)

NORTH, D. C. *Growth and welfare in the American past.* (New Jersey 1966)

ORTMANN, O. *The physiological mechanics of piano technique.* (New York 1962)

DEPARTMENT OF OVERSEAS TRADE *Reports on the market for musical instruments in Canada and India.* (1922) In Stephen Collection vol. 7.

PADEREWSKI, I. J. *The Paderewski Memoirs.* (1939)

PARIS EXHIBITIONS 1867 *Liste du jury internationale.* (Paris 1867)

   Rapports du jury. (Paris 1868)

   Complete official catalogue. (1867)

   Reports on the Paris universal exhibition. (1868)

   Report upon musical instruments by P. Stevens, U.S. Commissioner. (Washington 1869)

   1878 *Rapports . . . III par M. HERVÉ.* (Paris 1879)

   1889 *Rapports . . . II.* (Paris 1889)

PARRISH, C. 'Criticisms of the piano when it was new.' *Musical Quarterly* (October 1944)

PAUER, E. *A dictionary of pianists etc.* (1895)

PAUL, O. *Geschichte des Klaviers.* (Leipzig 1868)

PEACOCK, A. and WIER, R. *The composer in the market place.* (1975)

PEARSALL, R. *Victorian popular music.* (1973)

   Victorian sheet music covers. (1972)

PERKIN, H. *The origins of modern English society 1780–1880.* (1969)

PFEIFFER, W. *The piano key and whippen.* (Frankfurt 1965)

PIERRE, C. *Les facteurs d'instruments de musique.* (Paris 1893)

PIRIE, P. J. 'Fortepiano v pianoforte.' *Music and Musicians* (December 1973)

PLANTINGA, L. B. *Schumann as Critic.* (New Haven 1967)

PLUMB, J. H. *The commercialisation of leisure in 18th century England.* (Reading 1973)

POLE, W. *Musical instruments in the great exhibition of 1851* (1851.)

PONTÉCOULANT, A. Comte de *Douze jours à Londres: Voyage d'un Melomane à travers l'exposition universelle.* (Paris 1862)

   La musique à l'exposition universelle de 1867. (Paris 1868)

   Organographie: essai sur la facture instrumentale. (Paris 1861)

RICHARDS, J. *A treatise on the construction and operation of woodworking machines.* (1872)

RIMBAULT, E. *The pianoforte, its origins, progress and construction.* (1860)

RIMMEL, E. *Recollections of the Paris exhibition.* (1867)

ROBERTSON, R. M. *History of the American Economy.* (New York 1973)

ROOS, G. *Die Entwicklung der Deutsche Klavierindustrie.* (Ph.D. dissertation, Berlin 1924)

ROOSEVELT, B. *Life and reminiscences of Gustave Doré.* (1885)

ROSE, A. S. *A349, being the autobiography of a piano.* (1900)

On choosing a piano. (1903)

'Greater Britain musically considered.' *Irish Society of Musicians conference.* (Dublin 1895)

ROSENBERG, N. (Ed.) *The American system of manufactures.* (1969)

ROTH, E. *The business of music.* (1969)

THE ROYAL BLUEBOOK *containing the town and country residences of the nobility and gentry.* (1860, 1873)

RUBINSTEIN, A. My young years. (1973)

RUPPRECHT, M. *Die Klavierbauerfamilie Schiedmayer.* (Erlangen 1955)

RUSSELL, R. *The harpsichord and clavichord.* (1959, 1973)

RUTHARDT, A. *Das Clavier.* (Berlin 1888)

SACHS, C. *Das Klavier.* (Berlin 1923)

SAERCHINGER, C. *Artur Schnabel.* (1957)

SAUL, S. B. *Technological change: the United States and Britain in the 19th century.* (1970)

SCHAFER, W. J. and RIEDEL, J. *The Art of Ragtime: form and meaning of an original black American art.* (Baton Rouge 1973)

SCHAFHÄUTL, C. *Das pianofortebaukunst der Deutschen.* (Berlin 1854)

SCHIMMEL, K. *Piano-nomenclatur.* (Frankfurt 1966)

SCHMITT, H. *300 Etuden fur das pianoforte mit Janko'scher Claviatur.* (Vienna 1886)

SCHNABEL, A. *My life and music.* (1961)

SCHOLES, P. A. *The Great Dr Burney.* 2 volumes. (1948)

SCHONBERG, H. C. *The great pianists.* (1964)

SHAW, G. B. *London music 1888–89.* (1937)

Music in London 1890–94. (1932)

SHEPPARD, F. *London, the infernal wen.* (1971)

SIEVERS, G. F. *Il pianoforte.* (Naples 1868)

SMITH, F. M. *A noble art: three lectures on the evolution and construction of the piano.* (New York 1892)

SPELLMAN, D. and S. *Victorian music covers.* (1969)

SPILLANE, D. *History of the American pianoforte.* (New York 1890)

The piano: scientific, technical and practical instructions relating to tuning, regulating and toning (New York 1907)

STEARNS, M. W. *The story of jazz.* (1958)

STEINWAY *Family and business archives.* (New York)

STEINWAY, T. E. *People and pianos.* (New York 1953)

STEPHEN, J. L. *Collection of catalogues, drawings, trade tallies, blueprints, etc. relating to pianofortes.* (British Museum)

SUMNER, W. L. *The pianoforte.* (1966)

TEAHAN, J. 'A list of Irish instrument makers.' *Galpin Society Journal* (May 1963)

TEMIN, P. 'The relative decline of the British steel industry 1880–1913', chapter in Rosovsky (Ed.), *Industrialisation in two systems.* (1966)

TIMBS, J. *The industry, science and art of the age: or the international exhibition of 1862.* (1863)

TIMMINS, S. *Birmingham and the Midland hardware district.* (1866)

TIT-BITS 'How cheap pianos are made and sold.' (3 September 1887)

TRUE, L. C. *How and what to play for moving pictures.* (San Francisco 1914)

TURGAN, J. *Les grandes usines.* (Paris 1866, 1889)

TURNER, E. S. *The shocking history of advertising.* (1965)

UNITED STATES BUREAU OF THE CENSUS *Census reports on manufactures.* (Washington 1860–1939)

VIARD-LOUIS, J. *Music and the piano.* (1884)

VIENNA EXHIBITION 1873 *Report I: Oscar Paul, Wien officielle Ausstellung–Bericht vol. II.* (Vienna 1873)

    Report II: Ed. Schelle, Amtlicher Bericht über Wiener Weltausstellung. (Vienna 1873, 1875)

VIERLING, O. *Das elektroakustische Klavier.* (Berlin 1936)

VILLANIS, L. A. *L'art del pianoforte in Italia.* (Turin 1909)

WAINWRIGHT, D. *The piano makers.* (1975)

WALKER, A. (Ed.) *Franz Liszt, the man and his music.* (1970)

WALSH, C. I. 'An economic and social history of the pianoforte in mid- and late-Victorian Britain.' (MA dissertation, 1873).

WEBB, S. (Ed.) *Seasonal trades.* (1912)

WEBER, M. *The rational and social foundations of music.* (New York 1958)

WEITZMANN, C. F. *A history of pianoforte playing and pianoforte literature.* (New York 1897)

WELCKER VON GONTERHAUSEN, H. *Der Clavierbau in seiner Theorie, Technik und Geschichte.* (Frankfurt 1870)

WHITCOMB, I. *After the ball.* (1972)

WHITE, W. B. *Theory and practice of pianoforte building.* (New York 1906)

    Piano tuning and allied arts. (New York 5th edition 1946).

WIER, A. E. *The piano.* (New York 1940)

WINKLER, E. VON *Theory of the new keyboard . . . in use at the Paul von Janko conservatory of music.* (New York 1892)

WINTERNITZ, E. *Musical instruments of the western world.* (1966)

    Musical instruments and their symbolism in western art. (1967)

WOOLLARD, H. *The making of a modern pianoforte.* (1915)

YOUNG, T. C. *The making of musical instruments.* (1939)

ZELDIN, T. *France 1848–1945.* (1973)

ZUCKERMANN, W. J. *The modern harpsichord.* (1970)

Notes

Notes on Chapter 1

1. Broder, Colt, Gough, Melville, Pirie.
2. Dent.
3. Mackerness, 172.
4. Best, 260.
5. Landowska, 132.
6. Bach, 150.
7. Cf. recordings of Bach's orchestral suites conducted by Casals in 1966, and of the Brandenburg concertos led by Adolf Busch in 1935.
8. Boalch, 5–6.
9. Weber, 124.
10. Boalch, 46–7.
11. James, 52.
12. R. Harding, 67.
13. Parrish.
14. Gough, 41.
15. A. Einstein, *Mozart, his character and work.* (1946) 287.
16. Broder.
17. Letter to his father, 17 October 1777.
18. Scholes, I, 134.
19. R. Harding, 58.
20. Plumb.
21. Johnson, Teahan.
22. Parrish, 432.
23. A. G. Hess, *Galpin Society Journal.* 1953.
24. Hubbard, 159.
25. Boalch, 149.
26. Weber, 122.
27. Hubbard, 200.
28. Loesser, 388–392. Mackerness, 171–2.
29. Mould, 21.
30. Scholes, I, 35.
31. E. D. Jones, *Economic Crises* (1909) 44.
32. D. Beales, *From Castlereagh to Gladstone 1815–1885.* (1971) 84.
33. Letter to his father, 15 December 1781.
34. Schonberg, 49.
35. M Mag. June and July 1835.
36. MJ 11 February 1840.
37. MJ 7 January 1840.
38. MW 3 July 1845.
39. Melville, 66. C. E. Moscheles. *Life of Moscheles* (1873) I, 89.
40. Newman, 497.
41. Kennedy.
42. G. R. Hayes, quoted in James, 45.
43. D. F. Tovey, preface to Associated Board edition of Beethoven's Piano Sonatas, 7.
44. Dent, in James, loc. cit.
45. Walker, 51.
46. R. Harding, 158.
47. Matthews (Ed.) Ch. 5.
48. J. Harding.
49. Ortmann.
50. Backus, 302.
51. Briggs, Ch. 17.
52. Backus, 246–9.
53. Melville, 47.
54. MJ 2 June 1840.
55. Pirie.
56. Huneker, 56.
57. W. J. Santaella in *International Piano Library Bulletin*, I, 34, 4. (New York 1967.)
58. Badura-Skoda, 6.
59. Recorded by Badura-Skoda on a Graf piano of 1820.
60. Melville, 52.

Notes on Chapter 2

1. *Exhibition of the works of industry of all nations, 1851: official descriptive and illustrated catalogue* (1852). For English pianos see vol. I, class X. Foreign pianos are listed under country headings in vol. III. The jury report is in vol. II, class X. Visitors will have used the short catalogue (1851).
2. Dutton, 115 *et seq.*
3. Cf. Blackham, and Backus.
4. Backus is critical of Helmholtz on this point: 240–1.
5. R. Harding, appendix D.
6. Timmins, 592–3.
7. R. Harding, 237.
8. MW 1 December 1842.
9. Hipkins, R.S.A.
10. MW 9 June 1837. Cf. R. Harding, 297–8.
11. Smith, 58.
12. R. Harding, 179–82 and appendix E.
13. *Official catalogue*, III Austria No. 142.
14. *Harvard Dictionary of Music*, 575.
15. MO, August 1885.
16. Cf. pp. 125–6.
17. Krehbiel, 37.
18. Harding, 204.
19. Grafing.
20. *Official catalogue* III USA No. 458.
21. Loc. cit. Denmark No. 30.
22. *Official catalogue* II, 718.
23. Pfeiffer, 6.
24. Dodd, 9.
25. Sheppard, 170.
26. Pole, 16.
27. POD 1851.

28. POD 1855.
29. Dodd, 408.
30. Rimbault, 212–214.
31. Turgan.
32. By Pole.
33. Cf. Best's discussion of Booth's figures. op. cit. 84–91.
34. Pole, 18.
35. 'Special report of Mr Joseph Whitworth' in Rosenberg, 343.
36. 'Report of the Committee on the Machinery of the United States 1855'. in Rosenberg, 175.
37. Richards.
38. Aslin, 24.
39. MW May 1840 and 1841.
40. *Musical Directory, Register and Almanac.* (1855) Hopkinson advertisement.
41. MO October 1921.
42. MT September 1852.
43. MO March 1884.
44. Rimbault, 160–1 quoting *Chambers' Journal.*
45. Knight, 1335.
46. Pole.
47. Weber, 122.
48. R. Burley, *Edward Elgar: the record of a friendship.* (1972) 148.
49. D. Hudson, *Munby, Man of Two Worlds.* (1972) 51. The episode is described in Munby's diary 21 February 1860.
50. *The Royal Bluebook* 1860.
51. *The Royal Bluebook* 1873.
52. *The Guard.*
53. MS 12 June 1869.
54. Cf. Alexander, 161–2.
55. Landes, 186–7.

Notes on Chapter 3

1. T. E. Steinway, 11.
2. D. C. Burn, 'The genesis of American engineering competition 1850–1870'. *Economic History* January 1931.
3. Loesser, 484–5.
4. 'Reminiscences of William Steinway' in MO June 1896.

5. Schonberg, Ch. XIV, Chase, Ch. 15.
6. Fay.
7. Spillane, *History* . . . 216.
8. Rosenberg.
9. Saul, 171–2.
10. R. Harding, 187.
11. Spillane, *History* . . . 219.

12. MC 25 March 1896.
13. MTR November 1881.
14. MTR April 1888.
15. Steinway, diary for 15 and 17 November 1875.
16. McKendrick.
17. Loesser, 516–18.
18. See the tedious, ghost-written and unintentionally revealing *Memoirs*.
19. Steinway, letter dated Weimar 3 September 1893.
20. Loc. cit., letter to Metzdorf dated Weimar 27 September 1873.
21. Loc. cit., letter dated Weimar November 1883.
22. Clutton, 102.
23. Steinway, letter dated Bayreuth 11 April 1879.
24. Turner, 14.
25. Roosevelt.
26. T. Steinway, 33.
27. Hughes, 12. Curti.
28. Fétis, 262.
29. Loc. cit., 257.
30. *1862 International Exhibition* 5.
31. Pontécoulant, *Douze jours* . . . 66.
32. Op. cit., 143.
33. Op. cit., 150.
34. MS 15 December 1862.
35. Timbs, 149.
36. MTR August 1890.
37. Hemmings, Ch. IV.
38. MM 30 August 1892.
39. Pontécoulant, *La musique* . . . 219.
40. Cf. Pohl's statement that, as a juror at the Paris Exhibitions of 1867 and 1878, and the Vienna Exhibitions of 1873 and 1892, Hanslick 'did everything in his power to further the interests of the musical instrument makers of Austria'. *Grove* (1929).
41. *Paris Exposition . . . rapports*, 262. Cf. *Vienna Exhibition 1873 Report* I, 606.
42. *Paris Exposition . . . rapports*, 258.
43. Loesser, 512.
44. ME. 17 November 1867.
45. Pontécoulant, *La musique* 24 *et seq*.
46. R 21 April 1887.
47. Walker, 139.
48. ME. 3 November 1867.
49. Cairns, 111–12.
50. Steinway, letter dated Paris 25 September 1867.
51. Rimmel, 264.
52. MS 2 November 1867.
53. Paris exposition . . . reports, 197.
54. MS 7 December 1867.
55. Dolge, 318–19.
56. Vienna . . . report I, 634.
57. Loc. cit., 577.
58. NYMTR 18 February 1878.
59. R 30 January 1870. Cf. the comments on French pianos in Vienna . . . report II, 46.
60. Vienna . . . report I, 582.
61. The following account is based, except where otherwise indicated, on articles and correspondence in MTR between June and December 1878.
62. MC 12 February 1881.
63. MTR January 1881.
64. Interview reported in MC 12 February 1881.

Notes on Chapter 4

1. Fay, 206–7.
2. Roos. Dr Roos' scant treatment of statistics for the early period is indicative of their elusiveness.
3. MO October 1883.
4. This trend is further discussed on pp. 89–91.
5. MTR September 1881.
6. MTR June 1905.
7. Loesser, 586–91.
8. Bent.
9. MTR July 1882.
10. MTR September 1883.
11. These quotations are taken from translations of Mahillon's report which appeared in MTR 15 September 1884; MO 1 October 1884 and AAJ 20 September 1884.
12. Dolge, 235.
13. Bülow, letter to Klindworth, 1 May 1862. Subsequent references to Bülow are taken from this collection of letters, except where otherwise indicated.

14. ibid. 191, letter to Carl Bechstein.
15. ibid. 346–7.
16. ibid. 279.
17. Hirt, XXIV.
18. Blüthner and Gretschel.
19. AAJ 14 November 1885. MTR March 1884.
20. Ibach, 21.
21. MO January 1887.
22. Rupprecht; and in Z 1960, 83–7.
23. Z 11 May 1884.
24. MTR June 1883.
25. Roos, 22.
26. This exotic piece of information appears, without further elucidation, in M.
27. MTR and MO March 1883. MTR April 1883.
28. Z 1 and 11 August 1886.
29. Z 1 July 1884.
30. MTR 15 June 1878.
31. MO January and October 1883.
32. Stephen, vol. 6.
33. Loc. cit., vol. 4.
34. MTR 15 December 1878.
35. *Dresden Nachrichten*, 26 April 1880.
36. AAJ 11 December 1880.
37. AAJ 16 April 1881.

38. Melbourne Exhibition 1881: report of musical instruments jury, as published in MTR June 1882, and PDG August 1882.
39. Letter to MTR April 1882.
40. Letter to MTR August 1883.
41. Letter to MTR November 1885.
42. Letter to MTR December 1885.
43. Letter to MTR May 1884.
44. Colony of Victoria. *Report of Royal Commission on the Tariff Question*, quoted in MTR March 1884.
45. MTR May 1884.
46. MTR July 1884.
47. Z December 1883 and June 1884. Translated excerpts in MTR February 1883 and May 1884.
48. 1888–9 Centennial . . . 718.
49. MTR May 1888 and April 1890.
50. Letter to MO January 1889.
51. MO December 1890, quoting *The London Echo*.
52. MTR March 1894.
53. MO July 1898.
54. MO March 1898.
55. MO August 1899.

Notes on Chapter 5

1. MTR April 1878.
2. MTR September 1878.
3. MTR July 1878.
4. MTR May 1884.
5. *Stephen*, vol. 9.
6. Letter to MTR February 1882.
7. See, inter alia, MO November 1885 and March 1886; PO December 1887.
8. MTR January 1892.
9. MO July 1885.
10. Z February 1884.
11. MC 4 July 1883.
12. MO April 1885.
13. *British Medical Journal* 22 April 1899.
14. Letter to MO October 1892.
15. *Cassell's Household Guide* IV, 327. (1869–71).
16. Haweis, 525–6.
17. Rose, 'Greater Britain . . .'
18. *The Child's Guide to Knowledge*, 208–9. (*c.* 1870).

19. G. S. Haight (Ed.) *George Eliot's Letters*. (Yale 1954.) 6 October 1861; 9 May 1862; 19 January 1864.
20. B. Britten, *On receiving the first Aspen Award*. (1964)
21. MS 1 January 1866.
22. T. Hardy, *Far from the Madding Crowd*. (1874).
23. Nettel, 19.
24. MS 9 May 1868.
25. MTR December 1899.
26. MS 16 January 1861. Joachim, letter to Clara Schumann, July 1858.
27. Mackerness, 166–9.
28. Op. cit., 201.
29. Shaw, *London music*, 116.
30. Joachim, loc. cit.
31. J. J. Barnes, *Free Trade in books*. (Oxford 1964), 99.
32. MTR July 1887.
33. MTR January 1906.

34. Peacock and Weir, 33–48.
35. MTR April 1887.
36. Pearsall, *Victorian sheet music covers*; Spellman.
37. MS 15 December 1863.
38. MS 29 August 1868.
39. MT 1 December 1887.
40. Walsh, 33.
41. MTR February 1882.
42. P.P. 1901. *Teachers of Music Registration Bill*. House of Commons, 22 February 1901.
43. Perkin, 96.
44. T. Veblen, *The theory of the leisure class*. (1899), 85.
45. P.P. 1873, X, *Select committee on Coal, Minutes of Evidence*, 291.
46. MT 1 March 1885.
47. C. Booth, 3rd series, vol. 1 (1902) 16.
48. See, *inter alia*, J. Roebuck, *The Making of Modern English Society from 1850*. (1973), 131.
49. Jackson, 48.
50. Crowest, 5 *et seq*.
51. B. C. Hunt, *The development of the business corporation in England 1800–1867*. (1936), 13.
52. Cmd. 4596, *Report on Consumer Credit*. (1970.)
53. *Bethnal Green Times*, 5 January 1867.
54. MS 8 August 1868.
55. MS 31 July 1869.
56. MTR May 1878.
57. MO March–June 1888.
58. MTR May 1878.
59. MO May 1888.

60. DPM 1888, 44–5.
61. W. Booth, 217–18.
62. MTR January 1886.
63. MTR June 1885.
64. MO February 1887.
65. MTR October 1889.
66. MTR January 1890.
67. MTR November 1890.
68. MTR September 1891.
69. MO October 1892.
70. MTR June 1892 and May 1893.
71. MTR September 1893.
72. R. Lowe, *Sale of goods and hire purchase* (1968) 132–3.
73. MTR February 1894.
74. MTR June 1894.
75. FG July 1898.
76. *Truth* 12 January and 23 March 1899.
77. MTR June 1898.
78. FR 27 February 1903.
79. MO December 1902, quoting *Reynolds' Newspaper*.
80. Crowest, 201.
81. MTR February 1882.
82. Stephen, vol. 6.
83. Stephen, vol. 9.
84. MTR October 1885.
85. MO April 1886.
86. MTR October 1886.
87. MTR March 1893.
88. AAJ November 1886.
89. Report on Ajello v Worsley in MTR March 1897 and February 1898.
90. MU. April 1911.
91. Best, 261.
92. D. H. Lawrence, *Women in Love* (1916).

Notes on Chapter 6

1. Closson, *History* . . . 99.
2. G. P. Palmade, *French capitalism in the 19th century* (1972).
3. Pontécoulant, *Organographie*, 620–635.
4. Plantinga, 17.
5. Pierre, 180–2.
6. Pontécoulant, *Organographie*, 27.
7. See R. Harding, various references, and the long article in Fétis (Ed.) *Biographie universelle des musiciens* (Paris 1875).
8. Plantinga, 247.

9. Played by Ronald Smith on Oryx 1803.
10. *Erard's New Patent* . . .
11. Erard, *Exposition universelle* . . .
12. MC 11 September 1895.
13. Zeldin, 59–61.
14. MTR November 1881. AAJ August 1883.
15. MO October 1885.
16. Blom, 139.
17. AAJ 13 September 1890. MTR November 1890.
18. MTR February 1896.

19. MC 22 April 1885.
20. MTR August 1894.
21. MM 30 August 1894.
22. MTR June 1901.
23. Blondel, 2061–72.
24. MO February 1899, quoting AAJ.
25. London correspondents of NYMTR, 18 November 1877 and of AAJ 19 March 1881.
26. P. and R. Hume, 'The great Chicago piano war', *American Heritage*, October 1970. Cf. Loesser 558–60.
27. Rubinstein, 83.
28. Briggs, 34.
29. Shaw, *Music in London*, III, 97–100; criticism of a concert originally written in November 1893.
30. Paderewski, 253–4.
31. MC 31 July 1889.
32. On MacDowell's 'persistent Francophobia' see Chase, 348.
33. There were frequent references to the vigorous attack of modern, particularly American, pianists, in contrast to the quiet style of such players as Hallé. Cf. MM 30 April 1895, and J. Bennett, *Forty years of music 1865–1905.* (1908) 358.
34. PT. 28 October 1897.
35. MTR July 1878.
36. Stephen, vol. 11.
37. Dolge, 109–10.
38. MC 8 July 1896.
39. Advertisement in MTR February 1896.
40. Both reviews are reprinted in MTR November 1895.
41. Letters to MTR August 1896.
42. W, MTR August 1897.
43. In the *Biographie* (see note 7) Fétis praises his music extravagantly.
44. Cairns, 553–4. There is a portrait in Schonberg, 193.
45. Letter to Kumelski, 18 November 1831. Hedley, 93.
46. Schonberg, 110.
47. Grove (1929).
48. R 30 January 1870.
49. Vienna Exhibition, Report I, 582.
50. Turgan, 272–304.
51. Pierre, 176–80.
52. MO September 1894.
53. MM 30 November 1894.
54. MTR August 1879.
55. MTR February 1889.
56. MC 14 January 1885.
57. MTR October 1894.
58. MO December 1881.
59. MTR April and July 1888.
60. MTR January 1884.
61. Rubinstein, 128–34.
62. Paris 1889.
63. MM 15 October 1900.
64. NYMTR 25 August 1900.
65. P 9 August 1900.
66. MM 15 September 1901.
67. MTR September 1900.
68. MM 15 October 1900.
69. Marmontel, 204.
70. Pierre.
71. MM 30 September 1895.
72. J. B. Steane *The grand tradition* (1974) Ch. 8.
73. MM 30 October 1893.
74. MC 16 August 1893.
75. MM 15 and 30 July 1893. P 4 January 1894.
76. P 8 March 1906. NYMTR 10 March 1906.
77. MTR 15 November 1877.
78. MM 15 June 1898.
79. MC Trade Extra, June 1898.
80. MM 15 July 1889.
81. MM 15 March 1890.
82. MTR February 1891.
83. MM 30 August 1890.
84. MM 15 September 1892.
85. MM 30 September 1890.
86. MM 15 May 1892.
87. MTR 15 November 1877.
88. MC 11 September 1895.
89. Zeldin. 15.
90. Kriegelstein's improvement of Erard's grand action is described and illustrated in Harding, 175.
91. There are diagrams in Dolge, 88–96.
92. Dolge, 92.
93. MC 8 October 1881.
94. MC 28 February 1883.
95. MO December 1883.
96. The controversy is extensively reported in MC 19 March 1889; AAJ 29 March and 19 April 1890; and *The Indicator* 28 November 1894.
97. P 5 July 1900.
98. MM 15 August 1904.

Notes on Chapter 7

1. Benton.
2. North, ch. 2.
3. G. R. Hawke, 'The United States tariff and industrial protection in the late 19th century'. *Economic History Review* February 1975.
4. MTR February and July 1889.
5. MC 28 April 1886. AAJ 22 May 1886.
6. AAJ 25 December 1886.
7. AAJ 27 October 1883.
8. Martin, 172–4. *Making Music* No. 71, 1969.
9. Cf. *inter alia* Dutton, 88. Marwick, 116. D. Shawe-Taylor in the *Sunday Times*, 9 August 1970.
10. MTR April 1894. AAJ 27 February 1897.
11. MO November 1893. MTR February 1886, May 1895 and February 1896. MU. January 1900.
12. MTR October 1884. NYMTR 25 January 1879.
13. AAJ 14 May 1881.
14. MO August 1893.
15. Brady. 26. 76.
16. AAJ 23 November 1889.
17. MC 7 November 1888.
18. Whitcomb.
19. Loesser, 544–5.
20. Whitcomb, 7.
21. Joplin, 283.
22. A. Goldman, in *New Society* 30 May 1874.
23. Stearns, 140.
24. C. Hoffman, *The depression of the 1890s.* (Connecticut 1970) 151–2.
25. P 14 January 1904.
26. P 16 August 1894.
27. Advertisement in Stephen, vol. 10. MU. February 1900. P 23 July 1903.
28. Hume, *Clockwork music,* 257.
29. R. D. Chennevière, 'The rise of the musical proletariat'. *Musical Quarterly* 1920, 500–9.
30. Eg. Joseph Lhevinne, in advertisement, Stephen, vol. 10.
31. There is a fine collection in the London Piano Museum.
32. Letter to his wife, 20 November 1919, quoted in Schonberg, 353.
33. MU. July 1912.
34. PM August 1936.
35. Dolge, 180.
36. Spillane, *History.*
37. Loesser, 529.
38. MTR November 1899.
39. R. M. Robertson, *History of the American Economy* (New York, 3rd edition 1973) 345–53.
40. F. D. Abbot and C. A. Daniell, *The Presto Buyers' guide to the American piano.* (Chicago, 1899.)
41. PT. 2 April 1896.
42. V. S. Clark, *History of manufacture in the United States.* (New York 1929) III, 350.
43. MC 19 March 1889; 10 September 1890; 8 July 1891.
44. MTR March 1887.
45. MTR November 1887 and December 1888. AAJ 12 July 1890. MM 30 June 1898. Loesser, 523–5.
46. PT. 23 January 1896.
47. AAJ 12 December 1891.
48. MC 27 April 1892.
49. PT 10 August 1905.
50. AAJ 7 May 1881.
51. Z October 1881.
52. PT. August 1896.
53. Spillane, *History . . .* 298.
54. PT. 22 August 1895.
55. PT. 30 May 1907.

Notes on Chapter 8

1. Webb, 46. Jones, 377.
2. MC 17 October 1894.
3. MO March 1888.
4. MTR December 1891.
5. Boswell.
6. Hipkins.
7. MC 4 April 1883.
8. MC 1885.
9. AAJ 4 August 1883.
10. MTR March 1883.

11. Hipkins, *Journal*.
12. Coleman.
13. MTR July 1881.
14. MTR December 1890.
15. MTR February 1899.
16. PT. 19 July 1894.
17. MTR July 1893.
18. MTR November 1891.
19. MO February 1887. PO September 1887.
20. Bamberger, 141.
21. AAJ October 1891.
22. MTR 15 December 1878.
23. MTR January 1892. AAJ February 1892.
24. AAJ 30 November 1889.
25. MTR March 1901.
26. C. Booth, 55–7.
27. MTR January 1896.
28. PT. June 1896.
29. MTR February 1892.
30. *Tit Bits*, 3 September 1887.
31. MTR December 1898.
32. Court, *British economic history* . . . 431–2.
33. AAJ 29 January 1880.
34. MTR October 1882.
35. MTR June 1881.
36. MO August 1881.
37. MO December 1892.
38. *Daily Telegraph* 7 August 1886.
39. Loc. cit., 12 August 1886.
40. Loc. cit., 18 August 1886.
41. Court, *British economic history* . . . 447, 459.
42. MU. February 1910.
43. MTR February–April 1910. *Daily Chronicle* April 1911.

44. *The People* 11 October 1910.
45. MN May 1911 and October 1912. *Daily Express* 30 September and 7 October, 1913. PM 1913–14. Corporation of London, September 1912–December 1914.
46. MN October 1912.
47. PM October 1916.
48. MTR June–November 1887.
49. PO July 1887. MU. August 1896. MTR May 1900.
50. AAJ 16 January 1886.
51. MO 1 February 1886.
52. Cf. pp. 29–33.
53. AAJ August 1893. MC September 1894.
54. Hall, 74, 114.
55. MTR December 1884.
56. MTR September 1908.
57. MTR July 1899.
58. MO 1 October 1882.
59. MO March 1902.
60. MTR February 1910.
61. MTR March 1910.
62. MTR January 1884.
63. MO October 1912.
64. MO November 1912.
65. MU. July 1911.
66. *Economist* 23 August 1913.
67. MU September 1913.
68. MO October 1913.
69. Landes.
70. MO March 1910.
71. MO February 1910.
72. MTR November 1911. *Public Record Office* B.T. 31/15472/43797.
73. Bamberger, 238.

Notes on Chapter 9

1. *Observer*, 15 September 1918.
2. *British Trade Journal*, December 1914.
3. Court, *Scarcity and Choice* . . . 95.
4. MO February 1915.
5. *The Music Trade*, I, 1, 1917.
6. PM August 1914.
7. PM November 1915.
8. PM March 1915.
9. PM February 1915.
10. PM June 1917.
11. PM November 1914.
12. PM June 1915.

13. PM February 1915.
14. PM June 1916.
15. PM December 1915.
16. PM October 1916.
17. PM January 1917.
18. PM March 1917.
19. *Financial Times* 12 February 1917.
20. PM February 1917.
21. PM August 1917.
22. MO July 1916.
23. MU. February 1915. MN April 1915. MTR December 1916.
24. MU. March 1916.

25. PM May 1914.
26. Letter to PM June 1918.
27. Cf. Marwick, and Court, *Scarcity and Choice*.
28. MO October 1914.
29. MU. September 1914.
30. MO October 1914.
31. MO November 1914.
32. Letter to PM January 1915.
33. PM November 1916.
34. *The Times* 8 February 1916.
35. MO June 1915.
36. MO October 1914.
37. MO March 1915.
38. MO December 1915.
39. PM July 1917.
40. PM October 1916.
41. PM March 1915.
42. Invoice dated March 1915, in Stephen, vol. 4.
43. MO February 1915.
44. MU. June 1914.
45. PM August 1915.
46. PM April 1915.
47. Court, *Scarcity and Choice*, 93.
48. PM February 1915.
49. PM June 1915.
50. MO April 1915.
51. MO April 1916. PM May 1916 and February 1917.
52. PP 1915. House of Commons debate, 30 September and 20 October 1915.
53. MO November 1915. MU. November 1915.
54. PM March 1917.
55. *Ministry of Munitions Journal* April 1917. 'Restricted Occupations Order', 28 February 1917.
56. MTR September 1918.
57. MTR July 1908.
58. MTR November 1917.
59. MO August 1918.
60. MU. November 1917.
61. *Daily Mail* 1 February 1915.
62. *Manchester Guardian* November and December 1915.
63. The Equipment . . .
64. *The Music Trade* June 1917.
65. MU. March 1917.
66. MO January 1916.
67. PM April 1916. MO May 1916.
68. PM April 1918.
69. PM March 1918.
70. PM September 1918.
71. MO January 1918.
72. MO October 1915.
73. MTR January 1917.
74. PM July 1915.
75. PM January 1917.
76. PM March 1917.
77. PM February 1918.
78. PM August 1918.
79. *Pall Mall Gazette* 14 August 1918.
80. MU. July 1916.
81. 'Avion' in *The Motor* 28 May 1918.

Notes on Chapter 10

1. New York correspondent of MTR August 1919.
2. R. and S. Lynd, *Middletown* (1929), 244
3. Grangier, 8.
4. MTR April 1923.
5. Landes, 362.
6. Freygang, 91–2.
7. The prospectus is in PM August 1920.
8. PM March and November 1930. MTR April and December 1930.
9. *Star* 28 August 1919. *Nottingham Journal and Express* 30 August 1919.
10. MTR October 1919.
11. MO October 1919.
12. MTR September 1896.
13. MTR June 1896.
14. MTR January 1901.
15. MTR January 1879; July 1881; February 1892.
16. MTR 1919–1920.
17. On America: MO June 1920. On Germany: MTR June 1920, quoting *Deutsche Instrument Zeitung*.
18. PM February 1920 and September 1921. MTR February 1920 and April 1922. MO April 1921.
19. PM February 1920.
20. MO June 1922.
21. A. Marshall, *Industry and Trade*. (4th edition 1923) 131.
22. PM October 1913.
23. *The Times* 17 August 1917. Cf. Clay.

24. MI October 1923.
25. PM June 1919.
26. *Board of Trade Journal* May 1919.
27. MTR February 1921. On the 'never again' movement see PM throughout 1918. Cf. advertisements in Z 15 March 1919.
28. PM April 1923 and April 1924.
29. *Daily Express* 26 October 1928.
30. Loc. cit., 9 November 1928.
31. MTR 15 November 1928.
32. AAJ 8 October 1898.
33. PO July 1887.
34. MO August 1917.
35. *Music Trades Diary* 1921.
36. MO August, 1919.
37. MO March 1922.
38. MO June 1925.
39. MTR May 1924.
40. MTR May 1925.
41. MTR March 1921.
42. MTR December 1928.
43. MO June 1921.
44. PM June 1922.
45. MO November 1909, quoting *Chicago Indicator*.
46. PM December 1925.
47. MT November 1887.
48. Mu. March 1907.
49. Mu. June 1905.
50. MO August 1907.
51. Steane, 42.
52. Mu. December 1908.
53. PM September 1917.
54. MTR September 1921.
55. MO June 1928.
56. MTR March and September 1928.
57. MO July 1927.
58. Court, *Scarcity*, 122.
59. MTR January 1927.
60. MO July 1928.
61. PM October 1928.
62. MTR November 1929.
63. MO December 1927.
64. PM March 1929 and January 1931.
65. MO July and August 1928. MTR December 1928.
66. A. Briggs, *The History of Broadcasting in the United Kingdom* I (1961), 18–19. II (1965), 253.
67. MTR November 1929.
68. A. J. P. Taylor, *English History 1914–1945* (1965), 234. Briggs, II, 183. Cf., for example, Taylor's eccentric view of the BBC orchestra with Briggs's judicious account.
69. S. Pollard, *The Development of the British Economy 1914–1950* (1962), 225.
70. Freygang, 18. 90. Department of Overseas Trade, *Economic conditions in Germany to March 1936*. (No. 641), 145–6. MTR July 1929.
71. MTR March and April 1929; February 1930.
72. *New Survey*, 175.
73. Mu. May 1914.
74. MO June 1932.
75. MTR June 1928.
76. PM August 1933.
77. R. Stone (Ed.), *The measurement of consumers' expenditure and behaviour in the United Kingdom, 1920–1938* (Cambridge 1966) II, 17–18.
78. Wainwright, 155.
79. MO January and April 1936. Cf. Wainwright, 155–7.
80. Advertisements in MO February 1936.
81. MO July 1935.
82. PM August 1936.
83. MO February 1935.
84. MO April 1934.
85. PM April 1936.
86. *Consumer Bulletin*, 'The question on pianos: vertical or grand?' (New York October 1967), 9.
87. MO May to September 1939.
88. PM March 1939.
89. Patent 477, 297, June 1936 for soundboards. Patent 496, 082, May 1937 for ogee curve applied to rear of keyboard.
90. PM February 1939.
91. Briggs, II, 467.
92. PM December 1936 and January 1937. MO December 1936.

Notes on Chapter 11

1. PM November 1943. Cf. a tuner's complaints in PM April 1943.
2. Cf. remarks by Harrods' buyer, reported in PM August 1944.
3. *Consumer Bvlletin*, 'The question on pianos: vertical or grand?' (New York October 1967) 13.
4. W. P. Malm, 'The Modern Music of Meiji Japan', in D. Shively (Ed.) *Tradition and Modernization in Japanese Culture*. (Princeton 1971) 275.
5. MO February 1885.
6. NYMTR 5 and 20 March 1890.
7. A. S. Rose, 'Greater Britain . . .' 18.
8. AAJ 18 April 1896 and 27 February 1897.
9. PT. 16 September 1897. *Presto Yearbook* 1897 146.
10. NYMTR 26 August 1899.
11. NYMTR 24 November 1900. AAJ 1 December 1900.
12. ZFI reported in MTR December 1906.
13. PT. 3 January 1907.
14. ZFI reported in PT. 12 September 1907.
15. MN 20 January and 25 May 1907.
16. MO June 1907.
17. PT. quoted in MO August 1907.
18. MO May 1909.
19. MTR January 1910.
20. NYMTR September 1911.
21. MTR April 1916.
22. MO October 1919. MU December 1919. MI April 1926. MO November 1933 and March and April 1936.
23. Letter to PM December 1939.
24. *Sunday Times* 1 July 1973.
25. NYMTR September 1911. *Das Bechstein Bilderbuch* (Berlin 1927) 50.
26. Loc. cit., 12.
27. For a recent example see the *Observer Magazine* 4 May 1975.
28. MO July 1937.
29. Chapman, 31–2.
30. Roth, 85.
31. S. Bradshaw, in Matthews (Ed.) *Keyboard Music*, 316, 378.
32. H. Pleasants, *The agony of modern music* (New York 1955).
33. Loesser, 612–13.

Notes on Appendix III

1. K. F. Witte, 'letter from Barmen', in MC 18 July 1888.
2. MC 16 October 1889.
3. Winkler's manual has diagrams and fingering instructions. Cf. his article in MC 30 September 1891. Accounts of Janko's tours are in MO March, July and August 1887.
4. MO July 1888.
5. MC 16 October 1889.
6. MO January 1891.
7. MO February 1894.
8. MN 16 September 1900.
9. Witte, loc. cit.
10. C. Sternberg, 'Ad vocem, Janko keyboard', in MC 14 January 1891.
11. MO November 1923.
12. See review in *The Times* 18 December 1973.
13. MTR July 1890.
14. MO August 1933.
15. MO October 1933.
16. Galpin dates the neo-Bechstein 1936, but cf. note 14 and 15 above. Galpin, 130.
17. MO August and September 1938; October 1939.

Index

Index

Piano firms are listed without first names.